GOD'S KINGSHIP

STEVEN GILL
ANDREW HERBST
JEREMIAS ZUNIGA
of The Apostolic Classroom

GOD'S KINGSHIP

Truth
Book
Co.

God's Kingship
The Apostolic Classroom

All essays included in this volume were written (typed) in the author's own hand. No AI tools were used to synthesize passages, create thoughts, or produce information within the text. No attempt has been made by any of the authors of this volume to misrepresent content created by AI as their own work.

Published by Truth Book Company, LLC
Anderson, IN

ISBN: 978-1-965584-17-0, hardcover
ISBN: 978-1-965584-25-5, paperback

Cover Design: Jordon Frye
Typesetting: Uriah Fracassi

Unless otherwise noted, all scriptures are from the King James Version, public domain.

We hope you enjoy this book from Truth Book Company. Our goal is to provide high-quality, Bible-based books, curriculum, and resources to equip you to stand for truth.

For more information on our other books and resources, special discounts, bulk purchases, or hosting a live event, please visit www.truthbook.co.

Contents

Preface

For many Christians, studying the Doctrine of God can be overwhelming. The vast number of books, perspectives, and theological traditions can easily lead to paralysis by analysis; where does one begin? How does the average pastor, Sunday school teacher, lay minister, or church member grow in their understanding of God? These are questions we have frequently encountered while traveling to preach and teach across the country.

Individually, each of us had considered addressing the need for an accessible invitation into this topic. Those personal considerations culminated in the late spring of 2025, when we gathered to discuss the possibility of inviting regular church attendees into the kinds of conversations taking place in Bible college classrooms and other academic circles. The result of this discussion birthed the idea of the podcast, *The Apostolic Classroom*, and the essays collected in this volume.

This book aims to offer an introduction to a Biblical theology of the identity and nature of God. Because it is introductory, it is not exhaustive, nor does it attempt to answer every question a reader may have. Instead, we hope to invite readers into the broader theological discussion. Our primary audience includes ministers and students seeking to grow in their expression and articulation of God. Each essay reflects the distinct voice of its author as well as the thematic focus of the show. As a result, some readers may find certain essays more engaging than others. We encourage readers to engage the material at their own pace, working their way back into the more difficult material.

While introductory in scope, we believe even a more advanced reader could benefit from the material included in this book. For the reader seeking a more thorough exegesis, we recommend reviewing the resources in the footnotes. We are grateful for the opportunity to contribute these essays as an invitation to think more critically about how God is described in Scripture and pray that this work is beneficial to all who have supported this endeavor.

— *The Cohosts of The Apostolic Classroom*

WEEK ONE

Genesis and the Godhead – Foundations of Creation and Covenant

1

The Kingship of God in Genesis – An Examination of God's Self Disclosure

Steven Gill

Throughout the Pentateuch and the Old Testament broadly, there exists a gradual progression of the record and disclosure of God to His people. Often, Christian readers place primary emphasis on the use of certain Hebrew nouns throughout the Old Testament, such as *elôhîym* or *YHWH*, to articulate certain theological beliefs about the nature or power of the God of Israel.[1] Often, these lexical/syntactical examinations are done with Christological or ecclesiological views in mind – the interpretive practice of identifying Christ or His church in every aspect of the text.[2] Nevertheless, in many cases, modern Christian readings of the Old Testament, such as these, often do harm (even if well-intended) to the message of the Bible.

While it may be tempting for Christians everywhere to believe that the source of their claims about the nature and revelation of God comes directly from the

1. Among popular contemporary publications, this is seen most evidently in the *NIV Life Application Study Bible* as well as the *CSB Study Bible*. In the first, readers will find within the first few pages that the contributors introduce the possibility that the use of a plural noun in Genesis 1:26 was intended to disclose the trinity – a belief not widely held in Christian academia, as it requires the reader to approach the passage with later theological developments in mind. In the CSB Study Bible, the contributors say of the word *elôhîym*, "God is mysterious; though this particular Hebrew word for God is plural, the verb form of which 'God' is the subject is singular. This is perhaps a subtle allusion to God's Trinitarian nature." Once again, the contributors seem to acknowledge the singular verbs associated with these passages while disregarding their implications. For more on this, see:

"CSB Study Bible: Notes for Genesis 1:1." Life Bible. Last modified, 2017. Accessed April 15, 2025. https://lifebible.com/bible.

Life Application Study Bible (NIV): Zondervan, Grand Rapids, MI; Tyndale House Publishers Inc., Carol Stream, IL, 2007, p.6.

2. Richard B. Gaffin Jr., "The Redemptive Historical View," in *Biblical Hermeneutics: Five Views* ed. Stanley E. Porter, Beth M. Stovell (IVP Academic, 2012), 99-100.

scriptures, that belief assumes that all Christian traditions are themselves strictly biblical.[3] Of course, many lay readers will cede the point that this is likely not so. Living generations removed from the composition of the Bible, it is, perhaps, easy to forget how often post-biblical or extra-biblical ideas are read backwards into the text of the Bible. Using modern approaches to belief, such as philosophy, psychology, or certain forms of scientific inquiry, twenty-first-century readers may find themselves at odds with the intentions of the biblical writers. It is tempting to assume that all humans in every generation have approached knowledge and revelation the way we do today. Nevertheless, as David Baker states in his entry on the subject in *Dictionary of the Old Testament Pentateuch*:

> In the Pentateuch, narrator and narrative indicate understandings of aspects of Israel's God. Their genres include narrative, law and list, rather than theological treatise or philosophical discussion. Therefore, understandings often appear more obliquely, through story or statute rather than through a systematic analysis.[4]

Baker's observation is, perhaps, the first step to understanding misgivings about the revelation of God in the Old Testament and His role as king throughout the book of Genesis. While often read in light of modern discussions surrounding philosophy, theology, or metaphysics, the scriptures of the Old Testament exist independent of (even if related to) these disciplines.[5] Readers should resist the temptation to read back into the scriptures themes that were developed after – or perhaps even because of – the scriptures. Such eisegetical approaches will often lead to misunderstandings about original meaning. Language barriers and theological traditions can be significant hurdles for Christian thinkers who are not aware of their own presuppositions or biases.[6]

3. The advent of canonical hermeneutical practices after the fourth century often concretized certain beliefs and practices within the church that have no precedent in the New Testament, such as Marian veneration, prayers made to saints, the use of relics, etc.

4. David W. Baker, "God, Names Of," in *Dictionary of the Old Testament Pentateuch* ed. T. Desmond Alexander, David W. Baker (IVP Academic, 2003), 359.

5. In the book of Colossians, the Apostle Paul warned his readers regarding the danger of blending philosophical traditions with certain beliefs about Christ (Col. 2:8-9).

6. An example of these linguistic challenges may be shown in the development of vowels within western languages. In contrast to many languages of the Ancient Near East, western languages (Greek, Latin, English, etc.) incorporated the use of vowels, giving nouns stand-alone meaning. Without vowels, readers are more dependent upon the co-text to define the purpose

In the late thirteenth and early fourteenth centuries, a Franciscan friar named Nicholas of Lyra wrote many polemics to Jewish and Christian audiences, arguing in favor of certain Christian theological interpretations of the Old Testament.[7] Convinced that certain Hebrew nouns (particularly elôhîym) found in the book of Genesis proved his overarching claims,[8] Nicholas wrote adamantly that the Jews had either misrepresented or misinterpreted their own scriptures.

> In support of his arguments for the Trinity, Nicholas first refers to the Bible's use of a plural noun (*Elohim*) for God, as in the opening verse of Genesis, a noun often accompanied by plural adjectives and verbs. Although Jews deny the plural meaning of *Elohim*, Nicholas concludes that the "said excuse is false...".[9]

Attempting to defend the veracity of the Christian doctrine of the Trinity, Nicholas prioritized Old Testament passages of Scripture that could seemingly be used to support the claim that the God of Israel existed in three persons, just as the Christians had said. Believing he had correctly represented the Hebrew language to his Jewish audience, he insisted that the Jews of his time were in denial about the truth of the book of Genesis: That since creation, God existed in a plurality.

> Hence it is clear that it is not against the intention of the ancient Hebrew doctors that some plurality might be placed in God or the Gods while the unity of the

---

and form of nouns in a given sentence. Because Biblical Hebrew consists of nouns that use only consonants, stand-alone meaning must be nuanced by its incorporated meaning. In this way, the singularity and plurality of many nouns (as well as masculinity and femininity) are much more informed by the co-text. For more on the development of language and the significance of vowels in western thought, see: Jonathan Sacks, *The Great Partnership: Science, Religion, and the Search for Meaning* (Schocken Books, 2014), 41-47.

7. During the rise of the various mendicant orders of the Catholic Church, particularly in the fourteenth century, it was common for friars to write polemics opposing traditional Jewish readings of the Old Testament. Many of these polemics became the basis for later Christian opposition to perceived 'Jewish themes' in Christian doctrine, such as the oneness of God or a literal millennial messianic age. This development had a great impact on the Protestant Reformation as well and is seen most evidently in Luther's *On the Jews and Their Lies* as well as Calvin's *Response to Questions and Objections of a Certain Jew*.

8. In this case, Nicholas was arguing in favor of the claim that the doctrine of the trinity could be found in the Old Testament, provided the reader was not blinded by their Jewish biases.

9. Jeremy Cohen, *The Friars and the Jews: The Evolution of Medieval Anti-Judaism*, (Cornell University Press, 1982), 181-182.

deity is still preserved, which unity the Catholics most truly affirm.[10]

Yet the irony should not be lost on the reader here. While Nicholas was considered a prominent Christian Hebraist of his time, his arguments in favor of a plural God because of the biblical writer's use of elôhîym belies a fundamental understanding of the Hebrew language and exemplifies the linguistic pitfall that characterizes many modern examinations of biblical languages as well: Imposing the grammar rules of one's native tongue upon the languages of the Bible. While Nicholas was confident in his claims, the Hebrew language makes no room for Nicholas' theory.

> The form *elôhîym* occurs 225 times in the Pentateuch and refers to pagan gods (e.g., Ex 20:3; 23:13; 32:1; Deut 4:7, 28; 5:7 and eighteen further times in Deuteronomy) as well as to the God of Israel. Though morphologically plural, the word is regularly used as a singular when referring to Israel's God. This is shown by the regular use of singular verbs and adjectives in conjunction with the term...The purpose and meaning of the plural form is debated, with some seeing it as a plural of majesty, or royal plural...as an intensification or claim to exclusivity (Ringgren, TDOT 1.273; Fretheim, NIDOTTE 1.405) or as an honorific.[11]

Reading Baker's assessment, one understands that while the purpose of the use of elôhîym is disputed, the possibilities do not include, 'The noun is plural, therefore God is plural.' Such a reductionist reading lends itself too much to the habit of forcing Greek, Latin, or English (western languages) grammar rules upon Hebrew or Aramaic (eastern languages). Jeremy Lang has made this point in his entry on the issue in the Assemblies of the Lord Jesus Christ, General Ministry Conference Symposium of 2021, noting that

---

10. Cohen, *The Friars and the Jews*, 182. Polemical works by Nicholas and other writers like him include *Quodlibetum de adventu* (Questions About the Advent) and *Bibliorum sacrorum cum glossa ordinaria* (Holy Bible with Ordinary Gloss).

11. Baker, God, Names of, 361-362. Hebrew scholars have noted in many places that the Hebrew language contains plural majestic forms, as many languages do. For more on this, see Posner, Menachem. "Who was G-d addressing when He said, "Let US create man in our image?"." Chabad.org. Accessed March 27, 2025. https://www.chabad.org/parshah/article_cdo/aid/558595/jewish/Who-was-Gd-addressing-when-saying-Let-US-create-man.htm.

– while less common in western languages – eastern languages (particularly Hebrew) possess nouns, the singularity and plurality of which are sometimes dependent upon the verbs in a given sentence. Lang cites Genesis 1:26 as a primary example of these Hebrew grammar rules.[12] Thus, concurring with Baker, Lang dissents from Nicholas of Lyra's argument. The question of singularity and plurality becomes important for readers of the Bible, because it directly frames the reader's understanding of other biblical passages about God's lordship and sovereignty.[13] In short, Elôhîym is a dynamic term used in variety of ways throughout the Old Testament.[14]

As God's self-disclosure unfolds in the book of Genesis, readers are further acquainted with God as the *YHWH* (often pronounced in English 'Jehovah') of (Gen. 2:4).[15] If *'elôhîym* denotes heavenly or spiritual power/authority generally, *YHWH* identifies the 'who' of that power more specifically. It is often called, rightly I think, the 'proper name of God.' Known as the Tetragrammaton, this four-letter invocation is translated as LORD in the King James Version Bible. It possesses the nature of sovereignty, self-sustaining existence, and omnipotence. Yet, even in the disclosure of the name *YHWH*, the reader's relationship with the kingship of God in the book of Genesis is not complete. The sovereignty of God is not revealed in His names or titles alone, but by His action in the earth. 'God as king' is not merely something said, but something acted out.

> And Abraham said, My son, God will provide himself a lamb for a burnt offering: so they went both of them together...And Abraham stretched forth his hand, and took the knife to slay his son. And the angel of the LORD called unto him out of heaven, and said, Abraham, Abraham: and he said, Here am I. And he said, Lay not thine hand upon the lad, neither do thou any thing unto him: for now I know that thou fearest God, seeing thou hast not withheld thy son, thine only son from me. And Abraham lifted up his eyes, and looked, and behold behind him a ram caught in a

12. Jeremy L. Lang, "From the Foundation of the World: The Establishment of the Oneness in Genesis." in 2021 *ALJC General Ministry Conference Apostolic Doctrine Symposium*, ed. Nathan S. Whitley (Assemblies of the Lord Jesus Christ, 2021), 27-28.

13. Isaiah 43:11 is, perhaps, one example of this issue. The answer to the question, "Who is speaking is Isaiah 43?" will inevitably be informed by how one answers the *'elôhîym* question of Genesis.

14. This includes in reference to Abraham (Gen. 23:5-6) and the judges of Israel (Ex. 21:6).

15. Later, God is called *âdôni*, the Lord and master of His people in the sense of kingship, often displayed in earthly rulers, even in Genesis (Gen. 18:12;42:30 etc.).

> thicket by his horns: and Abraham went and took the ram, and offered him up for a burnt offering in the stead of his son. And Abraham called the name of that place Jehovahjireh: as it is said to this day, In the mount of the LORD it shall be seen.[16]

Here in Genesis, the narrative both discloses God's proper name and reveals His proper action. Believing God would "provide himself a lamb" to be offered in the stead of his son, Abraham steadfastly proceeded with his sacrifice. After God's intervention, the location of the sacrifice was renamed *YHWH iyr'eh* or, "Yahweh sees."[17] Far from being impersonal or in competition with another, God is present both in the mind of Abraham and in His movement at the place of sacrifice. His sovereignty is not disclosed in His name alone, but by His action in the earth. In Genesis, this is the repeated theme: The Almighty God who is, is also the Almighty God who acts.

---

16. Gen. 22:8;10-14 (KJV).
17. This form of conjunctive is also seen in Exodus 17:15 when Moses calls the place of his altar *YHWH nisiy* – God is my banner.

2

God and the Heavenly Host

Andrew Herbst

INTRODUCTION

Genesis 1:26 is often presented as an early Old Testament (OT) example of the revelation of the Trinity. However, a systematic approach to Scripture will show an alternate explanation. It will be demonstrated that angelic beings were present around God's throne and that God included them in His interaction with humanity. Therefore, Genesis 1:26 may be understood as depicting God speaking to angelic beings rather than speaking within the plurality of the Trinity.

HISTORICAL INTERPRETATIVE ISSUES

There are three passages in Genesis where God speaks of "us": Genesis 1:26, 3:22, and 11:7. Referring to Genesis 1:26, Gordon Wenham states that Christians have historically interpreted this verse as representing the Trinity, but it is "now universally admitted that this was not what the plural meant to the original author."[1] Therefore, it would be anachronistic to suggest that Moses intended to portray a divine Trinity within the Genesis "us" passages. The same can be said for the single "us" passage in Isaiah (Isa. 6:8).[2]

Victor Hamilton also questions the intention of the author of Genesis, stating that if Moses did indeed write Genesis 1, then it would be "going too far to call Israel's hero a trinitarian monotheist."[3] Moses was not combating issues within the Godhead, but he wrote against polytheism and the false gods of the ancient world. However, whereas Hamilton does not recognize the intention of

---

1. Gordon Wenham, *Genesis 1-15*, (Grand Rapids, MI: Zondervan, 2014), 82-83.
2. An *anachronism* is something that is out of place in time, such as a cellphone in the NT era.
3. Victor P. Hamilton, *The Book of Genesis, Chapters 1-17*, (Grand Rapids, MI: Eerdmans Publishing Co., 1990), 146.

Moses being connected to the Trinity, he does contend that Moses wrote theological language he did not fully understand. Meaning, Moses wrote Genesis 1:26 in opposition to false mythologies, but Hamilton argues that Christians can now understand the passage as a seedbed, or undeveloped doctrine, for later Trinitarian revelation found within the New Testament (NT).[4] However, just as the concept of a fully revealed Trinity was shown to be anachronistic within Genesis 1, so too should the concept of a Trinitarian seed be rejected.

Bruce Waltke plainly asserts that the "us" is a "reference to the heavenly court that surrounds God's throne."[5] For this to be an accurate interpretation, it must be demonstrated that angels were present at creation, that angels were present around God's throne, and that God included angels within His planning.

JOB 38

Job 38 is the primary Text that supports the presence of angels at creation. God spoke "out of the whirlwind" and began to ask Job a series of questions (Job 38:1).[6] The focus of the questions revolves around creation and elements of nature. For example, God asked Job, "Where wast thou when I laid the foundations of the earth?" (Job 38:4). Additional challenges demanded that Job answer who determined the measurements of the earth and to identify how the foundations are fastened (Job 38:5-6). Within this context of creation, God states that as these actions were unfolding, the "morning stars sang together, and all the sons of God shouted for joy" (Job 38:7). The first time Job mentions the "sons of God" is in Job 1, as they presented "themselves before the LORD." (Job 1:6). It is historically understood that these "sons of God" refer to angelic beings.[7] Therefore, the Book of Job portrays two elements from the thesis mentioned above, namely, that the angelic host was present at creation and that they continued to be in attendance around God's throne thereafter.

---

4. Hamilton, *Genesis*, 147.

5. Bruce Waltke, *An Old Testament Theology*, (Grand Rapids, MI: Zondervan Academic, 2007), 213.

6. Unless otherwise noted, all biblical passages referenced are in the *King James Version.*

7. An example of the general acceptance of the term "Sons of God" inferring angels in some texts is seen in in Longman's commentary on Job, although I disagree with Longman's conclusions regarding Enuma Elish. Tremper Longman III, *Job: Baker Commentary on the Old Testament,* (Grand Rapids, MI: Baker Academic, 2012), 427-28. Also, it should be noted that not every use of "sons of God" refer to angels. (e.g. Gen 6).

EZEKIEL AND I KINGS

Ezekiel 1 and 10 reveal angelic creatures in close proximity to God's throne. Ezekiel saw four of these creatures and identified them as cherubim (Ezek. 10:20). The cherubim were nearby, but there was only one on the throne, and only one who spoke (Ezekiel 1:28 and 2:1-2). As He sat on His throne, God told Ezekiel, "I send thee" (Ezek. 2:3). The plural language of "us" is absent, but its absence does not diminish the event's significance. The Ezekiel texts show angelic creatures near God's throne, and it is God who speaks and who acts. This concept is further developed in 1 Kings 22.

The context of 1 Kings 22 finds Micaiah sharing a heavenly vision with King Ahab. Micaiah "saw the LORD sitting on his throne, and all the host of heaven standing by him on his right hand and on his left" (1 Kgs. 22:19). God asked the host who would persuade Ahab to enter battle so that he would perish, and a lying spirit offered the solution that the Lord accepted (1 Kgs. 22:20-22). God approved of the spirit's plan, "I will go forth, and I will be a lying spirit in the mouth of all his prophets," but yet Micaiah concluded his message by stating that it was the Lord Himself who "hath put a lying spirit in the mouth of all these thy prophets" (1 Kgs. 22:22-23). Thus, Micaiah grants us three relevant observations: the heavenly host was around the throne of God, and they were included within God's interaction with humanity, but even though the host was included in the plan, it was God who performed the action.

ISAIAH 6

Isaiah 6 unites together the three elements of God's throne, the plural use of "us", and the Lord carrying out an action with the inclusion of the heavenly host. God is seen on His throne, and the angelic seraphim are observed worshipping "the LORD of hosts" (Isa. 6:1-3). After Isaiah's dread and subsequent cleansing, God asked, "Whom shall I send, and who will go for us?" (Isa. 6:8). It seems to be clear within the context that the "us" is God and those around the throne. John Oswalt, while taking I Kings 22:19 into consideration, affirms that "who will go for us?" is "an address to the heavenly host, either visibly present or implied."[8] God does the sending, but one who will go is going for the entire throne room.

---

8. John Oswalt, *The Book of Isaiah, Chapters 1-39*, (Grand Rapids, MI: William B. Eerdmans Publishing Company, 1986), 185.

The texts from Job, Ezekiel, 1 Kings, and Isaiah have shown that angels were present at creation, that they enjoy close proximity to God's throne, and that at particular times God has included angels within His plans regarding humanity. The final passages of study reside in Genesis, but this backwards progression need not cause concern. The same analysis could begin in Genesis and bear the same results. A systematic study should move forward and backward for the desired hope of consistency of understanding and interpretation.

GENESIS

In Genesis 11, humanity was unified in their rebellion against God and said, "let us make brick…let us build us a city and a tower…and let us make us a name" (Gen. 11:3-4). The humans began to build the Tower of Babel, but God said, "let us go down, and there confound their language…So the LORD scattered them abroad" (Gen. 11:7-8). Genesis 11 is similar to Genesis 1, in that both "us" statements are found with little surrounding information, which is why a systematic investigation is needed. To merely assume that the Trinity is the obvious answer does not do justice to the various passages that seem to provide a more consistent solution. Waltke postulates that the "us" going down to the Tower involves God and His angels who "superintend the nations" (Dan. 10:13) and "accompany the Lord in judgement" (Gen. 19:1-29, Matt. 25:31, and 2 Thess. 1:7).[9]

Genesis 3:22a states, "And the LORD God said, Behold, the man is become as one of us, to know good and evil…" Therefore, God drove Adam and Eve out of the Garden, and cherubim were placed as guardians at the Garden's entrance. Genesis 3:22 makes a distinction between two groups: the "us" and mankind. Man had come to know good and evil, but at this moment God separated them from immortality.

Even if man had retained immortality, that does not mean they were exactly like God. God is distinct as the Creator; everything else is creation. Therefore, the "us" must include those who could resemble God in a particular way that humans could also resemble God. The other members within the "us" are introduced in 3:24 as "he," God, placed cherubim "at the east of the garden of Eden." The "us" distinguished God and the immortal angelic beings from the humans.

9. Waltke, *Old Testament Theology*, 214.

Furthermore, God performed the action Himself, "So he drove out the man," and involved the cherubim in the event as He placed them at the entrance of the Garden (Gen. 3:24).

The primary verse in question will conclude this examination. Genesis 1:26a states, "And God said, Let us make man in our image, after our likeness..." Bringing all of the relevant texts together, it is consistent to understand God's plural statement to include Himself and the angelic host. The Hebrew construction of Genesis 1:26 may also bring more clarity to the situation.

Gary Pratico and Miles Van Pelt explain that within Hebrew, volitional imperfect verbs "are used to express a wish, request, or command."[10] This construction can be labeled as a volition of intent or cohortative, which means that the speaker is announcing or expressing their intention.[11] This concept continues to align with the passages mentioned above, as the next verse confirms the singularity of God creating, "So God created man in his *own* image, in the image of God created he him; male and female created he them" (Gen. 1:27). Some may argue that humans are not made in the image of angels, therefore, angels cannot be inserted into Genesis 1:26. However, the comment becomes pointless if the

---

10. Gary Pratico and Miles Van Pelt, *Basics of Biblical Hebrew Grammar*, 3nd ed., (Grand Rapids, MI: Zondervan Academic, 2019), 261.

11. Note offered by Jeremias Zuniga: Crucially, some grammarians have described the occurrence of the cohortative in this passage as a "plural of deliberation with oneself," see Paul Joüon and T. Muraoka, *A Grammar of Biblical Hebrew*: Third Reprint of the Second Edition, with Corrections (Roma: Pontificio istituto biblico, Gregorian & Biblical Press, 2011), 345-347 especially §114e. Also see Wilhelm Gesenius, Gesenius' Hebrew Grammar: Second English Edition Revised in Accordance with the Twenty-Eighth German Edition, ed. E. Kautzsch and A. E. Cowley (Oxford University Press, 1956), 398 §124g-n2. Importantly, this designation is not captured in all categorizations of the cohortative verb, see Christo H. J. van der Merwe, Jacobus A. Naude, and Jan H. Kroeze, *A Biblical Hebrew Reference Grammar*, 2nd ed. (Bloomsbury T&T Clark, 2017), 168-169 specifically 19.5.1.2. In Merwe, Naude, and Kroeze, they focus on the use of the cohortative as "Directive, Declaration of Intent, and Expression of wishes." In this way, the verb is not expressing internal deliberation, but either directing through proposal or request, declaring intention for self-encouragement, or strictly volitionally, which finds congruency with the note that "It provides a means of expressing the wishes or desire of the speaker in the first person...the plural form involves the speaker and one or more associate(s) (i.e., "Let us X")." See H. H. Hardy and Matthew McAffee, *Going Deeper with Biblical Hebrew: An Intermediate Study of the Grammar and Syntax of The Old Testament*, (Brentwood, TN: B&H Academic, 2024), 255-258 specifically 6.7.2, and 253n61. Additionally, this accords with the expression found in Nahum M Sarna, *The JPS Torah Commentary: Genesis*, (Philadelphia: Jewish Publication Society, 1989), 12. "The extraordinary use of the first person plural evokes the image of a heavenly court in which God is surrounded by His angelic host."

volition of intent was in focus, as God announced His intention to the host but He along did the creating.

CONCLUSION

This paper has analyzed Genesis 1:26 and relevant OT passages, and concluded that it is a faithful and harmonious interpretation to understand the "us" passages as referring to God and the heavenly host. Various stipulations were required for this conclusion to be accurate, and it has been demonstrated that the OT evidence supports the facts of angelic presence at creation and around the throne, as well as the heavenly host being involved in God's interaction with humanity. Therefore, one need not anachronistically place the Trinity within the creation account.

3

The Name of Our Divine King— The God of Genesis and Those Called His

Jeremias D. Zuniga

INTRODUCTION

In a cursory reading of Genesis, the observer will note the presence of the תולדות (*tôlᵉdôt = Generations or Records*) structure. This structure offers the reader an initial glance into the movements of Genesis, especially since it focuses on the centrality of beginnings and communicates origin and development (see Gen. 2:4, 5:1, 6:9, 10:1, 11:10, 11:27, 25:12, 25:19, 36:1, 37:2). While the structure is not superficial, a casual reading will result in missing the movement's motivations. Recognizably, it is important to identify each movement; however, there is a danger in overreading them as sections and disconnecting the new attention of a member of ancient Israel's lineage from their relationship to the book's overarching focus.[1]

In this essay, I will argue that Genesis' structure introduces and carries through each movement a theme central to understanding God's nature. That theme is God's kingship and how the use of His name reveals a pattern about a people in covenant; a pattern anticipated in Genesis and expounded in future books of the Bible. Since I will contend that kingship is essential in understanding the self-disclosure of God in Genesis, I want to focus on how Genesis 4:25-26 demonstrates His royal nature in correlation to people that practice some form of devotion to Him. To accomplish this, I want to present a few

1. Bill T. Arnold, *Encountering the Book of Genesis* (Grand Rapids: Baker Books, 2004), 17-18. While Arnold is no casual reader, I rely here on his accessible list and introductory efforts. My caution is to those in preliminary explorations of the text. Because Genesis has been wrest within the cultural debates, some works further create the illusion that these are disparate pieces that are inaccessible on the cultural level (see John H. Walton, *The Lost World of Genesis One: Ancient Cosmology and the Origins Debate* (Downers Grove: IVP Academic, 2009).

cultural elements that will work in contrast and comparison to the Bible's first book. Those elements will be divided between kingship and covenant and will serve to show the link between the *tôlᵉdôt (Generation)* passages.

KINGSHIP AND COVENANT

Today, the idea of kingship may provoke images of a figurehead; that is, a person with a lineage and the responsibility of representing a nation's philanthropic and constitutional work as a public figure.[2] While this perception and contemporary role show a small part of what kingship has been historically, the most ancient kings had a much greater involvement in state, military, and religious affairs. An example of this is evident in the legal code of Hammurabi, where his accession of the throne is claimed to be a result of the gods (i.1-40).[3] It is not simply that Hammurabi has been conceived of as receiving the crown by divine ordination, it is important to also note that the stele is concerned with his reputation and the memory of his name and his right to offer a code of law (v.15-25).[4] Additionally, the entirety of the epilogue champions Hammurabi—as a military man he is seen defeating foes, as a ruler he is divinely ordained to administer justice, his favor and position with the gods distinguish and set his name apart from the other kings.[5] Importantly, the relationship between the king's name and his deeds is essential in recognizing that for those in the ancient Near East (ANE), a king's name is related to his attributes and accomplishments. Thus, Hammurabi is not only qualified to issue

---

2. "*The Role of the Monarchy*," The Royal Family, accessed March 28, 2025, https://www.royal.uk/the-role-of-the-monarchy. This perception is common in western concepts of kingship, though long traditions exist that demonstrate a kings military and religious involvement. Yet, globally, the monarch has retained some military power (see "*The Royal Embassy of Saudi Arabia*," Government | The Embassy of The Kingdom of Saudi Arabia, accessed March 29, 2025, https://www.saudiembassy.net/government/?id=Skunk-3593-6229-42-4733).

3. Benjamin R. Foster, *Before the Muses: An Anthology of Akkadian Literature*, 3rd ed. (Bethesda, MD: CDL Press, 2005), 126-135. Importantly, Hammurabi receives his throne as given to him by Marduk. This identification is important as it will serve as a critical feature in the later enuma elish v 105-129 (see Johannes Haubold et al., *Enuma Elish: The Babylonian Epic of Creation* (London: Bloomsbury Academic, 2025), 71). For an overview and reference of the function of kingship also see Henri Frankfort, *Kingship and the Gods: A Study of Ancient Near Eastern Religion as the Integration of Society & Nature* (Chicago: Chicago University Press, 1978), 251-261.

4. Foster, *Muses*, 131.

5. Foster, *Muses*, 131-135.

edicts, but is destined to give the laws.

Similarly, ANE kings regularly relied on their reputation and the special relationship they had with their deities when establishing covenants with other rulers and people. As demonstrated in the prologue of *Mursili II's* treaty with a vassal nation, the reputation of a king and his relationship to people that would be brought into covenant with him were identified through that king's name.[6] Because of this, many ancient rulers adopted the name of their patron deity and were perceived as theophorically representing that deity's rule to the people of their nation.[7] That is to say, the nation-state was associated with its deity as the king bore that deity's name, and they were identified accordingly.[8]

6. "*Thus says My Majesty, Mursili, Great King, King of Hatti, Hero, Beloved of the Storm God,*" see Gary M. Beckham (Trans.), *An Ancient Treaty," in The Ten Commandments a Short History of an Ancient Text* (Auth. Michael Coogan, New Haven, Conn: Yale Univ. Press, 2014), pp. 135-141.

7. Frankfort, *Kingship*, 159-161.

8. It must be noted, that as power shifted throughout the ANE that transitions did not always reflect in name changes. However, while I focus on the king of Hattusa and the more ancient Hammurabi, what I call attention to here is the presence of Aššur and their allegiance to their deity, as they would also be called Assyria and many of their rulers would be named similarly as over two dozen Assyrian kings bear the nomenclature Aššur. See Adolf Leo Oppenheim and Erica Reiner, *Ancient Mesopotamia: Portrait of a Dead Civilization* (Chicago: University of Chicago Press, 1977), 343-346. I will refrain from drawing attention at this point to the Sumerian Kings List as it would expand the purview of this paper to treat it appropriately.

THE TEXT

25 And[9] Adam knew his wife again, and she bore a son,
and called his name Seth:
"For God set to[10] me another seed instead of Abel, for Cain killed him."
26 And to Seth, also, a son was born,
And called his name Enosh:
At that time,[11] men began to call on the LORD's name.

Genesis 4:25-26 are two verses commonly overlooked, given the pithiness of their message. For previous generations of scholarship, this short conclusion to the first *tôl^{e}dôt (Generation)* was challenging. The Challenge arose because of assertions that it may contradict the LORD's proclamation to Moses in Exodus 6:3, and those scholars claimed that Genesis 4 should be read as independent of the following genealogy in Genesis 5. Others have retorted, however, making the point that this represents something altogether different from a contradiction; that difference is worship.[12] Additionally, it must be noted that within the response, many have viewed this text as generic worship rather than something more relational. That view, of course, is related to splicing Genesis 4:25-26 apart from the following two chapters. I opine that splicing Genesis in that way misses a key movement in the preceding verses, the departure of Cain from God's presence, the bearing of his son, and the naming of a city (Gen. 4:16-17). In this way, Genesis 4 has supplied the link from *tôl^{e}dôt (Generation)* to *tôl^{e}dôt (Generation)*, and verses 25-26 serve as a distinction from the materialistic

---

9. Kittel, Rudolf, and Wilhelm Rudolph, eds. *Biblia Hebraica Stuttgartensia. Stuttgart: Deutsche Bibelgesellschaft*, 1997. All translations are based on my direct work with BHS unless otherwise identified.

10. The beauty of שת כי שת-לי is often missed, although others have noted the presence of the threefold קרא between verses 25-26. See Victor P. Hamilton, *Genesis: Chapters 1-17* (Grand Rapids: Eerdmans, 1990), 242-244. Hamilton's attention is on the twofold use in verse 26, noting that God's name is not given to Him, but invoked. More is said on this below. Additionally, Sarna nearly touches what I offer above when examining Seth's name, however his focus remains attentioned to cognate nouns. See Nahum M. Sarna, *The JPS Torah Commentary: Genesis: The Traditional Hebrew Text with the New JPS Translation* (Philadelphia, PA: The Jewish Publication Society, 1989), 39.

11. Hamilton, *Genesis*, 242n1.

12. Gerhard von Rad, *Genesis: A Commentary*, Revised (London: SCM Press, 1972), 112-113. Also see Claus Westermann, *Genesis: A Continental Commentary* (Minneapolis: Fortress Press, 1994), 338-341.

offerings of Cain and his descendants as they made names for themselves (Gen. 4:17-24) back to the spiritual focus of Seth's sons as they call on the LORD's name. After removal, Cain's lineage was industrious, among other things.[13] Contrastingly, Adam, the first man removed from God's presence in the garden, has another child whose son would contribute a return to the covenant name his family had turned away from.

The birth of Enosh and his ministry gave rise to the invocation of the LORD's name in worship, the first name not given but called upon.[14] This pattern of the use of the divine name is important, demonstrating that it was not entirely unknown. The text identifies that from Enosh onward, a group of humans were associated with the worship of the LORD in some way. The reader should observe in the opening texts of Genesis 4 that Eve names the initial child and claimed to have received him "from the LORD." The divine name is used, and the children of the first family appear before the LORD, giving offerings (Gen. 4:1-4). The absence of Adam and Eve from God's presence in the text is curious; she acknowledges that Cain is given by the LORD regardless of the couple being removed from the garden. Additionally, the two brothers appear in the LORD's presence, and Abel's offering is favorable while Cain's offering ultimately results in his turning away from the LORD. The children were still allowed access to the LORD's presence regardless of their parents' separation and expulsion from the garden. Subsequently, the conclusion of this *tôlᵉdôt (Generation)* reconnects humanity with the LORD and the following two *tôlᵉdôt (Generation)* movements outline the families of those that have a form of relationship to the covenant name (Gen. 5:22-24, 6:8-9).[15] This link is observable both in the genealogical focuses and the reiterated phrases:

> "ויתהלך חנוך את־האלהים"
> "And Enoch walked with God" (Gen. 5:22, 24)
> "את־הלהים התהלך־נח"
> "Noah walked with God" (Gen. 6:9).

13. Hamilton, Genesis, 251. Also see Matthew D. Jensen 2015. "*Noah, the Eighth Proclaimer of Righteousness: Understanding 2 Peter 2.5 in Light of Genesis 4.26.*" Journal for the Study of the New Testament 37 (4): 458–69. doi:10.1177/0142064X145581322.

14. Hamilton, *Genesis*, 244.

15. Westermann, *Genesis*, 357-359. Also see Sarna, *Genesis*, 43.

Returning to my thesis, it is not simply enough to claim that the presence of a name indicates some royal feature; it must also be shown how the calling of the name shows the LORD's kingship. In Genesis 4:25-26, it is essential to acknowledge that the name is not simply used ritualistically.[16] Had the intention been a generic ritualistic understanding, the proceeding lineage of Genesis 5 that contrasts with the preceding lineage of Cain in Genesis 4 would be rendered disjunctive. Of course, that is the error previous historical-critical methodologies encountered when exploring the text. However, the issue of disjunction finds resolution when the exegete observes that every occurrence of the name-calling in Genesis is associated with covenantal allegiance, and the statement "began" is no longer seen (Gen. 12:1-8, 13:1-4, 21:32-34, 26:24-25) since it has been established in Genesis 4:25-26.[17] Because the first family had become disconnected, a new allegiance was necessary to reestablish worship to the LORD. That allegiance would be accomplished by a group that is distinguished from the sons of men, as the appointed seed Seth is distinguished from the man Eve had previously received (Gen. 4:1, 25, 6:1-8). To this end, the invocation of the name is similar to that of ANE kings, as they were associated with the deity's name that was favored by them, though theophoric connections would not emerge until later periods in the Biblical text.[18]

CONCLUSION

While this essay explored cultural and Biblical texts, a central focus has preoccupied the purview of the examination: the name of a king. Additionally, I have argued that within the ANE the king's name and his accomplishments were essential. However, it was unimportant that the king's name be proclaimed

---

16. Sarna, *Genesis*, 40. Sarna indicates that the invocation of the divine name in this context is associated with prayer, and while this appears to be apart of future uses of the phrase, it does not seem to holistically include the relational aspect of the invocation (see my comments below).

17. It is not only important to note the uniqueness of this word's form, but also its absence in Genesis. I offer as an explanation that the חוחל serves as a sub indication of other greater beginnings, it is only intended to introduce the first occurrence insomuch as it is a solution to what had previously failed rather than an expression of organic emergence (Hamilton, *Genesis*, 242n2).

18. This reading also clarifies the similarities and differences between Genesis 5 and the Sumerian king list, as it may demonstrate humanity's long ages as related to their connection to the divine name. Although, a more thorough treatment of the relationship between Genesis 5 and the list would be required in light of this presentation.

unless he sought to connect himself to the divine or bring others into allegiance under his rule. Because of this, the reader should conclude that the Genesis 4:25-26 account is not the result of redactional sloppiness, but an anticipatory statement about the origin of humanity returning to covenant with the LORD as King, though not enacted in its entirety as demonstrated in future texts of the Biblical canon (Exodus 6).

WEEK TWO

Exodus and God's Kingship — The LORD, Pharaoh, and False Gods

4

The Kingship of God in Exodus—Sovereignty & Relationship

Steven Gill

If in the book of Genesis there exists a progressive presentation of God's self-disclosure from the general to the specific, in Exodus there is a portrait how that self-disclosure impacts God's relationship with His people. Even the phrase "His people" has a strong historical relationship with and is significantly dependent upon the materials of Exodus. More than many (perhaps any) book of the Old Testament, God's kingship in Exodus exists in juxtaposition to what most of the ancient world believed about the gods and man's relationship to them.

In the ancient world, the gods were not all-powerful. They could be opposed and, in some cases, even defeated.[1] When considering mankind's relationship to divine power in the Ancient Near East, it would be a mistake to assume that most cultures had any conception of an all-powerful, uncreated god who ruled over them, independent of other forces. Of the ancient Babylonian conception of the god Marduk, Nicole Brisch, Associate Professor of Assyriology at the University of Copenhagen, writes,

> One of the best-known literary texts [*Enūma eliš*] from ancient Mesopotamia describes Marduk's dramatic rise to power… In this narrative, the god Marduk battles the goddess Tiamat, the deified ocean, often seen to represent a female principle, whereas Marduk stands for the male principle. Marduk is victorious, kills Tiamat, and creates the world from her body. In gratitude the other gods then bestow 50 names upon

1. Victoria Donnellan, "The myth of the Trojan War." The British Museum. Last modified June 18, 2019. https://www.britishmuseum.org/blog/myth-trojan-war.

Marduk and select him to be their head.[2]

Typical of nearly all ancient literature about divine power is a consistent presentation of the gods as in conflict with one another, as well as humanity. In such a setting, it is not difficult to understand how human beings themselves could be conceived of as gods. If the ability to be all-powerful or all-knowing was not a barrier to entry in ancient pantheons, the pool of candidates for said pantheon becomes much more inclusive.

Because of the ubiquitous nature of this ancient perspective of pagan deities, the book of Exodus presents God in a way that could be considered radical for its time. In the book of Exodus, God is not only all-powerful, but He exists alone, independent, and unregulated by outside forces.[3] He expects to be worshiped alone, and He will not share His glory or worship with other gods. Because the book of Exodus is filled with prohibitions regarding idolatrous behavior, the reader quickly concludes that, before the commandments were given, the Israelites on whom the book centers were perhaps themselves given to the common practices of the ancient world, particularly with regard to image-making. It is also worth noting that – far from mere theological conception – the book of Exodus portrays the interests of God with regard to the pagan practices of the Israelites in practical terms as well.

> The first pages of the Pentateuch confront the reader with the beginnings of opposition to images representing deity. The order of creation and the concept of the *imago Dei* provide fodder for the polemic against the use of humanly fashioned objects to represent the presence of the deity. God fashioned humans in the image of God. Humans, in contrast, may not fashion God in the image of humans or anything else.[4]

---

2. Nicole Birsch, "Marduk (god)." Ancient Mesopotamian Gods and Goddesses. Last modified , 2019. https://oracc.museum.upenn.edu/amgg/listofdeities/marduk/.

Between these two entries is demonstrated a consistency in the ancient world over many centuries. From Babylon of the second millennium BC to Athens of the seventh century, beliefs about gods among pagan cultures remained largely static.

3. Throughout Exodus, these unique characteristics of God disclosing His special authority and relationship with mankind are demonstrated most clearly in Ex. 3:13-14; 12:12; 20:2-5; 20:11; 29:42-46.

4. Joel Hunt, "Idols, Idolatry, Teraphim, Household Gods," in *Dictionary of the Old Testament Pentateuch*, ed. T D. Alexander, David W. Baker (IVP Academic, 2003), 438.

The specific injunction against fashioning idols is distinct from the injunction against 'having any other gods before Him.'[5] In the book of Exodus, God is concerned with both. Furthermore, His role in the lives of the Israelites is presented in a way that heretofore within the Pentateuch is unknown. Apart from all other nations, God expected the Israelites to maintain a unique and sustaining covenant with Him that would be different from all other nations.

> And God spake all these words, saying, I am the LORD thy God, which have brought thee out of the land of Egypt, out of the house of bondage. Thou shalt have no other gods before me.[6]

The justification and prerequisite for the Israelites entering covenant with the Almighty God was framed around this understanding: 'I am the Lord that brought you out.' The use of the Tetragrammaton in this passage (*YHWH*) enjoins the identity of Israel's deliverer with the God of Abraham, Isaac, and Jacob.[7] It also brings the reader full circle from Genesis; the God who is, is the God who acts, and the God who acts is the sovereign Lord of His people.

> ...important elements of his [God's] character can be derived from Exodus 20:2, the introductory verse to the Decalogue: "I am the LORD [Yahweh] your God, who brought you out of the land of Egypt, out of the house of slavery." Yahweh has a personal relationship with his people, as shown by the personal pronouns employed. This is in an "I-thou" relationship of person with person; Yahweh is not some impersonal, cosmic force. Israel is particularly mentioned as having this relationship with him (e.g. Ex 3:18; 5:1; 6:7; Deut 1:6).[8]

---

5. Ex. 20:3. The command, "Thou shalt not make unto thee any graven image" is, of course, related to the general prohibition against idol worship. Still, Hunt's point is made evident – man was made in God's image, and are not, themselves, creators of any deity or force in the earth. Whatever proclivity mankind had for image-making, it was an unacceptable way to worship God.

6. Ex. 20:1-3 (KJV).

7. Ex. 3:15-16. In Exodus chapter three, the revelation of God's proper name, record, and fame, with the promise of Israel (past and future) is joined together in Moses' conversation with the LORD at the burning bush.

8. David Baker, "God, Names of," in *Dictionary of the Old Testament Pentateuch*, ed. T D. Alexander, David W. Baker (IVP Academic, 2003), 363.

So much is God's personal relationship with Israel emphasized in Jewish sources that it has often been debated what, precisely, constitutes the first commandment. Modern scholars have posited that the first of the Ten Commandments should rightly be understood as this pre-requisite phrase in stand-alone form: "I am the LORD thy God." On this understanding hangs all the words that follow.[9] Nevertheless, this prerequisite injunction extended beyond God's expectation of an internal acknowledgement by His people. Not long after the giving of the Decalogue, God expressed great displeasure toward Israel, not for who they worshipped, but for how they worshipped Him. Returning to the injunction against image making, Hunt remarks that Aaron and the Israelites revealed their own predilection for icons and idols during the fashioning of the golden calf, even if they believed their images represented Yahweh.[10] While Aaron announced that the celebration at the bottom of the mountain would be called "a feast to the LORD"[11] the celebration was not pleasing in the eyes of God. Far from honoring their worship, God demanded recompense for the Israelites' wicked behavior. Thus, in Exodus, it is revealed to the reader that, while sovereign, God is not a disinterested party; He desires obedience, not acknowledgement, from His people.

---

9. Joseph Telushkin, *Biblical Literacy* (William Morrow and Company, Inc., 1997), 421-422. According to Telushkin, the reason for this debate largely centers around a linguistics question. Aseret ha-Dibrot is the Hebrew phrase for what Christians call the Ten Commandments. However, this phrase rightly rendered in Hebrew is the "Ten Statements." Were the introductory injunctions of (Ex. Ch. 20) meant to be called the Ten Commandments, it ought to have been rendered *Aseret ha-Mitzvot* instead. Because of this, many Jewish scholars have suggested that acknowledgement of the Lord's place as sovereign God and deliverer of His people is the "first" of the "ten-statements." On the surface, this would seem to suggest there are not ten, but eleven commandments, however the second and third commands (1. Have no other gods 2. Make no graven images) are combined in this arrangement, reducing the number once again to ten.

10. Hunt, *Idols, Idolatry, Teraphim, Household Gods*, 438-439.

11. Ex. 32:5.

5

God's Kingship Over the False gods of Egypt

Andrew Herbst

INTRODUCTION

According to Scripture, worship is due unto God because of His identity and His mighty actions. In other words, humanity worships God for who He is and what He has done. The Lord is the Creator and King (cf. Ps. 19:1, Ps. 148, and Rev. 4:11), and He is the Redeemer of His people (cf. Exod. 6:6, Ps. 19:14, and Isa. 41:14). In the Old Testament (OT), God fully showed Himself to Israel as the Creator-King and Redeemer by bringing them out of Egypt. This paper will explore how He proved to the Israelites that He was the only true God by defeating and judging Egypt, and thus earning the allegiance of His redeemed people and becoming their King.

THE PLAGUES

The Lord accomplished this feat by sending the plagues upon Egypt (cf. Exod. 7-12). Those who deny miracles have attempted to explain away the supernatural significance of the plagues, claiming that each plague was a natural occurrence, originating from the Nile's over-flooding.[1] For a rebuttal of these assertions, see the analysis of Norman Geisler and Joseph Holden.[2]

There are others who challenge any historical foundation for the plagues, picturing the plague account as a mere myth or legend. However, one particular Egyptian document may help establish the historical veracity of the Exodus. The Ipuwer Papyrus records a tumultuous era in Egyptian history, with many of the descriptions bearing close resemblances to the Exodus plagues. The document

---

1. John H. Walton, *The IVP Bible Background Commentary: Old Testament,* (Downers Grove, IL: InterVarsity Press, 2000), 82.

2. Joseph M. Holden and Norman Geisler, *The Popular Handbook of Archaeology of the Bible,* (Eugene, OR: Harvest House Publishers, 2013), 225-28.

was written by a priest who was lamenting the chaos around him, reminiscent of Jeremiah in Lamentations.[3] Regarding the document, Egyptologists debate over its historical context and date of composition, with many secular scholars denying that the Ipuwer Papyrus has any connection to the Exodus at all.[4] However, the document does portray elements and descriptions that are similar to the Exodus plagues. Geisler and Holden present a graph of comparisons between the Ipuwer Papyrus and the Book of Exodus, and the similarities include a New Kingdom date, the Nile turning to blood, fire burning upon fields and crops, deep darkness, lamentations over children and sons of princes, and slaves wearing precious jewelry.[5]

If the plagues can resemble or connect to an existing historical account, then it is baseless to simply assert that the plagues are fanciful or mythological. Even if the lament within the Ipuwer Papyrus was reflecting on a time period prior to the Exodus, the details within bear matching historical similarities to Moses' day. It is not far-fetched to observe that Ipuwer's lament aligns with the Biblical record.

THE GOD OF ISRAEL AGAINST THE GODS OF EGYPT

The true God of the Bible has a long history of defeating false gods. Famous events include Dagon breaking and bowing down before the Ark (I Sam. 5) and the showdown against Baal on Mount Carmel (I Kgs. 18). Within the Pentateuch, it is clear from Exodus 12:12 and Numbers 33:4 that God targeted and defeated the entire Egyptian pantheon by sending the plagues. The plagues served two primary purposes, namely, to reveal God and bring His judgment. Both of these accomplished purposes then brought the deliverance of Israel. The Lord revealed Himself to Israel and Egypt alike, showing Himself to be the only true God and the redeemer of His people (cf. Exod. 6:7 and 7:5).

Each plague attacked one or more gods within the Egyptian religion, which would have affected all of Egyptian life. The Egyptian worldview completely interlocked life, religion, and nature together, so any disruption in one area

---

3. Holden, *Popular Handbook*, 223.

4. Many factors impact how this document may or may not be related to the Exodus. For example, there are issues within Egyptian chronology, as well as the Early or Late Date of the Exodus. For a robust analysis of the Exodus dating and support of the Early Date, see Michael Grisanti, *The World and the Word*, 194-207. For a brief analysis of the Ipuwer Papyrus, see Titus Kennedy, *Unearthing the Bible*, (Eugene, OR: Harvest House, 2020), 54-55.

5. Holden, *Popular Handbook*, 223-24.

greatly impacted the other two. Some scholars dispute any connection of the plagues to Egyptian gods, but the Biblical evidence seems to affirm the connection (cf. Exod. 12:12 and Num. 33:4).[6] It may not have been a distinct one plague to one god ratio,[7] but Michael Grisanti states that "it seems better to understand the plagues as a judgment against the entire pantheon of Egyptian gods," as well as against the pharaoh, "who ruled on behalf of the gods."[8]

A few specific examples in regard to the plagues and gods could be Ra (Re) and Osiris. Ra was the falcon-headed sun god and had a long and progressive history within ancient Egypt. He was the head of the Egyptian gods and "represented the sun in the fullness of his strength, combining all the forces of nature."[9] As the sun god, Ra was vital to Egyptian crops, order, and their very origin. The Egyptians developed a complex religious understanding of the movement and importance of the sun, with each stage of day and night carrying the weight of whether chaos would overcome order and bring destruction. Therefore, when God struck Egypt with darkness, a thick darkness that could be felt (Exod. 10:21-23), Ra would have been shown to be powerless and unable to protect his domain from what was viewed as cataclysmic. Furthermore, Ra was a primary "ally and protector of the throne" of the pharaoh.[10] This false god could not keep the darkness back, nor would he be able to protect the throne from the last plague. The final plague, the death of the firstborn, further demonstrated the weakness of Ra, but also attacked Osiris, Horus, and the pharaoh.

Osiris was the king and god of the underworld, the Duat. This Osiris example is multi-layered because of his connection with the pharaoh of Egypt. In the Egyptian worldview, the physical world mirrored the gods and the spiritual world. Osiris was king of the underworld, and his son Horus was the king of Egypt. In mirroring this dynamic, it was believed that when a pharaoh died, he became one with Osiris, allowing the dead ruler to remain a king in the afterlife. The deceased king's son then became the next pharaoh, reborn as Osiris' son,

---

6. For an example of dissent, see Victor Hamilton, *Handbook on the Pentateuch*, 2nd ed., (Grand Rapids, MI: Baker, 2005), 160.

7. For potential detailed connections, see Thomas Holdcroft, *The Pentateuch*, (Abbotsford, BC: CeeTeC Publishing, 2011), 118-123.

8. Mark Rooker, Michael A. Grisanti, and Eugene H. Merrill, *The World and the Word: An Introduction to the Old Testament*, (Nashville: B & H Pub. Group, 2011), 208.

9. E. O. James, *The Ancient Gods*, (London: Phoenix, 1999) ,71.

10. James, *The Ancient Gods*, 71.

Horus.[11] Therefore, the pharaoh was a living representation of Horus and would eventually become a representation of Osiris. This cycle of father to son positions continued with each pharaoh's death and birth.

The Passover night disrupted this important cycle, allowing chaos into the realm of Osiris and Horus, the domain of the living and the dead. Furthermore, Pharaoh's son literally died, and the visible Horus was judged. Pharaoh himself was judged, not because God hardened his heart immediately, but because the king rebelled against God's demands. When Moses confronted pharaoh the first time, issuing forth God's command to "Let my people go, that they may hold a feast unto me in the wilderness," (Exod. 5:1), the Egyptian ruler responded with, "Who *is* the LORD, that I should obey his voice to let Israel go? I know not the LORD, neither will I let Israel go" (Exod. 5:2). If Pharaoh did not know God then, he certainly would by the end of the plagues.

The final plague assaulted dead false gods and living false gods. The death of the firstborn brought the death of Pharaoh's son, who would have become the next image and embodiment of Horus. Pharaoh could not protect his offspring, the child of a god, and thus had put the future of Egypt, both in life and death, in jeopardy. One significant aspect of a pharaoh's rule was to maintain order and "harmony in the universe."[12] All of the plagues, especially the last one, had thrown Egypt into chaos, and showed that their spiritual and physical gods were not true gods at all. At this point, Pharaoh released the Hebrew slaves. The true God had revealed Himself, brought judgment, and redeemed His people.

CONCLUSION

After the Red Sea deliverance, the singers could justly proclaim, "Who is like unto thee, O LORD, among the gods?" (Exod. 15:11a). The Exodus redemption was one of the most significant events in Israelite history, and portrayed as such with the constant OT declaration that it was the Lord who "brought you out of the land of Egypt." God brought Israel out in order to bring them in, out of bondage and into the Promised Land. The Exodus event is the foundation for God's kingship over Israel, and it is upon this historical fact that the Lord provided the Ten Commandments (Exod. 20:2).

11. Alan Gardiner, *The Egyptians*, (London: Oxford University Press, 2001), 127.
12. Grisanti, *The World and the Word*, 208.

6

Who Will Be Your God—The God of Exodus and Those Called His

Jeremias D. Zuniga

INTRODUCTION

When exploring the texts of Exodus, no greater understanding aids the student of Scripture than first recognizing the text's connection to Genesis. The Genesis account concludes with the death of Joseph and his charge to carry his bones forward (Gen. 50:24-26), and just prior to that, we find the statement from Joseph to his brothers, "but you all, you thought evil upon me, *but* God thought it for good" (Gen. 50:20a). It is the impetus of this phrase that I want to explore in this paper, specifically, how a growing group of people come to learn of God's nature and identity from the statement made by Joseph. My argument is that Exodus details Israel's children as they struggle with faithfulness in acknowledging the Lord's kingship. That struggle could best be summarized by the following question: "Who will be your God?"

ANCIENT EGYPT

Within the culture of ancient Egypt, Pharaohs were regarded as more than kings; these human rulers were considered divine. This concept of the rulers as divine-kings emerges from the mythology of the Egyptians, where kingship ultimately came to belong to Horus as he united the lands of Lower and Upper Egypt (Memphis and Thebes).[1] During the Pharaonic dynasties, it appears that

1. John A Wilson, "*Egyptian Myths, Tales, and Mortuary Texts: The Theology of Memphis,*" *Translation, in Ancient Near Eastern Texts Relating to the Old Testament*, 3rd ed. (Princeton University Press, 1992), 4–6. This Egyptian text describes Horus's initial accession to the throne in Memphis and later unity of Memphis with Thebes. Also see Wilson's translation of "*The Contest of Horus and Seth for the Rule,*" *in Ancient Near Eastern Texts Relating to the Old Testament*, 3rd ed. (Princeton University Press, 1992), 14-17.

the kings of Egypt, like many in Babylonia, had their birth names and their Horus-inspired throne names.[2] Because of this divine status, the Pharaohs were deeply involved in the religious rituals of their land and it was not an unexpected thing for a Pharaoh to give a decree with the expectation of immediate adherence since they alone stood between the realms of human and divine (Exod. 1:22).[3] Additionally, the legal material from ancient Egypt is sparse, likely due to the fact that the Pharaoh's word was ultimate and considered to be a divine edict carried from dreams.[4]

This identification of Pharaoh's status as a god brings clarity to Exodus 7:1, when the Lord informs Moses, "See, I have made thee a god to Pharaoh…!" What will occur in the texts proceeding is not simply a dispute of judgment against the gods of Egypt; it is also a direct confrontation against who the people perceived Pharaoh to be, a god.[5] Moreover, the text of the Memphite Theology offers an important point for us to consider before moving into Scripture:

> The Great Seat, which *rejoices* the heart of the gods, which is in the House of Ptah, *the mistress of all life*, is the Granary of the God, through which the sustenance of the Two Lands is prepared, because of the fact that Osiris drowned in his water, while Isis and Nephthys watched. They saw him and they *were distressed* at him. Horus commanded Isis and Nephthys *repeatedly* that they lay hold on Osiris and prevent his drowning. (63) They turned (their) heads in time. So they brought him to land.[6]

---

2. See my essay on Genesis in this volume, and the related comments on the "theophoric" names of kings.

3. For a general description of the development and denigration of the Pharaoh's see Joshua J. Mark, "*Pharaoh*," World History Encyclopedia, October 3, 2022, https://www.worldhistory.org/pharaoh/. Interestingly, it is quite possible that Pharaoh's charge to kill the male newborns could be perceived as an offering to himself. I postulate this consideration given the later text of Moses and Aaron finding Pharaoh at the water's edge (Exod. 7:15-25), reflecting on Horus's call to rescue Osiris from drowning (see footnote 1).

4. G. Herbert Livingston, *The Pentateuch in Its Cultural Environment* (Grand Rapids: Baker Book House, 1987), 121-125, 173-179.

5. Gary Rendsburg, "*Moses as Pharaoh's Equal-Horns and All*," Biblical Archaeology Society, September 20, 2023, https://www.biblicalarchaeology.org/daily/people-cultures-in-the-bible/people-in-the-bible/moses-as-pharaohs-equal/. I must note, that my focus here compliments rather than contrasts with the essay addressing the judgment against the gods included in this volume.

6. Wilson, *Memphis*, 5.

For the Egyptians of this period, there was a relationship between kingship and prosperity. Further, it must be highlighted that if the god of granary suffered, it was quite likely that their crops would also be in danger. As was common in the ancient Near East, ritual and sacrifice were often connected with garnering divine favor, and the Egyptians were not entirely different in this regard, though distinctives exist. Magic, therefore, was a way for humans to engage with the divine realm. While the realm of magic remained separate, it could be characterized as having an influence on what occurred there through the use of mediums like talismans, idols, and amulets.[7]

PROVISION AND POWER

The time of the children of Israel in Egypt is not excluded from the texts of Genesis that I began our exploration with, although those texts frame what comes after. It is just as crucial that I highlight the tension experienced in Joseph's statement and what was experienced by his descendants. Notably, the Pharaoh following Joseph's death increased the burdens and affliction of the children of Israel (Exod. 1:11). This growing family would not cry out to God until that Pharaoh's death (Exod. 1:12, 2:23), which prompts God to return to His covenant with the patriarchs and visit Moses in Horeb (Exod. 3:1-9). Here, the question posed in my introduction finds its way to the surface, before the children of Israel can trust that what Pharaoh intended for evil, God thought for good, can Moses? Moses, having been drawn from a water initially intended to be his death and rejected by his kinsmen, now faces the LORD and questions:

> ויאמר משה אל־האלהים מי אנכי כי אלך אל־פרעה וכי אוציא את־בני ישראל ממצרִים:
> And Moses said to God, "Who am I that I will be going to Pharaoh, and that I should cause the children of Israel to come out from Egypt?" (Exod. 3:11).[8]

For Moses, it does not appear that he wrestled with an issue of deity; it does, however, appear that he felt insignificant in the eyes of his kinsmen. Amid this, the LORD would reveal His name to him (Exod. 3:14, 6:2-3) with the promise of fulfillment in a way unrealized by previous generations; the covenant-creator

---

7. See Livingston, *Pentateuch*, 168-183.

8. On the general conditional nature of this clause, see Victor P. Hamilton, *Exodus: An Exegetical Commentary* (Baker Book House, 2023), Exod. 3:11.

God who will deliver and establish His people.[9] This deliverance was not coaxed by the magic or rituals of the Egyptians that held the descendants of Joseph captive but was initiated by their sorrow and tears (Exod. 2:23-25). The LORD, Who could hear the calling of those before (Gen. 4:25-26), would now place His name on a people that He would deliver and call His own.[10] Incredibly, God not only kept His word to the patriarchs but also fulfilled His word to Moses and stood undefeated by the gods of Egypt (Exod. 12:12).

CONCLUSION

The LORD, unlike the gods of Egypt, could not be coaxed with magic, ritual, or sacrifice. Where the first Pharaoh called for the firstborn to be thrown into the river, the LORD allowed for Moses to be drawn out and the first plague to occur in the river as Moses met a Pharaoh at the bank; a Pharaoh who was determined not to be coaxed by the LORD's words (Exod. 7:14-25). Additionally, as David Dorsey has drawn attention to, Pharaoh would see the downfall of Egypt's might, as the firstborn males of his people would fall in the final plague and his army beside him in the Red Sea (Exod. 11:1-10, 14:27-31).[11] Certainly, what the first Pharaoh who perceived himself to be a god thought for evil when he commanded the extermination of the firstborn of Israel, the LORD, the true God, thought for good and would use waters to separate a people to place His name upon them; ushering them into a future He had covenanted with their ancestors to bring to pass.

---

9. Hamilton, *Exodus*, Exod. 6:2-4. Also see my previous essay.

10. See my previous essay in this book, "*The Name of our Divine King.*"

11. David A. Dorsey, *The Literary Structure of The Old Testament: A Commentary on Genesis-Malachi* (Grand Rapids, MI: Baker Academic, 2004), 66-67.

WEEK THREE

The Davidic Covenant—Kingship, Sonship, and the Promise Forever

7

The Davidic Covenant—Background and Implications

Steven Gill

Any considerations toward the Davidic Covenant presented in the Old Testament should, perhaps, begin with an examination of the king for whom the covenant is named. The David of the books of Samuel, Kings, and Chronicles has arrested the attention of Jewish and Christian scholars for centuries. Nevertheless, through the advent of biblical historical criticism (particularly in the twentieth century) it has become increasingly popular for readers to be skeptical of the reality of the David of the Bible. Did he exist? Was his kingdom a reality of the late eleventh and early tenth centuries BC, or is his life a fable of the Hasmonean era? How one answers these questions will greatly inform their understanding of later developments, particularly with regard to the New Testament and the Davidic Covenant on which the coming of the Messiah hangs.[1]

As many trends within the discipline of criticism, objections to the reality of David and his kingdom appear at last to be fading, however slowly, from the pages of academia. While certain scholars continue to raise objections to the historical veracity of the books of Samuel, Kings, and Chronicles, especially with regard to David and his life, these objections often represent an older body of scholarship that appears to be falling out of favor with many thinkers. Even

1. This covenant is born out in passages such as Second Samuel 23:5 and Second Chronicles 21:7, and it is coupled with Messianic prophecy in Zechariah 12:10 by many Christian scholars. In the New Testament, these connections become more pronounced with the words of John in the book of Revelation: "I Jesus have sent mine angel to testify unto you these things in the churches. I am the root and the offspring of David, and the bright and morning star" (22:16 KJV).

recent scholars who continue to voice certain objections, such as perceived discrepancies concerning when David first met Saul, rest their arguments on more on theological grounds than historical.[2] As Philip Satterhwaite says in his entry on the subject:

> Until recently it was widely held that the books of Samuel are composite, fashioned from different sources that can be at least partially reconstructed today...Many still hold these views, but others argue that the different sections of 1-2 Samuel are better integrated with each other than such views would imply. Even the common argument that 1 Samuel contains two accounts of how Saul first came to meet David (1 Sam 16:18-23; 17:12. 55-58) has been questioned...[3].

While quaint to some, these discussions are not meaningless. What one believes about the historicity of David and his reign will have a significant impact on how one receives the surrounding biblical materials concerning his covenant with God, his descendants, and Israel's standing among the nations. Interestingly, as archaeological evidence for the existence of the house of David becomes more pronounced, the tendency of many historical critics appears to be one of moving the goalposts concerning what constitutes evidence, rather than showing deference to the evidence itself. For more than a century after its discovery, critical scholars hung their hat on the claim that the popular Mesha inscription proved inconclusive evidence for the existence of King David.[4]

---

2. John Barton, *A History of the Bible*, (Allen Lane; Viking, 2019), 51. Here, Barton states, "...other narrative books also show signs of having been compiled from earlier materials, with inconsistent versions of the same story. How, for example, did David come to know King Saul? In I Samuel 16 he is introduced to Saul as a lyre-player, but in I Samuel 17, when he kills Goliath, it is clear that Saul has not met him before." Of course, many readers of the Bible will quickly note that it is *not* clear from reading First Samuel 17 that Saul had never met David before. First Samuel 17:15 acknowledges that David had indeed already been in the presence of Saul as chapter sixteen states, but he departed from Saul's presence at some point before the battle in the valley of Elah, later to return. Therefore, Saul's question, "Whose son is this youth?" to which Barton no doubt refers, is not a discrepancy, but a feature for readers to work out. The alternative – that chapter seventeen of First Samuel was written in two pieces by two authors unfamiliar with each other's work and glued together in obvious error – appears absurd.

3. Philip Satterhwaite, "David," in *Dictionary of the Old Testament Historical Books*, ed. Bill T. Arnold, H.G.M. Williamson (IVP Academic, 2005), 199.

4. The inscription borne on what is popularly known as the Mesha Stele was long believed to have mentioned king David, but many critics remained skeptical of the inscription due to

Nevertheless, in 2024, with the help of modern technology, a team of scholars led by Professor Michael Langlois were able to approach the stone with new eyes, confirming with a reasonable amount of certainty that the ninth-century BC stone now stands as strong evidence for the historical David.[5] When the Tel Dan Stele was discovered in 1993, reasonable scholars across the globe were stunned to realize that there existed yet another (and clearer) inscription bearing the name of King David, also from the ninth century BC.[6] Nevertheless, many critical examiners march on in their skepticism, despite the growing archeological evidence that seems to testify against them.

David's life and reign are crucial aspects of Christian doctrine because they greatly inform the biblical portrait of who the Messiah is. In the New Testament, Jesus is depicted as the legitimate descendant (and, therefore, heir) of the House of David.[7] With no literal King David to point to, the kingship of Jesus Christ becomes largely metaphorical and open to a great deal of interpretation. By contrast, those who readily accept the literal kingship of David see Christ through different eyes. If Jesus is the literal descendant of David, that makes Him the proper heir to the kingdom and the man on whom God's

---

its fragmentation and deterioration. Nevertheless, the advent of modern technology has helped decipher the stone, leading many scholars to the conclusion that the stone does, indeed, refer to the famous king of united Israel.

5. Armstrong Institute Staff, "Mesha Stele: The Second 'House of David Inscription'." Armstrong Institute of Biblical Archaeology. Last modified April 22, 2024. https://armstronginstitute.org/1051-mesha-stele-the-second-house-of-david-inscription. The stele was discovered in 1868. Known also as the "Moabite Stone," the Mesha Stele remains one of the most significant discoveries in biblical archeology to date. The stone was created by king Mesha of Moab who is mentioned in the book of Second Kings, and its inscriptions confirm the existence of other Old Testament figures such as Omri.

6. The BAS Staff, "The Tel Dan Inscription: The First Historical Evidence of King David from the Bible." Biblical Archaeological Society. Last modified June, 2024. Accessed April 16, 2025. https://www.biblicalarchaeology.org/daily/biblical-artifacts/the-tel-dan-inscription-the-first-historical-evidence-of-the-king-david-bible-story/. The inscription on the Stele describes an Aramean king celebrating his victory over one of the kings of Israel and the "king of the House of David." The fact that the stone refers to David's rule in dynastic terms signals the veracity of the Biblical account – that the kings of Judah (as opposed to Israel) were known descendants of David. The divided kingdom of the biblical narratives is also consistent with the record of other nations. Furthermore, the fact that the stele is a construction of an enemy kingdom as opposed to a memorial of Judah reveals the notoriety of David and his descendants among the surrounding nations.

7. Matt. 1:1-17. In Matthew's ancestry of Christ, readers are made to understand that the lineage of the House of David remained significant, both in the mind of God and in the heart of believers. David's place in Jesus' ancestry is pointed out again in Luke 1:27.

promise to David hangs (2 Sam. 7:16). Because of this, claims that the covenant between God and David was dissolved after the destruction of the kingdom of Judah become complicated.[8] If the challenge for critics of the historical David is to square their skepticism with archaeology, opposers of the eternal Davidic covenant are in no less dire straits; what is to be made of Jesus in the Gospels (to say nothing of Revelation) if the Davidic covenant was dissolved? Those inclined toward replacement theologies may find ways to reframe the subject using a sort of allegory, but the Bible in plain language signals an eternal, not conditional, covenant between God and His servant David. In the book of Second Samuel, when David desired to 'build a house for the LORD,' God responded to David's request by insisting that it would not be David but his son who would build such a house for the LORD to dwell in. In the concluding portions of the passage, the Bible says that God spoke to David and said,

> And thine house and thy kingdom shall be established for ever before thee: thy throne shall be established for ever.[9]

Prophecies attributed to the coming of Christ by the New Testament writers reveal the early church's belief that in Jesus of Nazareth, Israel had received its rightful Davidic heir. In the book of Luke, the writer signals the importance of Christ's association with David by emphasizing His birth in Bethlehem, the city of David.[10] As promised to David, Christ's kingdom is portrayed as an everlasting kingdom.[11] Concerning theological implications, there is probably some irony to the fact that, while many Jews of the first century denied that Jesus was the Christ on account of the fact that He had not yet restored the

---

8. J.J. Roberts, "Davidic Covenant," in *Dictionary of the Old Testament Historical Books*, ed. Bill T. Arnold, H.G.M. Williamson (IVP Academic, 2005), 208-209. Roberts discusses this possibility of conditionality in light of perceived uncertainties regarding the veracity of the covenant between God and David as it is depicted in the book of Second Samuel. Critics base their opposition largely on the belief that a later Deuteronomistic editor reframed or altered the covenant between God and David for later readers.

9. 2 Samuel 7:16 (KJV).

10. Luke 2:11. In the book of First Samuel, readers learn that Bethlehem is the hometown of king David. The narrative in Luke is to be compared with prophecies attending the coming of the Messiah in the prophets (Micah 5:2): "But thou, Bethlehem Ephratah, though thou be little among the thousands of Judah, yet out of thee shall he come forth unto me that is to be ruler in Israel; whose goings forth have been from of old, from everlasting."

11. Luke 1:30-33. Once again, this passage bears out the New Testament's emphasis on Jesus as the true heir of David and the literal Messiah on whom Israel awaited.

literal kingdom of Israel, there are many Christians in the world today who do not believe that Jesus will do so either.[12] Thus, the unbelieving Jews and certain Christians have something in common – a denial that Jesus will ever reign over the twelve tribes. These Christian beliefs are largely rooted in amillennialism or an ecclesiology of replacement[13] – the belief that the church of the New Testament has replaced natural Israel as God's chosen people.[14] Nevertheless, from the gospels and epistles alike, the fact remains apparent: Just as many Jews today continue to wait on the coming of their Messiah who will rule over them in a new kingdom, so, too, do many Christians await His return when He will reign in the earth, taking His rightful place as David's heir in Jerusalem.

---

12. Even the disciples of Jesus appear to have been confused about the matter. In Acts 1:6-7, the writer points out the disciples' own curiosity about when Jesus would restore the literal kingdom of Israel. Jesus did not dismiss their question as wrong-headed or doctrinally unsound – rather, He insisted that it was not for them to know when these things would be. Of course, His statement seems to imply that one day these things will indeed come to pass.

13. Replacement theology is a curious aspect of Christian doctrine that can be traced back to the New Testament itself. While many of the post-Apostolic and early apologist writers were advocates of the belief that the church had replaced the Jews as God's chosen people, the Apostle Paul shared no such view. In fact, the entirety of Romans eleventh chapter may be characterized as a caution against such beliefs. For early post-Apostolic, apologist, ante-Nicene and post-Nicene writings endorsing replacement theology, see:

Ignatius, *Epistle to the Magnesians* (CA 106-109).

Tertullian, *Against the Jews* (CA 197-220).

Eusebius, *The Life Of The Blessed Emperor Constantine, book III, ch. XVIII.* (CA 339).

14. Amillennialism – a theological view that denies there will be a literal millennial reign of Christ – appears to have gained some ground in Christian thought over the last century. Nevertheless, it is apparent that the New Testament writers presented the eventual reign of Christ as something literal. In this way, the writings of the New Testament are cohesive with Old Testament portraits of the restoration of the twelve tribes, particularly in Ezekiel chapter forty-eight.

8

The Davidic Covenant and the Sonship of Jesus

Andrew Herbst

INTRODUCTION

The events of 2 Samuel 7 unfold as David "sat in his house," free from warfare because God had given the king rest from his enemies (2 Sam. 7:1).[1] Consequently, David thought it right to build a house for God to dwell in, but the Lord rejected this desire. God was pleased with David's heart, but the Lord did not permit David to build His house. Instead, God gave David promises that would impact the future of the Kingdom of Israel and all of humanity. These promises are labeled as the Davidic Covenant.

COVENANTS

A covenant, in a Biblical and historical sense, is a relationship between two parties with legally binding agreements. Famous covenants from Scripture include God's covenant with Abraham (Gen. 12-17) and the Mosaic Covenant given at Mount Sinai (Exod. 19-20). Covenant relationships often included blessings for obedience and curses for disobedience. However, the Davidic Covenant was different, due to the emphasis placed on God's faithfulness to David and not upon the nation's compliance.

THE DAVIDIC COVENANT

The covenant promises God made to David are, 1) that David would have a son and that he would become the next king. This kingly line is important because God was promising David a royal house or dynasty. Saul was not given

1. Unless otherwise noted, all biblical passages referenced are in the *King James Version*.

this type of promise, but David was given a guarantee that his lineage would rule. 2) David's son would build the house for God's Name. This temple would ultimately fulfill Deuteronomy 12:5-6. 3) David's son would rule forever. Up to this point, no king in Israel had had a son to rule all Israel, much less rule forever. 4) God told David that his kingly son would not merely be the Son of David but that he would also be God's Son. According to Ronald Youngblood, the Davidic Covenant receives so much attention in the Old Testament (OT) that it is second in importance only to the covenant at Sinai, and that the covenant was the source of Messianic hope for OT prophets and psalms.[2]

David's son, Solomon, fulfilled a few aspects of the Davidic Covenant, but ultimately fell short. His sin and death carried on the hope of covenant fulfillment to the next generation. This transpired from king to king, father to son, all the way to the day of Jesus.

Gerhard von Rad explains that it was at the coronations of the kings from David's line that the Son of David entered "into a filial relationship" with God.[3] This is not to be viewed in a mythological sense, in comparison to the Egyptian pharaohs, but von Rad states that Israel understood "it in the sense of an historical legal act," as the "king was summoned" into a special covenant relationship with the Lord.[4] Meaning, as the Son of David was anointed as the king, he would then also be called the Son of God.

Due to the failures of David's sons and apparent destruction of the kingdom (cf. 2 Kings 25), Arnold A. Anderson explains that it was understood that God's promises to David "still retained its relevance for future generations."[5] Anderson states that Jews remained "confident that Yahweh would fulfill his promises," either in a current Davidic descendant, like Zerubbabel, or "in a future messianic figure."[6] Psalmists and prophets will look back to 2 Samuel 7 and the Davidic Covenant and then look forward in prophecy to the one who would fulfill the promises made to David (cf. Ps. 89).

---

2. Ronald Youngblood, *The Expositors Bible Commentary: 2 Samuel*, Frank E. Gaebelein ed., (Grand Rapids, MI: Zondervan Publishing House, 1992), 881.

3. Gerhard von Rad, *Old Testament Theology: Volume 1*, trans. by D. M. G. Stalker, (New York, NY: Harper and Row Publishers, 1962), 320.

4. von Rad, *Old Testament Theology: Volume 1*, 320.

5. Arnold A. Anderson, *Word Biblical Commentary: 2 Samuel, Volume 11*, (Grand Rapids, MI: HarperCollins Christian Publishing, 2000), accessed March 5, 2022, ProQuest Ebook Central. https://ebookcentral-proquest-com.ezproxy.liberty.edu/lib/liberty/detail.action?docID=5607921, 123.

6. Anderson, *2 Samuel*, 123.

OT PASSAGES REGARDING THE DAVIDIC COVENANT

Psalm 2 depicts a time when earthly kings will rebel against God and "His anointed" (Ps. 2:2). The "anointed one" comes from the terms *messiah* (Hebrew) and *christ* (Greek) and is connected to the Son of David and the kingly covenant. Psalm 2 continues with God speaking of His anointed, "Yet have I set my king upon my holy hill of Zion. I will declare the decree: the LORD hath said unto me, Thou art my Son; this day have I begotten thee" (Ps. 2:6-7). Therefore, it is evident that when the Son of David becomes king, he is also called the Son of God. Gilsun Ryu sees the Messiah as an exalted king, exalted to the extent that his "authority is considered to be divine."[7] This is due to the ruler receiving his power and kingship from God, who has "anointed, exalted, and installed him as king."[8] By the end of the chapter, the king is ruling the entire world, and all are submitted to His kingship.

Isaiah 11 is another passage that reveals the anointing, dominion, and accomplishments of the Davidic king. Both Psalm 2 and Isaiah 11 speak of the King being anointed by God; thus, the King would be empowered by God to rule: He was God's King for God's Kingdom. Isaiah 11 presents the future accomplishments of the Messiah's reign as a return to conditions that are reminiscent of the Garden of Eden. The King will defeat God's enemies (Isa. 11:4, cf. Ps. 2:8-9, Rev. 19:15), humanity will be at peace and harmony with nature (Isa. 11:6-8), and the entire "earth shall be full of the knowledge of the LORD" (Isa. 11:9). Furthermore, Gentiles will be invited into the kingdom as citizens (Isa. 11:10). The outcome of the work and dominion of the Messiah will truly be glorious and will return humanity back to the peace they had before the Fall of Adam.

Ezekiel 36-37 are also significant Messianic passages. While these two chapters are well-known for their prophecies regarding Pentecost, Ezekiel 37 states that God will reunite the split kingdoms of Israel and Judah (Ezek. 37:22), and that David would rule a united Israel again (Ezek. 37:24-25). Of course, the restoration of David's throne and kingdom is a reference to the Davidic Covenant.

---

7. Gilsun Ryu, "Messianism and Kingship in the Gospel of John: A Comparison Between the Fourth Gospel and the Royal Psalms 2, 72, and 110," *Journal of Religious & Theological Information*, 16:4, (2017), 125-140, DOI: 10.1080/10477845.2017.1317187, 127.

8. Ryu, *Messianism*, 128.

JESUS AND HIS DAVIDIC OFFICE

The Davidic Covenant answers why Jesus is called the Son of David and the Son of God. Jesus is the Son of David by blood, and the declared the Son of God by covenant anointing and power (Rom. 1:3-4). The phrases Son of David and Son of God strike at the heart of Biblical theology: the kingship of Jesus (cf. Isa. 9:6-7). Messiah, Christ, Son of David, and Son of God are all kingly phrases and are all connected to the Davidic Covenant (cf. Matt. 16:16, Mark 1:1, Luke 4:41, John 1:49, and John 20:31).

In the New Testament (NT) era, the Christ was to come and destroy God's enemies and re-establish David's kingdom, which would usher in a new age, as numerous OT texts prophesied. Jesus was announced as the anointed king at His baptism (see the author's Isaiah paper in the Prophet's Chapter). Further evidence of the beginning of Jesus' kingship can be observed in Matthew 11. While in prison, John the Baptist desired to confirm if Jesus was the Christ, and Jesus responded by quoting Isaiah. The prophet wrote throughout the Book that God would one day act to save and reconcile His people. Isaiah wrote that there would be proof of God's arrival and salvation (Isa. 35:4), and the evidence would show that the direct effects of the Fall were being undone and reversed. Specifically, the dead would be raised (Isa. 25:7-8), and the blind, deaf, lame, and dumb would all be healed (Isa. 35:5-6).[9] Jesus referenced the OT prophet to show that God had indeed arrived with salvation, and further revealed that the Christ was building God's kingdom and reversing the effects of sin and death.

Along these same lines, Blind Bartimaeus realized Jesus' identity as the kingdom builder and the one to bring restoration, so he cried out, "Jesus, *thou* Son of David, have mercy on me" (Mark 10:47). The Son of David, Bartimaeus understood, could heal blind eyes because He was the anointed King. This may be why Bartimaeus cast away his garment, because his faith was not tied to a guess or merely blind faith, but his faith was in the identity of who Jesus was. Jesus honored the blind man's faith and restored his sight (Mark 10:52).

CONCLUSION

Jesus has numerous titles described in Scripture, such as Son of Man, High

---

9. See D. A. Carson, *The Expositors Bible Commentary: Matthew*, ed. by Frank E. Gaebelein, (Grand Rapids, MI: Zondervan Publishing House, 1992), 262.

Priest, Suffering Servant, Messiah/Christ, Son of God, and more. Sometimes Christians use these terms as though they are interchangeable, but that is a mistake. Although Jesus fulfilled each of these offices or positions, and there is some unity between particular terms, many of Jesus' titles hold a specific and special meaning. The terms highlighted in this paper, Son of David, Son of God, and Christ/Messiah, have emphasized Jesus' kingship. Many OT prophecies regarding God's King were fulfilled at Christ's first coming, but there are still elements that must be fulfilled at His second coming. The King's return and the complete establishment of His kingdom are what the Church should be eagerly awaiting and preparing for.

9

Who is Rejected—
Was Kingship in Israel Against God's Will?

Jeremias D. Zuniga

INTRODUCTION

The question of kingship finds a prominent point of dispute amongst many Bible readers when they encounter the statement "Now, set to us a king to judge us like all of the nations" (1 Samuel 8:5b). Notably, it is this phrase that distinguishes a transition in Israel's history, especially as it follows Samuel's establishment of his sons as judges.[1] However, this transitional statement can be missed, specifically when 1 Samuel is read without the books of Exodus, Numbers, Deuteronomy, and Judges. Perhaps it initially seems like a bit much for me to state that in order to read 1 Samuel well, one must first wrestle with Israel's history in those four preceding books. However, I want to contend two things in this essay: First, that it was God's plan to provide Israel with a king. Second, that Israel errored in asking for the wrong kind of king. These two points I aim to demonstrate on the foundation of those four books, and it will be necessary that my reader refers to the essay included in this book on the Davidic Covenant, as I will argue here in tandem with Andrew Herbst's work there for the congruency of God's plan from Exodus to 1 Samuel.

ANTICIPATING A KING

It is no accident that 1 Samuel centers its introduction of the elders' petition to Samuel for a king around the failures of Joel and Abiah, the sons of Samuel who had recently been established as judges (1 Sam. 8:1-5). This designation is crucial when we consider the development from Exodus 18 and Numbers

1. Hans Wilhelm Hertzberg, *I & II Samuel, a Commentary*. Translated by J.S. Bowden (Philadelphia: Westminster Press, 1964), 71.

11:16-30, texts describing the appointment of elders to assist Moses in judging the growing tribes. The latter text informs us that Moses was distressed because of the complaints of the masses that he was burdened with, and pleads with God for a way forward (Exod. 18; Num. 11:10-15).[2] Gods answer is that the burden will be shared with the elders, though Moses' role as leader is not threatened by the prophesying elders (Num. 11:28-30). Further, in the retelling of the law, Israel is instructed to establish "שפטים ושטרים" or "Judges and Officers," who should be set in the gates of each tribe and were responsible for judging (Deut. 16:18). Three times the negative adverb לא (pronounced "low") is used to instruct the judges in the very next verse, an adverb that may be translated "Thou shalt not."[3] That adverb in certain legal texts carries the weight of "Never do this" (see Deut. 16:19), and those three prohibitions prohibit twisting judgment, showing favoritism, and accepting bribes. The prohibitions show that judgment should be carried out justly and through righteousness.

As Israel approaches the promise land, God prepares them to establish a government that will honor His law and protect the people from injustice. That is why Deuteronomy 17:9 looks to the time of the judges saying, "And to the Judges that will be in those days" and even more the LORD gives direction on establishing a king (Deut. 17:14-20). In these texts, the negative adverb is used 5 times to reference the king, three of which are informing the people of things the king should never do: amass horses (turning the people to Egypt), amass wives (turning his heart away from), and amass gold and silver for himself (Deut. 17:16-17). There are, of course, positive directions that are greater than the requirements given: when the coming king takes the throne, it will be his responsibility to make a copy of the law, and he must read from that copy until he passes (Deut. 17:18-20).[4] The above evidence, coupled with the covenant

2. That way forward in Moses' request is death, as though he had not received the direction from his father-in-law to appoint elders in Exodus 18.

3. Paul Joüon and T. Muraoka, *A Grammar of Biblical Hebrew*, Second (Roma: Pontificio istituto biblico, Gregorian & Biblical Press, 2011), §102J pg 306-307 & §160a-q 567-573. For the reader, Muraoka's translation and work with Joüon's previous grammar is technical and perhaps between an intermediate and advanced level of understanding Biblical Hebrew. For a more accessible beginner level see Gary Davis Pratico and Miles V. Van Pelt, *Basics of Biblical Hebrew: Grammar*, Third (Grand Rapids, MI: Zondervan, 2019), §15.8 & §15.9.5 pgs 160-161. It must be stated that "Lo" does not always offer absolute prohibition, although it is usually the case when appearing in a verbal clause with an imperfect verb.

4. Jeffrey H. Tigay, Deuteronomy = דברים: The Traditional Hebrew Text with the New

made with Abraham in Genesis 17:6b, "And kings will be coming out of you," shows that God not only expected His people to ask for a king (Deut. 17:14), but planned to make His people kingly themselves and to establish a king who would reign over them.

USURPING GOD'S TIMING

Considering the expectation of a coming king and the days of the judges, I want to move our attention beyond the Pentateuch toward the books of Judges, Ruth, and Samuel. I began this essay by highlighting the focus in Samuel on the disastrous lives of the two newly appointed judges, Joel and Abiah. I want you to note at this stage that Israel was supposed to have these judges as ruling governors in each tribe, and a central Mosaic-like leader to oversee the weightiest matters and ensure that the judges maintained the purity of the law. The sad account of Judges 17-21 shows that this system was failing, the largest contribution appears to us in these words:

> בימים ההם אין מלך בישראל איש הישר בעיניו יעשה
> In those days, there was not a king in Israel, a man could be doing what was right in his own eyes (Judges 17:6; 21:25).

We are informed by the Biblical author that Israel lacked national direction based in the law and when we read from Samuel, their priests were also not regularly hearing from God (1 Samuel 3:1). The instruction of the LORD was rare and God would call the young man to step into a role that had been neglected prior to his ministry, and that role leads us directly into our opening text, 1 Samuel 8:1-5.[5] As shown above, a king was anticipated throughout the promise of God to Abraham and the word spoken through Moses. When Moses and his successor Joshua ceased ruling, the days of the judges emerged without oversight, and Samuel would bring back the word of the LORD. When his sons failed to maintain his adherence to the law, the elders stood together to bring a centralized leadership back, while neglecting the requirements for that leader.

To this end, the issue was not that they asked for a king, but that their ask

JPS Translation (Philadelphia: Jewish Publication Society, 1996), 166-169. Tigay is helpful in showing that the LORD commanded for a king quite unlike the unchecked power hungry kings readily found in Mesopotamia.

5. Hertzberg, *I & II Samuel*, 41-44.

included the request to have a king "to judge us like all the nations" (1 Sam. 8:5b; Deut. 17:14b) without the protective and instructive prohibitions of the LORD's servant (Deut. 17:15-20). It is because of this that those elders did not reject Samuel; they rejected what he brought with him: God's word. It is no curious thing that God promised to Abraham and through Moses a king, but what should stand out to the reader is that the people ceased hearing from Him due to their pursuit of other gods. This point should stand out because once they receive the prophet Samuel, they are content, until he appoints the wrong judges, his sons. Instead of returning to the failure of the judges, they ask for a new system entirely, a king without the checks and balances that the law had specified. It should not be assumed from these texts that it was a prohibition from God for them to have a king, but a prohibition from God that they should have an earthly king who would not regard the laws that He had established for His people.[6]

CONCLUSION

What we learn from these texts is that the elders understood in part that a king was necessary; perhaps they even understood that it was a promise from God to His people. The issue is that they committed the dangerous crime of wresting a single clause without the protective elements from Scripture. I want to remind my reader that it is a dangerous thing to consider only a part of what God has promised and required of His people, pressing for progress and new methods, claiming these progressive efforts and innovations as emerging from Scripture, while only partially quoting the Bible to fit and further a very human agenda. It is this sin that was first committed by the questioning serpent who sought to upend God's rule over the first couple in the garden when he challenged the law of the King of the universe when he interrogated Eve, "And he said to the woman, 'Indeed, because God said you all should not be eating from every tree of the garden..."

6. The most helpful commentary on this subject that does not include the technical and often theoretical language some scholars have introduced is found in Victor P. Hamilton, *Handbook on the Historical Books: Joshua, Judges, Ruth, Samuel, Kings, Chronicles, Ezra-Nehemiah, Esther* (Grand Rapids, Mich: Baker Academic, 2008), 229-231.

WEEK FOUR

The Prophets and the Promise of the King

10

God's Kingship in the Prophets—Future Tense

Steven Gill

Despite long-standing disagreements between Jews and Christians over the matter, the disclosure of God's kingship throughout the books of the prophets cannot be easily separated from discussions surrounding the Davidic Messiah.[1] While for many Christian readers, the two bear natural harmony with one another, orthodox Jewish attitudes toward messianic promise and fulfillment are often presented in contrast to the Christian view.[2] The tension between these competing conceptions lies principally in disagreement over the nature of the Messiah, His purpose in the earth, and the fulfillment of the things that have been written about Him. Nevertheless, while many Jews await an earthly

1. Joseph Telushkin, *Jewish Literacy: The Most Important Things to Know About the Jewish Religion, Its People, and Its History*, (Willam Morrow and Co., 1991), 545-546. The impression readers may draw from Telushkin's work is that orthodox Jewish resistance to Jesus-as-Messiah has not significantly fluctuated in two thousand years. First-century unbelieving Jews were hesitant to accept that Jesus of Nazareth was the Messiah on the grounds that He had not yet restored the kingdom of Israel or ushered in a reign of peace (Ezekiel ch.48; Acts 1:6). For Christians, this objection is largely rooted in a misunderstanding of the full purpose of Christ. While many Christians believe that Jesus will indeed return to the earth to restore Israel and usher in an age of peace, they also acknowledge the purpose of His life as detailed in the New Testament was to pay the penalty for sin, granting access to Jew and Gentile alike to participate in the story of redemption.

2. David G. Firth, "Messiah," in *Dictionary of the Old Testament Prophets*, ed. Mark J. Boda, J. Gordon McConville (IVP Academic, 2012), 542. In this essay, Firth emphasizes the relationship between Yahweh's direct rule over His people and the promises detailed in the Davidic covenant. In the mind of the writer, the two cannot be separated. Thus, the tension between traditional Jewish interpretations of messianic promises (i.e., a literal king who will reign over literal Israel) and Christian views about the Christ (He is the Savior of both Jew and Gentile, Yahweh with us, and a spiritual redeemer) is, perhaps, unjustified; from the perspective of the prophets, the Messiah would be both.

king and many Christians boast a spiritual Savior, the books of the prophets make the subject less tidy for both parties. As Firth writes,

> A crucial element in the messianic understanding of the prophets focused on the continuation of the reign of David, and in particular on a representative of David's family who would provide a reign consistent with Yahweh's promise to David. Such a king's reign would be truly consistent with Yahweh's reign… As the prophets reflect on this theme, they stress that Yahweh is the one who brings restoration to and through Davidic kingship. Yahweh remains as the nation's savior, but the future king is integral to his purposes.[3]

While Firth is correct in his assertion that the books of the prophets preserve Yahweh's place as the Savior of Israel, readers should be cautious not to presume God's role to be merely titular. Far from being a distant arbiter who sends another to be His emissary in the earth, Yahweh's connection to the promised Messiah is intertwined with His own self-disclosure. On this issue hangs much of the Jewish/Christian debate concerning Jesus as the Christ of God.

In the book of Isaiah, the Messiah to come is called, "…Wonderful, Counsellor, The mighty God, The everlasting Father, The Prince of Peace."[4] The promise of His kingdom is eternal, and His reign is also without end (Isa. 9:7). Some scholars are quick to note that many of the honorifics attributed to the son-to-be in the book of Isaiah were common to the Ancient Near East, therefore too much should not be made of them; but this perspective misses the forest through the trees.[5] It is not the honorifics alone that reveal the uniqueness

---

3. Firth, 539-540.

4. Isa. 9:6 (KJV). While there remains dispute among scholars as to which son, precisely, is referred to in Isaiah's ninth chapter, it appears evident that suppositions about the prophecy relating to Isaiah's son are complicated by further reading: "Of the increase of his government and peace there shall be no end, upon the throne of David, and upon his kingdom, to order it, and to establish it with judgement and with justice from henceforth even forever. The zeal of the LORD of hosts will perform this" (Isa. 9:7 KJV). It is difficult to imagine a king of Israel in the days of Isaiah (or after) that this prophecy could have referred to, as no king established a never-ending government or peace in the land of Israel, nor was judgement and justice established forever. Living and writing long before Israel's first exile, these words do not appear applicable to Isaiah or his son.

5. Robert Chisholm Jr., *Handbook on the Prophets*, (Baker Academic, 2002), 39. Here, Chisholm presents the 'titles common to the ANE argument' and makes much of the claim that the subject of Isaiah 9:6 is obscure, juxtaposed to traditional Christian readings of the text which assume the passage to be about Jesus Christ. He highlights the notion that the honorific

of the kingship of this Messiah, but the unqualified nature of their attribution. In the prophets, no suggestion is made that the coming king is on contractual grounds with God, or that His reign may be interrupted by His own sinful behavior or that of His descendants, as other kings of the Bible had in the past.[6] In fact, there is no talk of this King's descendants at all, much less the possibility of His ruin. Instead, it is assumed as a state of fact that He will in every way reign as Yahweh Himself does. As Yahweh's perfect vessel, the Messiah who will come out of David cannot but execute right and perfect judgment; as Yahweh's arm in the earth, He cannot but reign forever.[7] It is for this reason that the attributes of Isaiah 9:6-7 are considered by many Christian readers to be something qualitatively different from what was familiar to the Ancient Near East. Much more could also be made of the nature of this Messiah's relationship to Israel and the rest of the world. Far from being a king over one nation or region, this King is presented as the sovereign over all the peoples of the world. Both Isaiah and Ezekiel speak of a time to come when Israel's Messiah will re-establish the twelve

'Mighty God' should likely be understood as "...divinely bestowed strength. Therefore the title 'Wonderful Counselor' probably depicts this warrior king as an extraordinary military strategist." It may be worth noting that the two titles unaddressed by the author are "Everlasting Father" and "Prince of Peace." This observation aside, I oppose Chisholm's reading for two reasons: First, it seems to ignore the plain sense of the text, which does not say "And his name shall be called wise military strategist and bestowed with divine might." Such a reading is possible, but it assumes facts not in evidence and demands the reader to imagine a context that is not self-evident. It is, therefore, a theological reading. Second, while Isaiah certainly speaks of a battle to come, he speaks of it as something qualitatively different from battles past ("For every battle of the warrior is...but this shall be...etc.") (Isa. 9:5). Furthermore, the promised child is certainly not referring to a son who would be born in the immediate future, as it is said of the promised son, "Of the increase of his government and peace there shall be no end, upon the throne of David, and upon his kingdom, to order it, and to establish it with judgement and with justice from henceforth even for ever" (Isa. 9:7 KJV). If this line is not read with the Messiah in view, I struggle to imagine what Old Testament verse might be.

6. In First Samuel 13:13, the reader is made to understand that, had Saul behaved himself properly, the LORD would have established Saul's kingdom "upon Israel for ever." In First Kings, Jeroboam is given similar assurance that "if thou wilt hearken unto all that I command thee, and wilt walk in my ways, and do that is right in my sight, to keep my statutes and my commandments, as David my servant did; that I will be with thee, and build thee a sure house, as I built for David, and will give Israel unto thee." (1 Kings 11:26-38 KJV).

7. Isa. 40:10. Here in Isaiah, the ruler-to-come is associated with God's own arm. Interestingly, in Isaiah 52:10, it is said that "The Lord hath made bare his holy arm in the eyes of all the nations; and all the ends of the earth shall see the salvation of our God." The witness of salvation through the 'arm of God' is extended into Isaiah 59:15-16 when the writer says, "...therefore his arm brought salvation unto him...".

tribes in the earth, ushering in a new age where Jew and Gentile alike come to make sacrifices of worship unto the LORD.[8] Furthermore, the King-to-come will cause Israel's standing among the nations to become glorious again.

> Therefore thy gates shall be open continually; they shall not be shut day nor night; that men may bring unto thee the forces of the Gentiles, and that their kings may be brought. For the nation and kingdom that will not serve thee shall perish; yea, those nations shall be utterly wasted. The glory of Lebanon shall come unto thee, the fir tree, the pine tree, and the box together, to beautify the place of my sanctuary; and I will make the place of my feet glorious. The sons also of them that afflicted thee shall come bending unto thee; and all they that despised thee shall bow themselves down at the soles of thy feet; and they shall call thee, The city of the LORD, The Zion of the Holy One of Israel.[9]

Yet, despite all that is said of the coming King's dominion in the prophets, it is never presented outside the context of God's own saving arm. In light of this, other statements attributed to the nature of the coming Messiah deserve equal attention, whether they readily highlight royal themes in the mind of the reader or not. In the prophets, the primary concern of the LORD is Israel's spiritual standing with God, not merely their place among the nations. Without exception, it is the spiritual depravity of Judah and Israel that brings about the very demise the Messiah is destined to rectify. Thus, a lay reader might expect that any act of restoration in the people of Israel would address both spiritual depravity and national sovereignty. In the prophets, these themes are constantly seen together. Israel is promised restoration, but the nature of their restoration is not isolated to a new kingdom; it is also restitution for the things that cost them their kingdom. As R. Mason says, "The condemnation…is followed immediately by a promise that this judgement will be reversed in every particular."[10]

---

8. Isaiah 66:18-24 and Ezekiel 47:21-23 both address the inclusion of certain Gentiles in their eschatological framework. In Ezekiel's closing chapter, the reader finds a detailed description of Israel's restoration in her own land. In that place where sacrifices are made and righteousness is restored, it is said, "and the name of the city from that day shall be, The LORD is there."

9. Isa. 60:11-14 (KJV).

10. J.G. McConville, "Micah, Book of," in *Dictionary of the Old Testament Prophets,* ed. Mark J. Boda, J. Gordon McConville (IVP Academic, 2012), 548.

> Who hath believed our report? and to whom is the arm of the LORD revealed?... Surely he hath borne our griefs, and carried our sorrows: yet we did esteem him stricken, smitten of God, and afflicted. But he was wounded for our transgressions, he was bruised for our iniquities: the chastisement of our peace was upon him; and with his stripes we are healed. All we like sheep have gone astray; we have turned every one to his own way; and the LORD hath laid on him the iniquity of us all.[11]

In this portion of the text, the King-to-come is not depicted as a mighty warrior, but as a suffering servant. Grief, sorrow, transgression, iniquity, and estrangement from God are disclosed as troubles of the people that the servant will rectify, known in the text as 'the arm of the LORD.' Here again, the anticipated neat divide between 'earthly savior' and 'spiritual savior' is blurred. In the prophets, God's kingship is disclosed, not with a man, but through a man. In this way, distinguishing between He-who-saves and He-who-is-responsible-for-the-saving becomes moot – they are presented together in one. By the time the reader reaches the minor prophets, the kingship of the promised Messiah who will reign over a restored Israel is indivisible from the kingship of the God of Abraham, Isaac, and Jacob who gave them commandments.

> In that day, saith the LORD, will I assemble her that halteth, and I will gather her that is driven out, and her that I have afflicted; And I will make her that halted a remnant, and her that was cast far off a strong nation: and the LORD shall reign over them in mount Zion from henceforth, even for ever.[12]

For Micah, the use of the tetragrammaton is not a discrepancy for readers to wrestle into position alongside other prophetic books; it is a feature to be worked out and understood by the reader. Thus, the King-to-come cannot rightly be separated from the King who was and is.

---

11. Isa. 53:1;4-6 (KJV).
12. Mic. 4:6-7 (KJV).

11

Isaiah and the Baptism of Jesus

Andrew Herbst

INTRODUCTION

The Baptism of Jesus is rooted in Old Testament (OT) theology and can be misunderstood if the OT background is overlooked. Jesus was not baptized to be an example for us to follow, for we are baptized for our sin, but He had no sin. Furthermore, Jesus' baptism was not meant to display a new revelation of the trinitarian Godhead. This paper will analyze the Baptism of Jesus through the prophecies of Isaiah, in order to properly understand that Jesus was anointed as the Servant and the King.

THE ANOINTED KING

Isaiah 11:1-9 anticipates an anointed figure coming from the line of Jesse (Isa. 11:1-2). He will rule the entire earth with righteousness (Isa. 11:3-5), and he shall bring peace through judgment and slaying of the wicked (Isa. 11:4-9). It is the anointed figure of Isaiah 11 that will bring restoration to Israel.

Restoring Israel, defeating the wicked, and ruling God's kingdom on earth would require this figure to be given power from God to accomplish this task (Isa. 11:2). Gerhard von Rad states that Isaiah does not attribute the "paradisal peace" and restoration of the king's reign to a contemporary anointed monarch, but the prophet looks forward to "one who is to come in the future."[1] Furthermore, in reference to the "stem of Jesse" (Isa. 11:1), von Rad proposes that Isaiah is not merely writing about a descendant of David. Rather, in speaking of Jesse as the father, a "new David" is in view, through whom God "will restore the glory of the original Davidic empire."[2]

1. Gerhard von Rad, *Old Testament Theology: Volume 2*, trans. by D. M. G. Stalker, (New York, NY: Harper and Row Publishers, 1962), 170
2. von Rad, *Old Testament Theology: Volume 2*, 170.

In contrast to other ancient kingdoms, von Rad reports, only in Israel was the monarch's call and authorization from the Lord "inseparably connected with the bestowal of the Spirit."[3] Furthermore, it was Isaiah who wrote of the anointed figure being spiritually endowed from God, which enabled him to "make the divine will for justice prevail in his kingdom."[4] The future figure became known as the Messiah, which comes from the Hebrew משיח, meaning "anointed one."[5] This "anointed" terminology is used throughout the OT for kings, priests, and a savior-figure (Lev. 4:3, Ps. 2:2, Isa. 45:1, & Dan. 9:25). Here, Isaiah uses the concept of God's anointed king to reveal how God will deliver Zion and His people. Geoffrey Grogan points out that the Spirit's anointing of the Messiah is shown to empower the king for every aspect of rule, and that the king would lack nothing in regard to knowledge and power from God.[6] During Isaiah's time, the monarchs of Judah had failed and not produced what the Davidic Covenant spoke of, but Israel's salvation lies in the future. It is God who will save Zion by raising up the anointed king.

THE ANOINTED SERVANT OF GOD

Isaiah 41 shows the power of God as He encourages and strengthens a weak Israel (Isa. 41:1-14), and it will be soon revealed that the anointed Servant will be God's instrument to bring security to God's people and God's rule upon the earth (Isa. 42:1-4). Isaiah 42 is considered the first servant song within Isaiah.[7] It begins by drawing attention to God's chosen "Servant" (Isa. 42:1), often called the "ebed of Yahweh," which Oscar Cullmann suggests is at "the heart of New Testament Christology."[8]

The Servant is well-pleasing to God, and the Lord anoints the Servant with His Spirit (Isa. 42:1 and 61:1). The Servant will bring covenantal judgment, and

---

3. Gerhard von Rad, *Old Testament Theology: Volume 1*, trans. by D. M. G. Stalker, (New York, NY: Harper and Row Publishers, 1962), 323.

4. von Rad, *Old Testament Theology: Volume 1*, 323 and 375.

5. William Holliday, *A Concise Hebrew and Aramaic Lexicon of the Old Testament: based on the work of Ludwig Koehler and Walter Baumgartner*, (Grand Rapids, MI: Eerdman's Publishing Company, 1988), 218.

6. Geoffrey W. Grogan, *The Expositors Bible Commentary: Isaiah*, Frank E. Gaebelein ed., (Grand Rapids, MI: Zondervan Publishing House, 1992), 88.

7. For a brief background of the history of identifying servant songs see Allan Harman, I*saiah: A Covenant to be Kept for the Sake of the Church* (Scotland, UK: Christian Focus, 2001) 283f3.

8. Oscar Cullmann, *The Christology of the New Testament*, trans. by Shirley Guthrie & Charles Hall, (Philadephia, PA: Westminster Press, 1959), 51.

he "shall not fail" until he has brought judgment to the entire earth (Isa. 42:3-4). Moreover, the Lord says that He has called the Servant "in righteousness" and the Servant himself will be given "for a covenant of the people, for a light of the Gentiles" (Isa. 42:6).

This is the same Servant that can be found in Isaiah 53. Often described as the "suffering servant," Isaiah prophesies that He would die on behalf of sinful humanity and bring redemption to the world. *The* obedient Servant would make it possible for there to be many obedient servants.

THE BAPTISM OF JESUS

The King (cf. Isa. 11:2 and Ps. 2:2, 2:7) and the Servant (cf. Isa. 42:1 and 61:1) would be anointed to fulfill their purpose from God. The New Testament (NT) reveals that Jesus, in His humanity, was anointed at His baptism and united these roles to fulfill God's plan for salvation. Christ's baptism focused on His humanity and what He would accomplish as a man, not to reveal the Trinity. This assertion can be supported by understanding the OT texts that were referenced at the Baptism.

When Jesus was baptized, the voice from heaven said, "This is my beloved Son, in whom I am well pleased" (Matt. 3:17). James D. G. Dunn reports that most scholars maintain that the heavenly voice uttered a combination of Psalm 2 and Isaiah 42.[9] "This is my beloved Son," comes from Psalm 2:7, and is directly connected to God's King.[10] The second reference, "in whom I am well pleased," is from Isaiah 42:1, and centers on the Servant of God.

The words from Psalm 2 and Isaiah 42, then, announce Jesus as the messianic king who will be obedient to the call and task of the Servant. This is clarified by the dove and the anointing of the Spirit. God does not need anointing power, but a human does. Jesus, in His humanity, needed power from God to complete His commission. Imagine a human having total divine power in the highest capacity, and that power remaining with the individual; this may be how to explain the anointing of the man Jesus in simplistic terms.

---

9. James Dunn, *Jesus Remembered: Christianity in the Making, Volume 1*, (Grand Rapids, MI: Eerdmans Publishing, 2003), 374.

10. See this author's essay on the Davidic Covenant for an overview of Psalm 2 and its foundation for the Baptism of Jesus.

Dunn states that the Spirit "equipped Jesus with power and authority for his mission to follow," and that this fulfilled Isaiah's prophecies about an anointed Messiah (Isa. 11:2, 42:1, & 61:1).[11] Cullmann adds that the voice emphasized sonship and servanthood, presenting Jesus as the only Son, who would fulfill the role of the servant of Yahweh, dying a sinless death for a sinful people (cf. Is. 53:12 & Lk. 22:37).[12] As the Son, Jesus could "depend upon miraculous divine power only if he is obedient to his divine commission."[13]

CONCLUSION

This study has provided the basic elements for understanding Isaiah's foundation for Christ's baptism. Jesus was not baptized to reveal the Trinity, nor was He baptized to be our example. Although Scripture affirms the deity of Jesus (John 20:28 and Col. 2:9), Christ's baptism focuses primarily on His humanity and what He would accomplish as a man. The voice from Heaven confirmed that the figures of Messiah and Servant are unified in the man Jesus. Jesus was baptized to be anointed and empowered to fulfill His ministry as the Servant and the King. He would bring redemption, reestablish God's kingdom, and then rule God's kingdom.

---

11. Dunn, James D. G., *Baptism in the Holy Spirit*, (Philadelphia, PA: Westminster Press, 1970), 24 and 27.
12. Cullmann, *Christology*, 284.
13. Cullmann, *Christology*, 284.

12

Preaching to Kings—While the Prophets Prophesied and Some Kings Were Passive

Jeremias D. Zuniga

INTRODUCTION

It can become lost to the modern reader that the Prophetic and Historical books of the Bible occur concurrently, especially given the presumed mysterious or difficult expressions found within these Prophetic books. Further, the immediate and future aspects of the prophets and their prophecies can become shrouded to the lay reader, assuming that it takes an expert to understand the "ins and outs" of these important works.[1] This separation between the Historic and Prophetic has created a pitfall where Scripture's readers have a challenge recognizing the reality of the prophets' messages, not just separating the immediate and future natures of these messages, but also casting a shadow over the contemporary perception of how the prophets functioned within ancient Israel and Judah. That challenge is usually seen in misperceptions of what it means to be a prophet today, which assume that prophecy is esoteric.[2]

---

1. An introductory example of the various categories that scholars have taxonomized "divination" in the ancient world can be seen in the recent overview by John W Hilber, "*Israelite Prophecy in Its Ancient Near Eastern Context,*" essay, in *The State of Old Testament Studies: A Survey of Recent Research* (Grand Rapids, MI: Baker Academic, 2024), 132–46. While these works are helpful in introducing students to the academic landscape, their purpose is necessarily for the pew. That is the point I want to raise here, that a popular level work is not always as nuanced or expansive, and well researched works often fall well outside of public consumption.

2. This is evidenced in the New Apostolic Reformation (NAR) movement that has been readily condemned by many Cessationists (see "*A New 'reformation' That Many Don't Realize They've Joined,*" Biola Magazine - Biola University Blogs, July 2, 2025, https://www.biola.edu/blogs/biola-magazine/2015/a-new-reformation). However, while the Cessationists are correct in highlighting the unbiblical nature of this movement and do well to focus on NAR's abuse and manipulation of others, they would be incorrect in claiming that Pentecostalism as a whole has participated in this movement and Pentecostals would benefit from drawing clear boundaries

Because of this bifurcation, I want to pose the following claim as my topic of exploration: when the prophets describe the LORD their King, it held both an immediate and future expectation as they challenged failing leaders and their nation(s). In an effort to remain concise, I want to observe the occurrence of the phrase: אני י-ה-ו-ה...מלככם or "I am the LORD ... your King" in Isaiah 43:15 while centering the exploration on both the immediate context and the anticipation expressed in the wider passage.[3]

THE SITUATION

As recognized above, there are times when readers disconnect the Historical and Prophetic books, neglecting the wider context of the prophecies within these books. To begin, it is important to recognize that Isaiah's book opens by identifying the kings he had engaged with when delivering God's word, "The vision of Isaiah, son of Amoz, which he saw about Judah and Jerusalem in the days of Uzziah, Jotham, Ahaz, and Hezekiah, kings of Judah" (Isa. 1:1).[4] These are the kings of Judah Isaiah would minister to as well as to the people of Judah who had been divided from the Northern kingdom of Israel (see 1 Kgs. 11:28-12:24). Naturally, the kings of Judah overlap to the extent that Uzziah is the father of Jotham, grandfather of Ahaz, and great grandfather of Hezekiah.[5] It

---

to protect against the falsehoods of these spurious groups. For a more thorough critique of the NAR movement see Holly Pivec and R. Douglas Geivett, *Counterfeit Kingdom: The Dangers of New Revelation, New Prophets, and New Age Practices in the Church* (Brentwood, Tennesee: B&H Publishing Group, 2022).

3. My claim considers the dissenting voice of the well research Martti Nissinen, who argues that prophecy in ancient Israel was not unique. See Martti Nissinen, *Ancient Prophecy: Near Eastern, Biblical, and Greek Perspectives* (New York: Oxford University Press, Incorporated, 2017), 144-167 & 257-280. While I consider Nissinen's claim and ultimately argue contrastingly, I must note the important of the following phrase, "Comparable radical conflicts between the prophets and the king or the kingdom have not been found so far." (261) which is a quote from Erich Zenger et al. 2012. Einleitung in das Alte Testament, Eighth edition, ed. C. Frevel. Stuttgart: Kohlhammer. And while Nissinen disputes the claim that is based on the foundation of his own work, the evidence provided is scant at best.

4. The reader should note that all translations throughout this paper are my own, and while it is not my intention to offer unique translations, I understand the astute reader will have their Bible open as they are reading this book. I hope to provide this note to eliminate the frustration of attempting to find the translation I have used as they will not differ substantially or at all from a faithful translation of the OT text like that found in the King James Bible.

5. For an easily understood list of the kings recorded in Chronicles see Victor P. Hamilton, *Handbook on the Historical Books: Joshua, Judges, Ruth, Samuel, Kings, Chronicles, Ezra-Nehemiah, Esther* (Grand Rapids, Mich: Baker Academic, 2008), 480-482. Although I disagree that Jotham

is important to note this because when Isaiah begins to prophecy, he is prophesying during the reign of Uzziah (Isa. 1-6), a king who had been promised and received prosperity so long as he sought the LORD (2 Chron. 26:1-5). Clearly, the good beginning of Uzziah took a turn; he transgresses, is struck with leprosy, and eventually dies in isolation (2 Chron. 26:16-23). Isaiah's prophecies against Judah are not favorable in the opening six chapters of his book, as the latter years of Uzziah's life of separation from the temple of God and isolation are demonstrative of the people's condition.

It is from the example of Uzziah's goodness, however, that Jotham learns and lives. While relatively little is captured about the sixteen years of Jotham's reign, it does not appear that there was an issue of personal paganism that would overshadow his reign. However, the presence of the phrase "Only, he never entered into the LORD's temple. And still the people did corruption" (2 Chron. 27:2) should cause the reader to pause.

Interestingly, Isaiah's writing transitions from the death of Uzziah (Isa. 6) into a series of prophecies against Ahaz, who was entirely pagan (2 Chron. 28:1-4; Isa. 7ff) while Uzziah was not directly prophesied against. Further, there appears to have been a co-regency between Uzziah and his son, Jotham, who allowed the people to continue in their corrupt ways. Thus, the transition in Isaiah 1-6 from Uzziah to Ahaz includes within it a description of how both Uzziah and Jotham allowed the people to live. Critically, Isaiah proclaims in his vision of the temple, a place where Uzziah had been removed and where Jotham would not go, "I also saw the LORD, sitting upon a throne" (see 2 Chron. 26:18-27:2; Isa. 6:1), and later declares the uncleanness of the people as he stands before the King (Isa. 6:5). This foundation of Uzziah's and Jotham's kingly apathy is crucial, because Ahaz goes further than the apathy of his predecessors and outright adopts idolatrous practices for himself. Later attempting to progress the Judahites into an alliance with the Assyrians, Ahaz plunders three houses, the LORD's, the king's, and the princes', assuming that these precious gifts would bring the support of the much larger Assyrian army: that assumption was wrong and his efforts were pointless, the loot was taken without any help offered in return (2 Chron. 28:16-24; Isaiah 7:17-8:8).[6] The threat of Assyria descending

has no marring language related to his rule, this disagreement is discussed below as his apathy.

6. Hamilton, *Handbook on the Historical Books*, 492.

upon the people of Judah was not simply bad news, it should be understood that it was the worst possible news. The Assyrians were nearing the height of their strength, and they would, in the generation after Ahaz, return to claim Judah as their own (2 Chron. 32:1).[7]

While the Assyrians positioned themselves to overtake Jerusalem, Isaiah and Hezekiah pray to the God who Hezekiah had just reestablished worship to (2 Chron. 29:5-31:21). Because of these reinstitutions, the LORD responds to the Assyrian threat and weakens Sennacherib's army (2 Chron. 32:21). This downfall of Sennacherib is important for us to consider, because while the previous kings were apathetic or in direct opposition to proper worship of the LORD, Hezekiah was not and corrected the errors by returning to what his fathers let go of. Nonetheless, Hezekiah is tested by the LORD, and his heart shows that he can be just as flippant as his fathers in the matters of foreign policy. He welcomes ambassadors from Babylon and invites them to see every piece of treasure the LORD blessed him with (2 Chron. 32:25-33; Isa. 39), resulting in the prophecy that Babylon will attack and overthrow Judah.[8]

THE HOPE EXPRESSED

The apathy and political maneuvering of these kings bring the impending doom of the Babylonians, news that would terrify most of the ancient Near East. However, it must also be observed that in a time when those kings vacated the temple, the King was still on the throne. It is at this point that I will begin to merge the historical with the prophetic, turning to the second portion of Isaiah's prophecies and our opening textual focus.[9]

---

7. A most helpful outline of the history of the Assyrians and Babylonians can be found in Bill T. Arnold and Brent A. Strawn, eds., *The World around the Old Testament: The People and Places of the Ancient near East* (Grand Rapids, MI: Baker Academic, a division of Baker Publishing Group, 2016), 31-137. The book is composed of articles covering a number of ancient civilizations in an overview approach that is both accessible and while not exhaustive it remains thorough enough to cover the rise and fall of various people groups.

8. For a more thorough discussion on a *Babylonian invasion see Gary V Smith, "Cyrus or Sennacherib? Historical Issues Involved in the Interpretation of Isaiah 40-55,"* essay, in *Bind up the Testimony: Explorations in the Genesis of the Book of Isaiah* (Peabody, MA: Hendrickson Publishers, 2015), 175–193. Additionally, it is important to recognize that it possible Hezekiah ultimately corrected his way. Especially if Isaiah 39 is read as chronologically occurring prior to Isaiah 36-38.

9. This turning of attention is not to explicate that the opening focus of Isaiah does not include the foretelling nature of prophecy, it is only that I am focusing on that aspect from chapter 43.

The various kings reigned respectively for a combined 113 years (see Isa. 1:1). Naturally, this does not account for the overlap of time where co-regency occurred, but it does give me the room to raise for discussion the link between Isaiah 6 and Isaiah 43. If Isaiah 6 occurs at the end of Uzziah's 52-year reign, the remaining time of the other kings is an estimated 59-61 years. The ministry of Isaiah does not shift in those 60 years, as we find him yet again speaking God's word to the people in Isaiah 40-42, only this time he is bringing encouragement. On this foundation we see him raise the following, "Thus said the LORD, your Redeemer, the Holy One of Israel, for your sake I myself sent Babylon, and will bring all of them down as fugitives, and the Chaldeans wailing in the ships" (Isa. 43:14).[10] This notice to the Judahites was crucial, the LORD had not made a promise from a position of powerlessness. The fact is, the LORD had made that promise from where He had always been, the place where Judah had abandoned Him, His throne. As such, Isaiah's prophecy continues, "I am the LORD, your Holy One, the Creator of Israel, your King" (Isa. 43:15).

CONCLUSION

How is that hope, that the LORD could send a threat as great as the Babylonians against Judah? That is the promise, as Assyria had grown in power, and with Sennacherib's assault, the only hope was an overthrow from their flank. The Babylonians were geographically just south of Assyria, and during the years of Israel and Judah's exile, they would team up with the Medes to overthrow the Assyrian empire. Isaiah communicated both warning and promise to the people of God, captured in the same texts. The LORD was and will be on His throne; He is the King who cannot be overthrown. Because of His rule, it is a warning to those who make Him their enemy, and a promise to those who worship Him as the King He is and always will be. Sadly, the nations of Judah and Israel did not correct their ways and would be carried away as captives. However, the promise that God would bring down their captors remained, and God was faithful to His word. It is in the challenge of the very immediate that the LORD used Isaiah to speak to the immediate and future, and because of this, we will see the King return in glory, another theme present in Isaiah's prophecies.

---

10. For the difficulties in translating this verse see Allan M. Harman, *Isaiah: A Covenant to Be Kept for the Sake of the Church* (Fearn, Ross-shire, Scotland: Christian Focus, 2011), 300-302. Harman's commentary is also highly recommended as a fantastic single volume work on Isaiah for non-technical readers.

WEEK FIVE

The Gospels and the Godhead—The Word Made Flesh, Sonship, and Kingship

13

The Godhead in the Gospels—Reframing the Gospel of John

Steven Gill

Often in contrast to Matthew, Mark, and Luke, John is commonly presented as the gospel which most thoroughly discloses the divinity of Jesus Christ.[1] Those who defend the absolute oneness of God often call upon John's fourteenth chapter for assurance that Jesus' divine nature is indivisible from God the Father.[2] For those of the trinitarian persuasion, John's opening materials complicate the oneness reading; chapter one signals the mysterious nature of the divine trinity – God's unified three-ness.[3] Nevertheless, while

---

1. Craig Bloomberg, *Jesus and the Gospels*, (B&H Academic, 2009), 186. Here, Bloomberg points out that while the Gospel of Mark shares John's language of Sonship, the two gospels represent different perspectives on what Sonship means. According to Bloomberg, the Sonship of the book of John is something divine, as opposed to other gospels, in which it is presented in especially human terms. He writes, "But 'Son' for John is even more clearly identified with a heavenly figure than in the Synoptics. John 3:31-36 is a key Christological passage that sums up important Johannine themes: 'The one who comes from above is above all…For the one whom God has sent speaks the words of God, for God gives the Spirit without limit. The Father loves the Son and has placed everything in his hands…". Of interest is Bloomberg's use of John 3:35 as a sort of proof-text for his chief claim – that the Sonship of Jesus Christ is displayed differently in John's gospel than in the synoptics. Yet, much like Mark's use of the term, the Sonship of Jesus in the aforementioned passage is characterized as submitted, obedient, and not an independent actor from heaven.

2. John 14:6-10. In this passage, Jesus' words "…from henceforth ye know him, and have seen him [the Father]" and "…he that hath seen me hath seen the Father; and how sayest thou then, Shew us the Father?" are often called upon as proof texts to point out that the neat 'division of persons' created by the doctrine of the trinity are more complicated than its adherents may, perhaps, be inclined to believe.

3. John 1:1-3. The question often raised by this passage regards the disposition of "the Word" which is described as being both "God" and "with God." "In the beginning was the Word, and the Word was with God, and the Word was God." Trinitarian thinkers often hang their hat on the 'with-ing' of the verse, while oneness adherents rely more upon the 'was-ing.' While both parties agree that the Word should be understood as something not different from God in any

John's materials are often lauded for presenting the highest Christology of the gospels, his book does not (in this regard) necessarily represent a radical departure from the others as has been, at times, supposed.

While survey examinations of the gospels are often framed around the way each writer presented the earthly ministry of Jesus of Nazareth, John's work is frequently left out of these examinations. Often, this is done on the grounds that the Gospel of John does not use the chronology of Matthew, Mark, and Luke nor are its narratives identical to the other three. Still, the Christology of John should probably not be interpreted as crowding out other dominant themes of the book, many of which Matthew, Mark, and Luke share. To participate in any sound discussion concerning the role of Christology in John, the reader must first answer a too easily neglected question: Precisely what is meant by "Christology"? For trinitarian theologians, the study of the incarnation of Christ is often viewed through the lens of the theology that informs all discussions about the nature of God; Jesus is the incarnation of God the Son, second person of the triune God.[4] Because of this, portions of John's gospel often

---

material way, they disagree upon what, precisely, is meant by the word "God." For trinitarians, the Greek word θεός (*theos*) should be understood as "God the Father" by implication – the first person of the trinity and not God in His total disclosure. For those who embrace the oneness of God, *theos* is a generic Greek term for God used in a ubiquitous way throughout the New Testament (see Matt. 12:28; Luke 1:47; Luke 3:6; John 17:3-4; Rom. 8:9-11; 1 Cor. 1:21; 1 Cor. 3:23; Eph. 5:20; 1 Tim. 3:16; Col. 2:1-2; Col. 2:8-9; Col. 3:17; 1 Thess. 2:3; James 1:27). These passages and others complicate the notion that theos can (or must necessarily be) understood as the first person of the trinity, God the Father. Of particular interest are (Eph. 5:20; Col. 2:1-2; Jam. 1:27) which seem to create a marked distinction between these terms (God and Father) in much the same way trinitarians identify the distinction between Father and Son in the New Testament. From the oneness persuasion, these passages suggest that, had John intended to disclose a trinity in his opening remarks, the verse should, perhaps, have included further distinction (i.e. 'In the beginning was the Word, and the Word was with God the Father and the Word was God the Son' etc.). Furthermore, the trinitarian reading requires further clarification, as it is the third person of the trinity – God the Holy Spirit – who is left out of the reading.

4. This perspective was articulated by Athanasius, of whom Servetus said, "…he teaches that the Son of man should be understood as the human being whose body was assumed [by God] and not the actual Son of God. He says that the Son of man was filled with the Son of God." This he defended on the grounds that Athanasius, apart from believing that Jesus was the incarnation of God truly, was only the incarnation of God's genuine and eternally begotten offspring which was co-eternal with the Father. Athanasius stated explicitly that "…but the Son Himself is not the Son by participation, but is the Father's own Offspring. Nor again is the Son in the Father…" Earlier he wrote, "Perish the thought; the Triad is not originated…the Son was ever; for He is eternal, as is the Father, of whom He is the Eternal Word…". While Servetus was writing as a dissenter against the doctrine of the trinity in the sixteenth century, his framing of

described as possessing a 'high' Christology, may be read differently by oneness theologians.[5] For these, Jesus of Nazareth is a man in whom the fullness of God dwells. In this way, His Sonship is neither co-eternal nor metaphysical; in fact, it is especially human. In light of the latter reading, Christological passages are first examined with God's oneness in view. Thus, for oneness believers, Jesus is not the incarnation of God the Son, second person of the trinity, but He is 'God manifested in the flesh'[6] and 'God with us.'[7] Concerning Christ's divinity, He is truly God; Concerning His humanity, He is truly man. While these distinctions are no doubt quaint to some, they carry some significant ramifications. How one understands the Sonship of Jesus Christ will greatly impact their view of the book of John. When discussing the divinity that is disclosed in the opening chapter of John, competing perspectives are often framed around determining the nature of the incarnation of the Son. Such discussions become complicated by the author's use of the Greek word λόγος (*logos*) translated as

---

Athanasius' words in the fourth century does not appear to be a mischaracterization. In chapter four of his first discourse in Against the Arians, Athanasius defended the co-existent Son with the Father again, using John's first chapter as his proof text.

For Servetus: Michael Servetus, *The Restoration of Christianity*, Book I

For Athanasius: Athanasius, *Against the Arians*, Discourse I, Ch. VI; Discourse III, Ch. XXIII

5. This sort of Christology is sometimes called 'The Doctrine of Eternal Generation' or a variant of it. For more on this, see: Smith, Brandon D. "Eternal Generation According to Athanasius." The Center for Baptist Renewal. Last modified September 21, 2021. https://www.centerforbaptistrenewal.com/blog/2021/9/20/eternal-generation-according-to-athanasius.

6. 1 Timothy 3:16. Perhaps due to the obscurities raised by the use of the term theos in other passages of the New Testament, early trinitarian writers suggested that none of the persons of the trinity were the full disclosure of God. Augustine wrote, "...since we have said the Holy Spirit is so called relatively, not the Trinity itself, but He who is in the Trinity...we do not speak of the Father of the Holy Spirit, lest the Holy Spirit should be understood to be His Son...we do not speak of the Son of the Holy Spirit, lest the Holy Spirit be understood to be His Faither." Readers of the New Testament may question the writer's meaning here. From Augustine's perspective, Christ is within God (triune) but God (triune) is not necessarily within Christ; The Holy Spirit proceeds from the Father and Christ, yet He is distinct from both of them. The dizzying logic is only complicated by comparison of Augustine with the New Testament writers. In Matthew 1:18, readers are told that Mary was "...with child of the Holy Ghost." The statement is repeated in verse 20. In Second Corinthians, Paul said that "...God was in Christ, reconciling the world to himself." These passages and others complicate Augustine's chief claim, that there exist neat divisions of labor (even if only functionally) between the persons of the trinity.

For Augustine: Augustine, *On the Trinity*, Book V ch. XIII.

7. Matthew 1:23. Here again, the use of the term theos must be sorted out for the trinitarian. Is the Christ child the "fulness of the godhead bodily" as Paul said, or is He Emmanuel, 'God [by implication the Son] with us,' as Augustine seems to suggest?

"Word" in English Bibles. While it is often taken for granted that this "Word" can become interchangeable in the reader's mind with the "Son" described throughout the scriptures, readers should be cautious not to under-interpret John's use of *logos*. Had the writer wanted to say, "In the beginning was the υἱός (Son), and the Son was with God, and the Son was God," it stands to reason that he could have. John used this term frequently throughout his gospel; yet in John 1:1, the writer chose a different term entirely. The reader may rightly wonder as to why this is the case. Confusion about the incarnation may be born out of a sincere attempt to rationalize John's meaning; he does not speak plainly of two persons in any proper sense. Instead, John wrote of the incarnate Word, which is itself the personification of communication.[8] Communication (even divine communication) is not generally understood to be a person, but the expression of a person. Far from being distinct from the speaker, the Word is the revelation of the speaker himself – the manner by which the speaker is disclosed to his listeners.

This portrait of the incarnate Word is born out throughout the scriptures, which often speak of Jesus as the fulfillment of the Law and the Prophets (Matt. 5:17), the emissary of God's will (John 4:34; 5:19; 5:30; 8:28), and He who teaches heavenly doctrine (John 7:16). A modern reader's attempt at framing John's opening text might be presented thus: Far from an ambiguous characterization of an ever begotten or eternal Son, the logos that was made flesh is the Word of God that was, from the beginning, made manifest to the world. In this way, Jesus is truly the incarnation of all that was spoken in the Law,

8. C.S. Keener, "John, Gospel of," in *Dictionary of Jesus and the Gospels* ed. Joel B. Green (IVP Academic, 2005), 428. Keener's comments on John's compatibility with the contemporary Jewish psyche is interesting. He writes, "John's image moves beyond Wisdom or Torah…Nevertheless, he clearly plays on this line of Jewish tradition, which often personified Wisdom as God's agent… Although grace and truth were present in the law (Ex 34:6), Jesus explicitly reveals these aspects of God's character in a fuller manner than Moses' law had (Jn 1:17)…The law revealed God's character partially; Jesus has revealed it completely." Thus, for Keener, it appears that personification is not merely a literary device for John; it is an accurate depiction of God's self-disclosure to man, seen first in His written Word, and later at an appointed time through His living Word.

the Prophets, and the Writings;[9] He is, as Hebrews says, 'the living Word.'[10] From this perspective, the Word is not understood as a second person who is somehow both co-eternal yet ever begotten,[11] but as the incarnation of God's earthly disclosure. Therefore, we do not have God the Father and God the Son; rather, we have God, and God revealed.

The distinction between these portrayals of Christ is important. If He is the earthly disclosure of God the Son, second person in the trinity who is co-eternal and co-equal with God the Father, then much of John's supposed 'high' Christology becomes not very high at all. In fact, the doctrine of the trinity may be characterized as in conflict with many of John's chief claims, namely that Jesus is sent to do the will of the Father (John 4:34), can do nothing of His own accord (John 5:19), and does not seek His own will (John 5:30). Each of these descriptions of Jesus contradicts the doctrine of co-equality if Sonship is understood in eternal or spiritual terms. Far from being a second person of the Trinity who co-existed co-equally with God the Father throughout eternity, the Son of God is described as a man who is submitted to God, obedient to God, and taught by God. Trinitarian adherents may be quick to suggest that the submission of Jesus Christ is merely a disclosure of His humanity and should not be interpreted as in conflict with His divinity – but then the question begs, what further need have they of a doctrine of three eternally divine persons? If the Son is a man in whom God dwelt, then none need speak of God in any divided terms.[12] If Sonship is viewed through the lens of Christ's humanity, God is an omnipresent Spirit who dwells in the heavens above and the earth

---

9. Keener, 428. In his entry on the subject, Keener parallels all that is pictured in Exodus chapters 33-34 with John 1:14-18. Here, Keener says, "...Jesus is the logos, usually translated as the 'Word.' In John's day this title was rich in nuances...the most important background that John shared with his audience, however, was the Greek translation of earlier Scripture, in which God's 'word' involved especially prophetic revelation and Scripture itself, most notably the Torah." I concur with Keener's portrayal of John's use of "word" in his prologue. From this perspective, Jesus is understood as the incarnation of God's Word in a proper sense. God disclosed Himself to mankind through His spoken Word in the beginning, and that Word is incarnate in Christ.

10. Hebrews 4:12.

11. Brandon Smith, *Eternal Generation According to Athanasius*, (The Center for Baptist Renewal, 2021).

12. Another alternative may be something like: God the Son temporarily gave up co-equality with God the Father to become the Son of God. Still, if this were the case, trinitarianism would be more Arian than trinitarian – the fourth century belief that Jesus is less than God but more than man.

below; He need not be divided into persons eternal, but distinctly revealed in the man, Jesus Christ. From this perspective, both the positive and negative Jewish responses to Jesus throughout the New Testament become clearer. The Son of God is an especially human term with which John's readers would have likely been familiar. As Winn writes:

> The OT uses the concept of divine sonship to describe three different groups: angelic beings, the people of Israel (or the collective nation of Israel) and Israel's kings (particularly those kings descended from David.)...The identity of the king as God's son conveys a variety of meanings: the king as the recipient of God's paternal faithfulness to and love for the king (2 Sam 7:14-16; Ps 89:24; 28-37); the king as God's agent who exercises God's authority on earth (Ps 2); the king as the heir and the recipient of God's inheritance (Ps 2:7-8); the king as the recipient of God's paternal discipline (2 Sam 7:14; Ps 89:20-27); and God's role as the progenitor of the king, since it is God who called and established Israel's kings.[13]

Thus, Sonship within the New Testament is not a concept self-evidently intended to introduce any notion of 'God the Son,' nor should it be understood as a term that was novel to its hearers. With the oneness of God in full view, John's portrayal of Christ differs very little from Matthew, Mark, and Luke, all of which describe Jesus as the Son of God (Matt. 16:16; Mark 15:39; Luke 4:41), who is also the Son of David (Matt. 1:20; Mark 18:48; Luke 18:38), doer of His Father's will (Matt. 26:39; Mark 14:36; Luke 10:22), and one who is pleasing to the Most-High (Matt. 3:17; Mark 9:7; Luke 9:35). Concerning the Godhead, John is in harmony with his contemporaries as well; God is one, and Jesus Christ is the image of the one invisible God (John 20:28). Rather than pointing His followers forward toward novel revelations about a triune God, Jesus consistently pointed His followers back to teachings of the Law of Moses and the God of their fathers (Matt. 19:17; Matt. 22:31-32; Matt. 24:36; Mark 7:8; Luke 4:8; Luke 10:27). Thus, Jesus' statement within the book of John, "Before Abraham was, I am" (John 8:58) should not be read as a departure from everything else Jesus said and taught, nor should it be understood as a

---

13. Adam Winn, "Son of God," in *Dictionary of Jesus and the Gospels* ed. Joel B. Green (IVP Academic, 2005), 886.

contradiction against Matthew, Mark, and Luke. Far from representing a departure from the gospels, the statement in John is harmonious with the portrayal of the Savior introduced at the beginning of the New Testament; Jesus, who is the Christ, is "Emmanuel," God with us (Matt. 1:21-23).

14

John's Gospel and the Fullness of God's Revelation

Andrew Herbst

INTRODUCTION

Trinitarians identify John 1 as a foundational passage to display evidence for the doctrine of the Trinity. The goal of this paper is to analyze the work of eminent trinitarian scholars and articulate that John 1 does not demand a trinitarian interpretation. John 1 is rather a passage about God fully revealing Himself and His plan of redemption to humanity.

THE LANGUAGE OF DISTINCTION AND IDENTITY

Within Scripture, there are moments when the focus is centered on Christ's humanity (Matt. 26:39), and other moments that emphasize His deity (John 20:28).[1] Most confusion regarding the Godhead revolves around misidentifying which aspect of Christ's ministry is being highlighted. Language of distinction and language of identity must be properly understood for the ministry of Jesus to be clear. Language of distinction can be found in texts that point to what Jesus accomplished in His humanity. As a man, there is a distinction from what Jesus did as God. Texts with language of identity recognize who Jesus was: He was the God of the Old Testament (OT) manifested in the flesh (John 8:58). We must observe and understand distinction while remaining faithful to the Text of Scripture, meaning, neither the humanity nor deity of Christ should be ignored.[2]

---

1. Unless otherwise noted, all biblical passages referenced are in the *King James Version*.

2. For more on understanding the significance of Jesus in His humanity, see Hendrikis Berkhof, *Christian Faith*, trans. by Sierd Woudstra, (Grand Rapids, MI: Eerdmans Publishing Company, 1979), 286-293.

JOHN I

The opening of John's Gospel reminds us of the very beginning, "In the beginning…" (Gen. 1:1). F. F. Bruce states that Genesis 1 presents the history of the old creation, but John 1 announces the "story of the new creation."[3] Creation and order occurred when God spoke in Genesis, but through sin, that world was fallen and in disorder. John's new creation account tells the story of God's plan for restoration. Thus, the apostle begins by introducing the Word (John 1:1-2).

The English translation "Word" comes from the Greek word *logos*, but these terms should not be confused with simply meaning "a word in a sentence" or merely as "reason." Bruce explains that particular Greek philosophers taught that the logos was the reason and order at work within man and the universe, but it is not with the Greeks that John aligns his theology; John draws from Hebrew OT revelation.[4]

According to Bruce, the word of God in the OT signified "God in action, especially in creation, revelation, and deliverance," and in John, this concept is continued as God fully "expressed Himself."[5] James D. G. Dunn further describes the Word as "a way of speaking about God acting. The Word is the expression of God, the unspoken thought of God coming to verbal expression."[6] Moreover, the Logos, the Word, is about the invisible becoming visible, as Dunn affirms, stating that "Jesus is the clearest expression of God's immanence, the one who makes visible the invisible God."[7] In short, issues of God's expression are connected to His self-revelation, or how He makes Himself known to humanity. It is specifically through the Word that God has ultimately spoken and revealed Himself to mankind. Craig Keener notes that John is recognizing the Word as "the embodiment of all God's revelation in the Scriptures and thus encourages his Jewish Christian hearers… that only those who accept Jesus truly honor the law fully" (John 1:17).[8] Thus, the essentiality and significance of the Logos is grounded in God's redemptive plan and action, and how man can truly

---

3. F. F. Bruce, *The Gospel & Epistles of John*, (Grand Rapids, MI: Eerdmans Publishing, 1983), 28-29.
4. Bruce, *The Gospel & Epistles of John*, 29.
5. Bruce, *The Gospel & Epistles of John*, 29.
6. James D. G. Dunn, *Did the First Christians Worship Jesus?*, (Louisville, KY: Westminster John Knox Press, 2010), 120.
7. Dunn, *Did the First Christians Worship Jesus?*, 120.
8. Craig S. Keener, *The IVP Bible Background Commentary: New Testament*, (Downers Grove, IL: InterVarsity Press, 2014), 249.

know and experience a holy and redemptive God. The Word made flesh, Jesus, the Son of God, is the full revelation of who God is and how God will provide salvation to humanity (cf. Heb. 1:1-4).

THE UNITY OF GOD

Texts such as "In the beginning was the Word, and the Word was with God, and the Word was God," (John 1:1), "The Word was made flesh," (John 1:14), and the Son being the "express image" of God's person (Heb. 1:3), all seem to show a unity with God, the Word, and the Son. Bruce confirms that "the deeds and words of Jesus are the deeds and words of God."[9] Dunn adds that the early Christians believed that "to be in the presence of Jesus was to be in the presence of God," and that Jesus was "the human face of God, as the one who made the unseen God known and known more clearly and fully than he had ever been known before."[10] Dunn continues, "Jesus is the Word, God's creative speech, God's revelatory and redemptive action, become flesh," and "You will see the unseen God in and through Jesus; you will encounter God in and through Jesus."[11] These admissions articulate what the Bible proclaims regarding the identity of Jesus, "For in him dwelleth all the fulness of the Godhead bodily" (Col. 2:9). Scripture does not claim that a person within the Godhead became flesh, but that God Himself was manifest in the flesh (1 Tim. 3:16). John carries over the OT tabernacle and temple language of God dwelling with His people and states that the Word "dwelt" or tabernacled among men (John 1:14).[12] The revealed Son was the "express image" of God's person (Heb. 1:3), and thus the single person of God became a man.

Regarding the Godhead and Christ, unity and distinction can be held at the same time by acknowledging that the OT prophesied that God would come unto humanity (cf. Isa. 9:6 and 40:3) and that the New Testament (NT) understands Jesus as that fulfillment (Matt. 3:3, 1 Tim. 3:16, and Rev. 22:3-4). However, this is where trinitarians stop short. Bruce and Dunn both affirm the deity of the Son, but only as an additional person within the Godhead. Dunn comments that the

---

9. Bruce, *The Gospel & Epistles of John*, 31.

10. Dunn, *Did the First Christians Worship Jesus?*, 122-23.

11. Dunn, *Did the First Christians Worship Jesus?*, 122.

12. See Andreas Köstenberger's "*John*" in Gregory K. Beale and Donald A. Carson, eds., *Commentary on the New Testament Use of the Old Testament,* (Grand Rapids, MI: Baker Academic, 2007), 422.

Logos was affirmed to be as "close to God as possible," honored as the Father is honored, and that the "Logos was truly God himself speaking and acting."[13] And yet, Dunn claims that John portrayed distinction, not just as Christ in His humanity, but also within the Godhead as well. As mentioned above, the language of distinction should be comprehended as what God did in the flesh. However, Dunn asserts that John "endeavored to maintain a balance between the thought of Jesus both as God and as not God the Father."[14] This statement stops short of the Biblical evidence. Yes, John's Gospel teaches distinction in Christ's humanity, but both John 10 and John 14 emphasize the unity of deity within the Godhead. Jesus confirms that He and His Father are one (John 10:30), and He further affirms what has been stated above, that when one sees the Son, they see the Father (John 14:9). Trinitarians claim these passages are centered on Jesus' will being aligned with the Father's will.[15] However, if these proclamations of Jesus were about unity of the wills between Father and Son, then it seems out of place that the Jews would desire to stone Jesus (John 10:31). In addition, the Jews explain their reasoning and it was not about unity of will, but because Jesus, "being a man" made Himself God (John 10:33).[16]

Andreas Köstenberger notes that John 10:30 echoes Deuteronomy 6:4, and, although he attempts to keep the Trinity in focus, Köstenberger admits that "there is more in view than a mere oneness of will between Jesus and the Father."[17] Köstenberger postulates that the unity of Father and Son is not just in function (their wills), but that Jesus' statement means that unity in being "seems to be presupposed."[18] In other words, it may have been presupposed that the Father and Son share the same being. This is an incredible admission for a trinitarian to make, but Köstenberger can only articulate a possible presupposition here, because if the Father and Son share the same being then he would lose the Trinity.

---

13. Dunn, *Did the First Christians Worship Jesus?,* 123.
14. Dunn, *Did the First Christians Worship Jesus?,* 123.
15. Gregory K. Beale and Donald A. Carson, eds., *Commentary on the New Testament Use of the Old Testament,* (Grand Rapids, MI: Baker Academic, 2007), 464.
16. See John 5:18 also.
17. Gregory and Carson, eds., *Commentary on the New Testament Use of the Old Testament,* 464.
18. Gregory and Carson, eds., *Commentary on the New Testament Use of the Old Testament,* 464.

CONCLUSION

As the Word in flesh, Jesus revealed the one face and one image of God. John's textual evidence reveals distinction when God acted in His flesh, but the unity and oneness within the Godhead is completely affirmed. Furthermore, in the New Jerusalem, there will be one throne, one on the throne, and there will be one face to be seen (Rev. 22:1-4).[19] The language of distinction and language of identity are unified in Revelation, which John also wrote, as God and Lamb, deity and humanity, will be seen in the face of Jesus.

19. See this author's essay on Revelation for an expansion of how Jesus is portrayed in the Book of Revelation.

15

John and the King of the Exodus

Jeremias D. Zuniga

INTRODUCTION

John's Gospel demonstrates an incredible explication of Old Testament theology through his experience of walking with Christ as Jesus lived, died, and resurrected. Because of how John alludes to the Old Testament, it can be missed. Regardless of these misses, it is recognized in most commentaries that John's Gospel offers substantial theological reflection, mentioning the Passover more than the other Gospel accounts.[1] While this is useful in orienting the reader to the importance of understanding the theology undergirding the book's presentation, the question of what informs that theology is what I have highlighted above as being missed. One reason that the importance of the Old Testament in John is missed is due to interpreters offering quite late dates for the Gospel, speculating that John's theology develops much later than the other Gospel accounts. Consequently, this causes some to claim that primitive Christians had not developed a more robust or refined Christology.[2] That view requires both a later date for John's Gospel (c. 95-140), and a heightened focus on potential Greco-Roman philosophical views that could be present when John potentially wrote.

---

1. Raymond Edward Brown, *The Gospel According to John: A New Translation with Introduction and Commentary* (Garden City, N.Y: Doubleday, 1984), XLVIII-XLIX & 114. Also see F. F. Bruce, *The Gospel & Epistles of John: Introduction, Exposition, and Notes* (Grand Rapids, Mich: Eerdmans Pub. Co, 2002), 73.

2. For a brief yet helpful overview of this older notion that John's Christology is higher and impacted by Hellenistic thought see Brown, "*The Gospel According to John*," LXXX-LXXXVI. Additionally, it would be a benefit to the reader to consult a work directly addressing the continuity between John's Gospel and the Old Testament. A work I recommend is Richard Bauckham, *The Testimony of the Beloved Disciple: Narrative, History, and Theology in the Gospel of John* (Grand Rapids, Mich: Baker Academic, 2008), 28-29 & 239-252.

In this essay, I want to present the Old Testament purview of Jesus in John's Gospel that might be missed by a casual reading. Especially highlighting that Jesus was understood in John's Gospel to be anointed as King, and identified as inaugurating a kingdom that reflects an Old Testament theology. That Old Testament theology is seen in the LORD, who led the mixed multitude out of Egypt during the Exodus. Because my efforts will explore the Old Testament theology of John's Gospel, it will be outside of my focus to present an earlier dating than the current consensus. However, it is my view that the Gospel of John should receive an earlier dating with less focus on the potential Greek philosophies that it could have engaged with and more of a focus on the nature of the development of Old Testament theology through the life of Christ historically.[3] To the theological end, I offer the exploration below.

JOHN'S USE OF THE OLD TESTAMENT

Critically, John's Gospel opens with an immediate allusion to the Old Testament when he writes, "In the beginning was the Word, and the Word was with God, and the Word was God" (John 1:1), which alludes to Genesis 1's creation account.[4] In alluding to this text, John does not offer a formula or inform the reader that he will be drawing the allusion.[5] John assumes his audience has knowledge of the Genesis record, and continues to show his readers just how the life of Jesus demonstrated He was God with us. John showed this by including allusions to the tabernacle when he wrote, "And the Word was made flesh, and dwelt among us, and we beheld His glory" (John 1:14a). The language of "dwelling" is ἐσκήνωσεν (*eskēnōsen*), a word indicating tabernacling when the reader recognizes that beholding His glory refers to Exodus 25:8 and Exodus 40:34-35's description of the LORD's presence filling the tabernacle.[6] While these allusions appear more obviously to readers, I posit that John's understanding of the Old Testament had been opened through his interaction with Christ in a way that may be missed by the reader that has disconnected the

3. George van Kooten, *The Pre-70 ce Dating of the Gospel of John: 'There is (ἔστιν) in Jerusalem … a pool … which has five porticoes' (5.2).* New Testament Studies. 2025;71(1):29-55. doi:10.1017/S0028688524000213

4. Bruce, *The Gospel & Epistles of John*, 28-31.

5. Gregory K. Beale and Donald A. Carson, eds., *Commentary on the New Testament Use of The Old Testament* (Grand Rapids, MI, etc.: Baker Academic etc., 2009), 415-420.

6. Bruce, *The Gospel & Epistles of John*, 39-42.

Old Testament from the New Testament. Because of this, it is crucial that I first encourage the reader to sit and read John 2 entirely before I offer an exploration of John 2 and reintroduce the Exodus account.

THE KING OF THE EXODUS

There are some monumental moments that I want to raise from John 2, the first is the wedding in Cana. When Jesus and the disciples arrive, they encounter an issue; there is a lack of provisions customarily enjoyed at wedding celebrations. After a short interaction with His mother, she instructs those that are present with them, "Ὅ τι ἂν λέγῃ ὑμῖν ποιήσατε" or "Whatever He says to you all, do [it]" (John 2:5b).[7] It is upon this charge that Jesus commands the filling of the waterpots, and He transforms the water into something entirely new, wine (John 2:6-11). This transformation demonstrated that Jesus had full control over the water, He was not just able to command the servants to bring it, but could command the waters themselves to become something new.[8] Importantly, the text describes this as the beginning of Jesus's miracles in Cana before visiting Capernaum and subsequently leaving for Passover in Jerusalem with His disciples (John 2:11-13, 17). While the celebration of Passover commenced, Scripture brings back into focus the miracles of Christ and the belief of the disciples that had been following Him by clarifying through word play, "πολλοὶ ἐπίστευσαν...αὐτὸς δὲ ὁ Ἰησοῦς οὐκ ἐπίστευεν ἑαυτὸν" or "many believed... but Jesus did not himself believe" (John 2:23-24a).[9] The resolution of Jesus's lack of belief is found in the fact that He knew the hearts of each person, and it was unnecessary for anyone's insight; Jesus was the one able to read the hearts of all (John 2:24b-25). These observations are crucial because in the very next few verses, Jesus offers a response that might puzzle a reader that has not recognized

---

7. This phrase is noted as a verbal parallel to Genesis 41:55 in Beale and Carson, *Commentary*, 430-431.

8. L. Michael Morales, *Exodus Old and New: A Biblical Theology of Redemption* (Downers Grove, IL: IVP Academic, an imprint of InterVarsity Press, 2020), 161. Morales notes that, "Jesus' first sign of turning water into wine at a wedding recalls Moses' opening sign of turning the Nile water into blood—and also anticipates the blood and water that will pour forth from Jesus' pierced side in his passion (John 19:34), the only other scene where his mother is present." This is a critical point, especially as the entirety of the chapter expands the motif in light of the life of Christ.

9. Colin G. Kruse, *John: An Introduction and Commentary* (Downers Grove, IL: InterVarsity Press, USA, 2017), 109-111.

His understanding of the human heart. Jesus proclaims the necessity of two things if someone is to enter the kingdom of God: they must be born of water and Spirit (John 3:3, 5).[10]

In my essay on Exodus, I focused on God's kingship as He used the Egyptians' evil for good. In that essay's conclusion, I briefly mentioned the connection between Pharaoh's command to throw the Hebrew boys into the water, the first plague where the water was transformed into blood, the final Passover plague where the firstborns of Egypt were struck, and the judgment of the passing through the waters. Having summarily reviewed John 2-3:5, there are some features of the Exodus that I would like to further draw attention to as Jesus fulfilled these before proclaiming to Nicodemus what the new Exodus would require. First, we encounter the transformation of the water into something entirely new. Under the former covenant, it was deathly (blood), and as Jesus inaugurated the kingdom, it was abundance (wine).[11] Further, the reader is led to the Passover feast, where it is announced that Jesus knows all (John 2:24-25). It should stand out that the elders of Israel were to prepare the houses for the evening when the passing over would occur (Exod. 12:21-28), and at midnight the LORD accomplished His word by striking Egypt in judgment (12:29-30). Israel flees from Egypt and we read, "And I will harden Pharaoh's heart, and he will follow after them" (Exod. 14:4a), "And Pharaoh's heart was overturned and his servants against the people" (Exod. 14:5b), finally "And the LORD hardened the heart of Pharaoh, king of Egypt" (Exod. 14:8). Just as the King caused His people to exit from Egypt through the waters and led them in the cloud (Exod. 13:18-22), Jesus proclaimed knowing that Nicodemus had not hardened his heart "Except one is born of water and the Spirit, he cannot enter into the kingdom of God" (John 3:5).

CONCLUSION

Interestingly, in the Exodus' account of the LORD offering freedom to those that would be His people, that freedom was available to anyone that refused to allow their heart to harden by rejecting His words and those that left Egypt were a mixed multitude (Exod. 12:38). In John's report of

---

10. Bruce, *The Gospel & Epistles of John*, 78.

11. I must note, that while Jesus speaks of and inaugurates the coming kingdom, His reign fulfillment will not be realized until the Millennium.

Jesus's life, I want to highlight that we see Jesus fulfilling this invitation to Nicodemus, a ruler of the Jews in much the same way that the elders were to prepare their house. While midnight was the crucial moment in Exodus, in John, nighttime is when Nicodemus comes to Jesus and hears the reminder that the LORD is still redeeming those who have an open heart. Perhaps this is why Paul declares, "[our fathers] were all baptized unto Moses in the cloud and in the sea" (1 Cor. 10:1-2). Certainly, it was Jesus's command that if one is to be a part of His kingdom, they would have to pass through the waters and be baptized of the Spirit.

WEEK SIX

Acts and the Godhead—Pentecost, Kingship, and the Birth of the Church

16

The Godhead—Christ's Kingship in The Acts of the Apostles

Steven Gill

While contested by certain scholars in modernity, the narrative unity of the book of Luke and the book of Acts is, perhaps, the best place to begin discussions surrounding the attitude of the author of the book of Acts toward our subject. If the gospels represent the biographical framework around which the Messiah is presented to the world, the book of Acts may be considered an epilogue to the biography. The kingship of Christ that is disclosed within the book of Acts, then, should not be considered distinct from its presentation in the gospels, but as something dependent upon them – specifically, the testimony of Luke.

Although sometimes framed as a treatise in which its author reimagined or re-created the history of the people involved, the book of Acts contains both biographical and historical information that is congruent with what can be known about the time-period.[1] Furthermore, the evidence that Acts was meant to be read as a companion volume (and, therefore, in much the same way) as the book of Luke is notable.

Along more constructive lines it is important to note that the division of Luke-Acts into two volumes does not signify that one account had ended and a new one begun or that volume 2 would turn to a different subject matter.

1. Craig Keener, *The IVP Bible Background Commentary*, (IVP Academic, 2014), 316. Here, Keener remarks, "By ancient standards, Luke is meticulously careful with his sources in the Gospel (Lk 1:1-4), and we may regard him as no less trustworthy in Acts, where we can often check him against letters of Paul (few of which would have been available to Luke)." While it has become increasingly popular to criticize the historical veracity of Luke's account of the church in Acts, it is apparent that his work represents a much more thorough and complete assessment of the early church than has been sometimes assumed.

Rather, as a matter of physical expediency ancient authors divided their lengthy works into "books," each of which fit on one papyrus roll. The maximum length of a papyrus roll extended to thirty-five feet, and Luke's two volumes, the two longest books in the NT, would have each required a full papyrus roll...Both narratives begin in Jerusalem; the Gospel ends and Acts begins with commission narratives associated with reports of Jesus' ascension; the time span covered by each volume is approximately thirty years...Luke has regularly developed parallels between Jesus in the Gospel of Luke and his disciples in the Acts of the Apostles...Similarly it is critical that we understand that incidents in the Gospel anticipate aspects of the story narrated only (finally) in Acts.[2]

Assessing the trustworthiness and narrative unity of Luke-Acts is important because it informs how a modern reader may interpret certain passages which detail the early church's doctrine about Christ, His kingship, and the church's role in the earth. The book of Acts opens with the anticipation of a prophetic fulfillment – the outpouring of the Holy Spirit on God's chosen people (Acts 1:4-5; 2:16; Joel 2:28-32). This event is anticipated by the writer in Luke 24:45-50 and detailed in Acts 2:1-11. The promised event appears first relegated to the natural descendants of Abraham, leading even certain Apostles to miss the full significance of the event (Acts 10:9-16). Later, it is revealed that the events of Acts 2 would not remain with the Jews only but would be extended to the Gentiles as well. In Acts' tenth chapter, the gift of the Holy Ghost that was poured out upon the Jews[3] is extended to the Gentiles first through one Italian centurion named Cornelius (Acts 10:44-48). While the inclusion of the gentiles in Christ's kingdom was, at first, perplexing for many Jewish Christians (Acts 11:1-3), in Luke's writing, the gentile event was anticipated by the Law and the

---

2. Joel Green, "Acts of the Apostles," in *Dictionary of the Later New Testament and its Developments*, ed. Ralph P. Martin, Peter H. Davids (IVP Academic, 1997), 12-13.

3. At various points in the New Testament, the Holy Ghost is described as 'seal upon the life of a believer' (Eph. 1:13; 4:30; Rom. 4:11). This theme is particularly emphasized among Reform theologians who insist that the essence of this analogy of a 'seal' is to emphasize the fact that the believer's spiritual condition remains in an unalterable state. Nevertheless, its use throughout the scripture is more related to the mark of a royal figure than to something unalterable. Of its use in Ephesians, Keener writes, "A wax seal would have a mark of ownership or identification stamped in it, identifying who was attesting what was inside the container that had been sealed...The Ephesians must preserve their attestation for the day when their redemption would be complete (the Old Testament 'day of the Lord,' when he would judge the world and vindicate his people)."

For Keener, see: Keener, 544-550.

Prophets (Deut. 32:21; Hos. 2:23; Acts 11:17; Acts 28:28). Many writers have commented on a perceived fixation upon the gentiles by Luke within the framework of his gospel, but this gospel priority harmonizes with all that Luke was to write in the book of Acts as well. In this regard, it is their congruence, not their disparity, which offers clarity to our subject: Over whom, precisely, would Christ be king?

Concerning the ascension of Christ, Luke is the only gospel writer to include the question posed to Jesus by His disciples: "Lord, wilt thou at this time restore again the kingdom to Israel?" (Acts 1:6). This question appears to be posited from the contemporary Jewish understanding of who the Messiah would be and how He would be king in the earth. Many Jews of the first century anticipated a soon-coming king who would throw off the oppression of God's people by surrounding nations.[4] This anticipation became so fervent during the Roman occupation of Judaea that even prominent rabbis such as Akiva were led to believe that certain military governors were indeed the Christ.[5] Nevertheless, while Jesus did not dismiss the validity of the question posed by the disciples, Jesus forewent offering any answer that might have seemed satisfactory (Acts 1:7). In many ways, the brief exchange neatly summarizes misconceptions about the coming king shared by both believing and non-believing Jews at that time:

---

4. Throughout the gospels, the "kingdom of God" is an oft contested phrase by modern scholars. Some might easily wonder if the kingdom that Jesus taught about was something that had already come (Mark 1:15) or something that was coming (Matt. 26:64). Thompson writes that the, "...the kingdom of God," was, "a common but undefined expression for Jesus' message in Luke's Gospel (e.g., 4:43; 6:20; 7:28; 9:2; 10:9; 17:20-21; 18:16-17; 22:16, 18). This same expression also describes the message of the Christian preaching in Acts (e.g., 8:12; 14:22; 19:8; 28:23, 31). In Jesus' day, people hoped for the kingdom of God in the distant future. However, in both the Third Gospel and Acts...it expresses how God had presently entered into human experience through Jesus."

Richard Thompson, *Acts: A Commentary in the Wesleyan Tradition,* (Beacon Hill Press, 2015), 59.

5. "Bar Kochba." JewishHistory.org. Accessed November 4, 2025. https://www.jewishhistory.org/bar-kochba/. In his entry on the subject, C.A. Evans writes that tensions between Christians and Jews increased during this period because "Simon was regarded as the Messiah...Christian allegiance to Jesus as the Messiah contradicted Simon's claims and undermined his authority." Indeed, Eusebius also notes that the Bar Kochba Revolt represented a significant shift in Jewish/Christian relations, leading church to become eventually dominated by gentiles.

For Evans: Craig Evans, "Christianity and Judaism: Parting of the Ways," in *Dictionary of the Later New Testament & Its Developments*, ed. Ralph P. Martin, Peter H. Davids (IVP Academic, 1997), 165.

First, that the savior-king described by the prophets was first and primarily concerned with destroying the earthly adversaries of His people; Second, that the savior-king would rule exclusively over God's people, the Jews. To the first point, much of the dispute between Jewish and Christian conceptions of the Christ hangs upon the issue of purpose: From what, precisely, do the people of God need salvation? For the New Testament writers, through the death, burial, and resurrection of Jesus, one can know with assurance that He is the Christ, as His life disclosed the fulfillment of the suffering-servant passage of Isaiah. This does not negate the kingship of Christ but is the necessary precursor to it. Because He paid the penalty for our sins, Jesus has saved us from sin (Isa. Ch.53). Cullman writes:

> The Acts of the Apostles offers us the strongest proof of the fact that in the most ancient period of early Christianity there existed an explanation of the person and work of Jesus which we could characterize somewhat inaccurately as an *ebed Yahweh* [servant of God] Christology…We may even assert that this is probably the oldest known solution to the Christological problem. The account of the conversion of the Ethiopian eunuch (Acts 8:26 ff.) shows that in the first century Jesus was explicitly identified with the *ebed Yahweh*…We may conjecture, by way of summary, that the *ebed Yahweh* concept very probably dominated the Christology of the Apostle Peter…If this is the case, he, who had wanted to divert Jesus from the way of suffering, who had denied him at the decisive moment of the passion story, would be the first after Easter to grasp the necessity of this designation *ebed Yahweh*.[6]

This 'servant of God' who, according to Isaiah, would suffer for the sin of His people was a fixed feature of Christian beliefs about the Christ (Acts 2:29-36; Acts 7:47-53; Acts 8:27-36). This is important to our subject, as it is only in this context that the reader can rightly understand the grafting-in of the gentiles to God's plan detailed in the book of Acts. Sin was not just an Israelite problem, but a global problem. From this perspective, it becomes clearer how the Christ of the Old Testament would be the king – not just of the Israelites – but of the whole world (John 3:16; 1 John 2:2). In Acts, the grafting in of the gentiles

6. Oscar Cullman, *The Christology of the New Testament,* (The Westminster Press, 1963), 73-75.

signaled God's concern for restoring the sons of God – all the children of Adam – back to a relationship with him.[7] Thus, in reconciling the first disparity concerning views about the Christ, light is shed upon the second. The Gentiles were brought into the covenant, not to replace the Jews, but to be saved from sin just as Israel needed to be saved from sin. That the gentile event mirrored Jewish entry in the kingdom of God is seen most evidently by their shared experience with regard to the Holy Ghost, as well as their participation in water baptism. In each case, the experience of the Jews, diasporic communities, Samaritans, and gentiles is consonant (Acts 2:4-6; 8:12-17; 8:36-38; 10:44-48; 19:1-6). Entry into the kingdom of God was signaled by 'calling upon the name of the Lord' in water baptism and reception of His Spirit as the evidentiary seal upon the heart. In every case, the entry of the people of God into the kingdom found within the book of Acts reflected fulfillment of and obedience to Christ's commission in Luke's gospel: "...that repentance and remission of sins should be preached in his name among all nations, beginning at Jerusalem." (Luke 24:49).

7. In light of this understanding, it is, perhaps, easier to grasp in what manner Luke's genealogy of Christ is truly distinct from Matthew's. Matthew, beginning with Abraham, offered the ancestors in descending order down to the Christ. By contrast, Luke, beginning with Christ, works his way not back to Abraham, but to Adam. For more on this, see: Steven Gill, *The Last Man*, (Biblical Hebrew Academy Online, 2023), 29.

17

Apostolic Identity and the Words of Scripture

Andrew Herbst

INTRODUCTION

Attacks have been made stating that Luke was a faulty historian, recording errors and inconsistencies. Another line of criticism attempts to cast doubt on the sermons in Acts, claiming that Luke summarized or crafted the 'speeches' in Acts to match his own theological agenda. We must analyze Luke and the Biblical evidence more closely to determine whether or not these assertions carry weight. Although Luke and Acts are in focus, the other three Gospel accounts would be impacted as well, because the sermons and events rely on firsthand eyewitness testimonies.

LUKE AS A HISTORIAN

Because of postmodernism and the culture of the day, it is popular to claim that authors always have a bias or an agenda behind everything they write. When this concept is applied to the Bible, it is called *narrative criticism*. This position would deny that Luke wrote Acts as a historian, and deny or diminish the working of the Spirit upon Luke as an author. Rather, Luke wrote 'narrative history' with a desire to use the stories to create a propaganda work. Some critical assertions may sound like this: 'Luke re-constructed the speeches, not inventing from scratch, but summarized them to match his own theological purposes.' In other words, the sermons may not be totally accurate, but they were crafted by Luke to portray certain ideas to his readers. Some would refuse to use the word *propaganda*, but that is what Acts becomes within narrative criticism.

Sir William M. Ramsay (1851-1939) was a skeptic who set out to disprove Luke's writings. Considered an expert in multiple historical and archaeological fields, he made several journeys throughout Biblical lands and uncovered numerous archaeological artifacts. The evidence of Luke's accuracy was so overwhelming that Ramsay was thoroughly persuaded of the New Testament's reliability. Gasque summarized Ramsay's conclusion,

> The author of Acts is not to be regarded as the author of historical romance, legend, or third- or second-rate history. Rather he is the writer of an historical work of the highest order, a work to be compared with that of Thucydides, the greatest of the Greek historians.[1]

Several points can be observed to demonstrate Luke as a high-class historian. Looking at the missionary journeys alone (Acts 13-28), there are approximately 84 verified facts.[2] These facts include geography, local politics and officials, local customs, and more. Specifically, the terms asiarchs (Acts 19:31) and *politarchs* (Acts 17:6),[3] which were titles for political leaders, have been found on coins and stone inscriptions near the Biblical locations.[4] In addition, the correct location of the Island of Clauda (Acts 27:16) is recorded, which is in contrast to other experts of that era who incorrectly identified the island's location.[5] The exact precision of these details relates to us that Luke was present at the event(s) in the Book of Acts, or spoke to someone who was.

How could Luke gain information he was not present to see himself? Luke did his research (Luke 1 and Acts 1), and he was an eyewitness to the events of the second half of the Book of Acts (cf. the 'we' passages).[6] In addition, he had access to the apostles, especially Paul. It seems that Luke could have spoken with the apostles themselves, and the Holy Ghost moved on him to faithfully write down what the apostles relayed to him.

---

1. W. Ward Gasque, *Sir William M. Ramsay: Archaeologist and New Testament Scholar*, (Grand Rapids, MI: Baker Book House, 1966), 28.
2. See Colin Hemer, *The Book of Acts in the Setting of Hellenistic History*, (Winona Lake, IN: Eisenbrauns, 1990).
3. Unless otherwise noted, all biblical passages referenced are in the *King James Version*.
4. Joseph M. Holden and Norman Geisler, *The Popular Handbook of Archaeology of the Bible*, (Eugene, OR: Harvest House Publishers, 2013), 353-56.
5. Hemer, *Book of Acts*, 331.
6. Luke had access to eyewitness accounts for his Gospel and the first half of Acts. Beginning in Acts 16, the author introduces the 'We' passages (Acts 16:9-10, 20:6, 21:1-8, 27:1-2). These passages indicate that the author was present and personally witnessed the events within the latter half of the Book of Acts.

Furthermore, the firsthand accounts of Jesus were numerous, many of which had seen Jesus resurrected and were still alive in the mid-50s AD (1 Cor. 15:6). This is significant considering Luke finished writing Acts around AD 62. Thus, at a minimum, Luke may have had a decade or so of time to interact with first-generation Christians before writing his books.

An important note, and perhaps the most worthy of attention, comes from John 14:26. Jesus articulated that the apostles would have perfect and total recall of memory for what Jesus had taught. This promise of supernatural memory should lead us to understand Jesus' sermons as faithful word-for-word accounts. Moreover, if the Gospels, especially Luke's, correctly preserved the words of Jesus, then we can confidently believe the words of the apostles in Acts to be preserved as well. Therefore, doubting Luke's sermons seems unnecessary: if the Spirit could assist in preserving the words of Jesus, then the Spirit could assist in preserving the apostle's words as well.

Luke's circumstances were different from, say, Thucydides. As Thucydides recorded the facts surrounding the Peloponnesian War, the Greek historian said he was documenting events that spanned multiple decades and stretched across a wide geographical range. Thucydides admits he was not always able to gain direct testimonies and that some sources may have been secondhand, but he attempted to be as accurate as possible.[7] Even though Thucydides is praised as one of the greatest historians of the ancient world, Luke's status should be even higher. His firsthand experiences, access to eyewitnesses, and the inspiration of the Holy Ghost all contributed to his composition of Luke and Acts. With all of these elements combined, Luke should not be demoted to the same authorial status as a non-spirit-filled historian. Everything we can verify in the Gospels and Acts has been shown to be truthful; therefore, we have no logical reason to doubt the historical events or the sermons.

SERMON LENGTH

Another critical argument could be, 'because ancient speeches were always long, and sermons in Acts are short, it follows that Luke summarized the sermons.' However, this is faulty reasoning. We know that some sermons were

---

7. Robert Strassler and Richard Crawley, *The Landmark Thucydides*, (New York: Free Press, 2008), 15.

long (Acts 20:7), but Luke gives us clues when he is not telling us every word that was spoken. For example, in Acts 2:40, Luke tells us directly that he has given the main idea of how Peter concluded his sermon, but without every sentence. Seeing this indicator, the first section of Peter's sermon should be understood differently than the latter half: the first section should be interpreted as it is written, "then Peter said" is actually what Peter said.

CONCLUSION

To be Apostolic means we follow the doctrines and practices of the apostles. They held to the very letters and words of Scripture as God's revelation to humanity. We must have a reliable history if the revelation and doctrine are to be any use to us. If we cannot trust the words, then what we practice from those accounts becomes unfounded. Attacking the words of God has occurred from the beginning (Gen. 3) and will continue until He returns. The evidence shows that Jesus and the apostles did not consider the Bible to be conceptually Scripture or merely theologically God's Word, but every word, letter, and recorded event to be inspired. To be Apostolic, one must adhere to these beliefs without reservation and hold fast to every word that proceeds from the mouth of God.

18

The Promise of a King—The Prophetic Nature of the Psalms in Acts 2

Jeremias D. Zuniga

INTRODUCTION

Arguably, the Psalms are among the most important portions of Scripture a believer can commit to memory.[1] As a young person, I recall being "voluntold" that I would be in Bible quizzing. As a young boy, my competitive side was thrilled. It was because of this choice, to memorize the Scripture for sport, that I was first introduced to the Psalms. While the motivation of a child may not have been to learn Scripture for Scripture's sake, as a 5-year-old, the exposure to the nearly 200 verses was impactful. Interestingly, it was not until I was much older that I realized I did not understand what had been memorized, although these verses and others have not been forgotten almost 25 years later.

Importantly, I am aware that this essay must cover Acts and that the reader may be questioning just how this relates to the account of the Spirit and Apostles' activities in establishing the early church. That is the point. As a child, I was entirely unaware of the connections between the Psalms and Acts. Because of this disconnection, I want to raise a challenge to an assumption, an assumption that causes a critical misunderstanding of the psalter. My claim is that Old Testament kings could be used to prophecy or serve in priestly functions, though their chief roles may have remained as king. Naturally, this offers nuance

1. This point is well made in the work following, Dennis F. Kinlaw, *Old Testament Theology Lectures: Thirty Six Lectures* (Wilmore, Ky: Francis Asbury Society, 2003). Kinlaw includes full texts repeatedly with the aim of causing the reader not to rush through references, to slow down and engage the Scripture that is being written about. To this end, I encourage the reader of this book to keep your Bible close, as it is imperative to use this work only as a reference to it, not a replacement.

to the claim that only Jesus can hold the "*munus triplex*."[2] And while I do not aim to show that David was a prophet, priest, and king for the entirety of his rule in Israel, I will demonstrate that while being a king, David was a prophet. While it would be optimal to demonstrate the priestly and prophetic functions robustly, my purview does not permit me to at this time. However, the reader should refer to 1 Samuel 14:3, 21:9; and 2 Samuel 6:14 for the garments of a priest and David's use of the ephod.

THE HOLY ONE

Throughout the Old Testament, there occurs and reoccurs the statement, "Holy One" (e.g., Deut. 33:8; 2 Kings 19:22; Ps. 16:10; Is. 43:14-15).[3] It is interesting to note that each of these verses utilize distinctive Hebrew phrases to indicate "Holy One," which is not always recognizable if the reader does not read closely. In Deuteronomy 33:8 the phrase "לאיש חסידך" (*ləʾîš ḥasîḏekā*) or "to your holy one," focuses on a "לאיש" literally "to a man/one" which should be understood as the tribe personified as one that has lived piously. That is to say, the Levites are collectively described as being loyal in their devotion and thus consecrated.[4] Whereas in 2 Kings 19:22, "על־קדוש ישראל" (*ʿal-qəḏôš yiśrāʾēl*) or "against the Holy One of Israel" is describing God as the Holy One responding to the Assyrian king Sennacherib and uses the word normally translated as "Holy," or "Holiness."[5] Naturally, since Isaiah was the prophet delivering God's word in 2 Kings, Isaiah 43:14-15 also uses the same phrase as 2 Kings 19:22 "קדוש ישראל" (*qəḏôš yiśrā'ēl*) or "the Holy One of Israel," with a small adjustment in verse 15 to include that the Holy One is the creator. Noticeably, Deuteronomy uses a different word than Isaiah חסיד (Deuteronomy) versus Kings and Isaiah's קדוש. Isaiah uses the word normally translated "Holy," and Deuteronomy uses a word that stems from another root, meaning loyal.[6]

---

2. This term refers to the offices of prophet, priest, and king.

3. While this volume is not intended to be read start to finish, it will be beneficial if the reader first engages with my earlier essay "Preaching to Kings," and the essay addressing the Davidic Covenant written by Andrew Herbst.

4. Jeffrey H. Tigay, Deuteronomy = דברים: The Traditional Hebrew Text with the New JPS Translation (Philadelphia: Jewish Publication Society, 2003), 324.

5. D. J. Wiseman, *1 and 2 Kings: An Introduction and Commentary* (Nottingham: Inter-Varsity Press/IVP Academic, 1993), 300-302.

6. The word in mind here is חסד, a word commonly translated "mercy," "kindness," or "loyal love," see Tigay, *Deuteronomy*, 67. Tigay connects the two words as well in 324n55, as he comments on Deut. 33:8.

Having considered these, Psalm 16:10 offers something only slightly different from Deuteronomy 33:8. However, while Deuteronomy is reflecting on the Levites, the Psalter has one in focus. In the Psalter, the following occurs, "לא־תתן חסידך לראות שחת" or "never will *ḥasîḏekā* be given to see corruption" (Ps. 16:10b). Here, the Psalter is expressing the loyalty that the LORD has to those who have shown loyalty to keeping covenant.[7] The LORD will not allow the Holy One to see corruption, a reference to death, because the Holy One has been set apart by His faithfulness to Him.[8] This fidelity is critical as we consider Psalm 16:11, especially the indication that this Holy One would be at the right hand forever. Additionally, Psalm 16:8 informs us that the Psalter has been strengthened because the LORD is set before him, as the "right hand" of the Psalter indicates power to remain strong despite the severity of the situation at hand.[9] Also, the idea of God's right hand in verse 11c should not escape the reader as here it denotes that the LORD will reposition the Holy One to a beautiful place.

ACTS 2:27-30

Gathered there in Jerusalem at the feast of Pentecost were Jews and others who were devout, people who would be expected to understand the Scriptures (Acts 2:5). It is on this occasion that Peter stood to preach to the multitude of amazed doubters and mockers (Acts 2:12-13) and begins by referencing the Old Testament texts. Beginning his sermon, Peter tells his audience that he is quoting from the prophet Joel (Acts 2:16), then in Acts 2:27, he starts to quote from David. The text selected by Peter was Psalm 16:8-11, which is why it is crucial to recognize the focus I highlighted in the Psalm above. After reciting the Psalm in the ears of his audience, Peter calls David two things: Patriarch

7. John Goldingay, *Psalms 1-41*, vol. 1 (Grand Rapids, Mich: Baker Academic, 2006), 227m. Goldingay translates the text, "you will not let someone committedm to see the Abyss." And notes, '"*ḥāsîdkā*; perhaps "someone to whom you are committed."'

8. This is not a prophecy concerning Christ's "peccability" or "impeccability," terms discussing whether Christ could have sinned or not. This text is focused on whether the Holy One would remain dead given the focus on Sheol.

9. This is well captured in the following, "He uses another anthropomorphic expression: "He is at my right side." The right side is idiomatic for the place of strength, support, and honor." See Allen P. Ross, *A Commentary on the Psalms: 1-41*, vol. 1 (Grand Rapids, MI: Kregel Academic & Professional, 2011), 408. Additionally, "The right hand is the position of support, and Yhwh's being there encourages the suppliant to stay faithful." Goldingay, *Psalms 1-41*, 232.

and Prophet (Acts 2:29-30). He recognized that when David wrote about the nature of God, he wrote proleptically, though David himself might have been experiencing immediate threats to his life. David understood that God would not suffer the Holy One, the One who remained faithful in all things, to remain dead but would reposition Him to sit at His right hand. An astute reader should recognize that the Psalter does not include the language of a throne, although that is implicit in the favorite New Testament Psalm, Psalm 110, and appears to be understood in Peter's statement that "knowing that God had sworn with an oath to him, that of the fruit of his loins, according to the flesh, he would raise up Christ to sit on his throne;" (Acts 2:30 KJV).[10]

Further, Peter does not say, "David, who was used in the prophetic" or even, "David, who prophesied at times" (see 1 Sam. 10:10-13). Rather, he offers a definitive role concerning the LORD's use of David, "Accordingly, he was a prophet" (Acts 2:30a). There is little room for ambiguity, king David, who God had promised would have a son that would reign forever, was able to write prophetically, and often of what God would do for that coming son.[11]

CONCLUSION

It should not surprise the reader that the New Testament describes David in this way, nor should the prophetic nature of the Psalms. Historically, it is common to refer to some of the Psalms as "messianic," which is simply acknowledging that they prophecy of the coming Messiah, the anointed One. Further, it was Jesus who lived a life unlike any other human and remained faithful to covenant without falling to temptation, regardless of the pressure before Him. As David prophesied of a situation so dire, he knew that the strength of the LORD is with the faithful, and as Jesus suffered and died, it was a sure promise that He would resurrect and ascend to the throne awaiting, with a promise of His return (Acts 13:16-43; Heb. 5:5-10).

10. Craig S. Keener, *Acts: An Exegetical Commentary Introduction and 1:1-2:47*, vol. 1 (Grand Rapids, MI: Baker Academic, 2012), 948-954.

11. See the footnote above for Keeners comments.

WEEK SEVEN

Paul and His Epistles—The Law, the Godhead, and the New Creation

19

The Godhead—Reframing Paul

Steven Gill

Christianity is sometimes presented as a movement born out in two stages: The first is generally framed as 'The Jesus era' in which Christianity maintained much of its Judaic foundation – emphasizing God's oneness, upholding the Hebrew scriptures, and embracing a unique prioritization of the nation of Israel. The second, often called 'Pauline Christianity,' is the era in which Christianity drastically departed from its Jewish roots – abandoning or modifying the Old Testament conception of God, introducing novel interpretations of the scriptures, and advocating for the active replacement of God's chosen people.[1] Nevertheless, this two-stage framing of Christianity represents a mischaracterization of the New Testament, often forcing its readers into isolated readings of the biblical text that do not square with the whole. This is, perhaps, never more apparent than when discussing the godhead in Paul's letters.

Any discussion surrounding the epistles of Paul should begin with the historical background in which those letters were written. Thus, the Paul of the letters

---

1. This view is articulated by Jewish and Christian thinkers alike, such as rabbi Joseph Telushkin and Joshua Schachterle.

For Telushkin, see: Joseph Telushkin, *Jewish Literacy*, 129. "Paul radically redefined this small Jewish sect into a new religion...". In this entry, Telushkin insists that Paul's teachings reflect a near-hostility toward Jewish Law and signal his misunderstanding of the basic tenants of Judaism. "According to him [Paul], what mattered to God was not observance of the Torah, but faith in Jesus...Jesus' brother, James...ordered Paul to observe Jewish law (Acts 21:24). Paul rejected James's command." Telushkin's portrayal of Paul's attitude toward the Torah is misleading, as examples of Paul's adherence to many of the basic tenants of Jewish life are discussed throughout this paper. Furthermore, Acts 21:26 states that Paul did, in fact, take heed to James' request in Acts 21:24.

For Schachterle, see: Joshua Schachterle, *Paul's Christianity: How the Apostle Molded the Christian Faith*, accessed 6/2/2025. Here, Schachterle emphasizes his belief that Paul's teaching represented a significant departure from the teachings of Jesus Christ, a view that is, to say the least, highly disputed.

to the Corinthians, Colossians, and Ephesians cannot be separated from the Paul of the book of Acts. When readers are first introduced to Paul,[2] he is a young man who is an official of the Pharisees and responsible for the harassment and arrest of Christians (Acts 7:58-8:3). Paul's intensely religious background is important to his later influence within the church. While sometimes thought of as a Jew who, upon his conversion to Christ, abandoned his Jewish life, the Paul of the New Testament is much more complex than contemporary Christian thinkers might imagine. Cohick states,

> It is common to think of Paul as having converted from Judaism to Christianity, but the situation is more complicated. Paul describes a vibrant, zealous religious life as a Pharisee before he believed...(Phil 3:4-6), not a life of fear or dread before God. He contrasts that time with his work as an apostle to the Gentiles as before and after his encounter with Christ Jesus. Thus if convert means "change belief about Jesus as Messiah," then Paul converted...However, because Paul continued to embrace the Jewish Scriptures, to participate in synagogue worship, and to self-identify as a Jew, we should not conclude that Paul "converted" to Christianity as if he left Judaism altogether.[3]

Although a believer by the ninth chapter of the book of Acts, Paul still behaved as a Jew throughout the course of his life. In in the eighteenth chapter of Acts, Paul is found having taken a vow,[4] shaving his head after the custom of the Jews

---

2. I use the familiar iteration of Paul's name throughout this paper. While Paul is sometimes imagined as a Christian who, much like Peter, underwent a dramatic name-change intended to disclose his conversion, this is not the impression of his name that one takes from the New Testament. Early in the book of Acts, Luke, writing in Greek, translates Paul's name from Hebrew to Greek (Σαῦλος) (Transliteration: *Saulos*). In English, this Hebrew word is rendered "Saul." Later, Luke uses the presentation of Paul's name more familiar to his gentile audience – the Latin derived Greek word (Παῦλος) (Transliteration: *Paulos*). These are not two different names, but two iterations of the same name, translated from two different languages. Hence, as Luke says, "Then Saul, (who also is called Paul,)..." as the apostle was likely familiar to Christians by both names (Acts 13:9 KJV).

3. Lynn Cohick, "Paul and Judaism," in *Dictionary of Paul and His Letters*, ed. Scott McKnight, Lynn H. Cohick, Nijay K. Gupta (IVP Academic, 2023), 772-773.

4. This likely refers to a Nazir vow, during which it was customary for the adherent to abstain from certain foods and behaviors, leaving their hair uncut until the conclusion of the vow in accordance with Numbers chapter six. While some Christians resist the notion that Paul participated in such a vow perhaps due to perceived tensions regarding certain beliefs about the

(Acts 18:18). Before his arrest, Paul traveled to the temple in Jerusalem, fulfilling a rite of purification at the request of James and the brethren, an act wholly consistent with Paul's Jewish identity (Acts 21:17-27). Long after his conversion, the reader of the book of Acts finds Paul hastening to Jerusalem, attempting to make it to the city in time for the Jewish holiday of *Shavuot* (Acts 20:16).[5] Although critical of believers who prioritized circumcision as a means of justification, Paul insisted upon Timothy's circumcision before adopting the young man as a traveling companion (Acts 16:3).[6] While commonly known as the apostle to the gentiles, it is important to note that Paul made habit of frequenting the synagogues first in his travels. Throughout the entirety of the book of Acts, Paul

---

role of the Law of Moses in Paul's life, it is apparent from later reading in Acts that Paul took no issue with such vows of purification. In Acts 21:26, Paul took Christian brethren with him into the temple to complete vows to fulfill "...the days of purification, until that an offering should be offered for every one of them." This passage shores up the notion that Paul took no issue with his place as a Jew and lived in accordance with that identity. If the vow of Acts 18:18 was not the biblical Nazir vow, it would be difficult to sort out why Paul would have participated in an extra-biblical vow of a similar sort. Paul warned against participation in 'Jewish fables' in his pastoral epistles in Titus (1:14). This phrase is certainly not used in reference to the Law of Moses, but it likely refers to extra-biblical traditions that some have suggested certain believers participated in. My hesitancy toward this idea leads me to believe that Paul's vow was likely the Nazir vow of Numbers.

For the Nazir Vow, see: Menachem Posner, *The Nazir and the Nazirite Vow*, 2025.

5. In each of the three aforementioned cases, Paul's posture as a Jew is seen after his conversion. Even Paul's statement that he was a 'Hebrew of Hebrews' gives lie to the claim that his life represented a Hellenized version of Judaism that parted ways with the traditions of his fathers; nearly the opposite appears to have been the case. As F.F. Bruce states, "...in reference to visitors to Corinth who tried to undermine his position in the eyes of his converts there, he [Paul] says, 'Are they Hebrews? So am I' – and the context suggests that 'Hebrews' has a more restricted sense than 'Israelites' or 'descendants of Abraham' (2 Corinthians 11:25). In Acts 6:1 'Hebrews' is used in contradistinction to 'Hellenists', although both Hebrews and Hellenists were Jews...The distinction was probably linguistic and cultural: the Hebrews, in that case, attended synagogues where the service was conducted in Hebrew an used Aramaic as their normal mode of speech, while the Hellenists spoke Greek and attended synagogues where the scriptures were read and the prayers recited in that language." Thus, Paul's perspective of his own life was one of a Hebrew who – juxtaposed with many of his fellow Israelites – faithfully followed the scriptures and teachings of their forefathers.

F.F. Bruce, *Paul: Apostle of the Heart Set Free*, (Paternoster Press, 1977), 42.

6. This action by Paul is often characterized as a simple means to an end; the Jews would not have received Timothy had it not been for his circumcision. Nevertheless, it is not Paul motive for the action, but the action itself which gives lie to the claim that Paul rejected circumcision wholesale as a defilement to Christian life. Whether as an ordered regard for Timothy's Jewish identity or a means to an end, Paul found utility in circumcision. This fact disrupts the popular notion that Paul sought to distance Christianity from Judaism in every way.

prioritized his ministry within the synagogue before his preaching outside of it (Acts 13:5; 13:14; 14:1; 17:2; 17:10; 17:17; 18:4; 18:7-8; 18:19; 19:8).[7] All of this suggests a Paul who, far from abandoning his Jewish identity, insisted upon harmony between that identity and his faith in Christ.[8]

When Paul discussed the nature of God and the incarnation in his epistles, he did so in a manner that was consistent with a traditional Hebraic approach to the scriptures. For Paul, God is one, and the one God is both omnipresent and omnipotent (Eph. 4:4-6). Concerning Christ, Paul's attitude was that the believer's conception of God was not a radical departure from the Hebrew scriptures, but the fulfillment of them (Acts 13:29-33). Far from distancing himself from the doctrine of the Jewish scriptures, Paul displayed an intimate familiarity with the Old Testament, using it to bolster his teachings about Christ, the church, and the place of the Jews in God's master plan.[9] For Paul, Jesus is the Son of God who was promised to come in the writings of the prophets and fulfilled at the Bethlehem birth (Acts 13:22-23). Just as Jesus prayed that His disciples would be found 'in Him and He in them,' (John 17:21-23) so too did Paul instruct the churches: "For as many of you as have been baptized into Christ have put on Christ" (Gal.3:27). In disclosing the mystery of God's Law written upon the hearts of men (2 Cor. 3:3 Heb. 8:10), Paul called this Spirit "Christ in you, the hope of glory" (Col. 1:27). The Spirit's coming foretold in (Jer. 31:31-33; Ezek. 11:19-20), Paul's presentation of the nature of the Holy Ghost is in harmony with the prophets. Although perhaps depicted otherwise by later trinitarian interpreters, Paul's use of the prophets' imagery is born out most clearly in Romans, in which Paul variously calls the Spirit within the believer the "Spirit of God,

7. It is important to note at this juncture – while gentiles were certainly present and sometimes converted within the synagogues (Acts 17:12; 18:4), Paul's ministry to the gentiles is presented as something at least nominally distinct from his ministry within the synagogues. This is seen most clearly in the eighteenth chapter of Acts, when Paul concludes that there is no more value in his presence among the Jews in that place and states, "...henceforth I will go unto the Gentiles" (Acts 18:6, KJV).

8. Steve Walton, "Paul in Acts," in *Dictionary of Paul and His Letters*, ed. Scott McKnight, Lynn H. Cohick, Nijay K. Gupta, (IVP Academic, 2023), 782.

9. Between Romans tenth and eleventh chapters, Paul quoted no less than seven books of the Old Testament thirteen times in less than two chapters of reading [10:5 Lev.18:5] [10:11 Isa. 45:17] [10:13 Joel 2:32] [10:15 Isa. 52:7] [10:16 Isa. 53:1] [10:19 Deut. 32:21] [10:20 Isa. 65:1] [10:21 Isa. 65:2] [11:2-3 1 Kings 19:9-10] [11:4 1 Kings 19:18] [11:8 Jer. 5:21] [11:9 Psa. 69:22] [11:26-27 Isa. 59:20-21].

Spirit of Christ, Christ in You, and the Spirit of Him that raised up Jesus from the dead…" (Romans 8:9-11).[10] Generally critical of Hellenism and objecting to its theological compatibility with the scriptures, Paul warned believers against allowing philosophy and extra-biblical traditions to influence the Christian view of the Godhead (Col. 2:8-9). For Paul, life in Christ was not only compatible with his Judaism but dependent upon it (Rom 9:4-5). Far from introducing extra-biblical works into his epistles as one might expect of a Hellenistic-inclined theological pioneer, on numerous occasions Paul called upon the text of Genesis to illustrate his beliefs about the nature of the Son of God and the purpose of Christ.[11] Among the most significant contributions of Paul to Christian doctrine is found in his insistence that one day the ministry of the Sonship of Christ will cease "…that God may be all in all" (1 Cor. 15:28), a view not held by many Christians in the world today.[12] Thus, in many ways, Paul's epistles do not represent a radical departure from the teachings of the Hebrew Bible, but they do, perhaps, present challenging questions for the twenty-first-century church. The question may rightly be asked, how compatible is contemporary Christian thought with that of the first-century apostle? Concerning the godhead, Paul's writing finds much more harmony with the Old Testament that preceded him than with the canonical Christian teachings that followed him.

---

10. Paul's presentation of the form and function of the Holy Spirit is not easily harmonized with later trinitarian developments. In trinitarian theology, the Holy Spirit is the third person of the triune God and fulfills a distinct purpose/function within the trinity that is distinguishable from the other two persons. The Holy Spirit is the person of God who dwells within the believer, not the Father or the Son. Nevertheless, Paul spoke of the Spirit within the believer interchangeably as the Holy Spirit, The Spirit of Christ, Christ Himself, and the Spirit of Him that raised Jesus from the dead. In another place, Paul wrote that it is the 'Father who is in all' (Eph. 4:6) illustrating that these distinctions were not as clear as later Christian thinkers supposed.

For the traditional trinitarian view on the third person of the Trinity, see: Yves Congar, *A Theology of the Third Person of the Trinity*, (Church Life Journal, 2023). In Congar's entry, "Catholics say, 'who proceeds from the Father and the Son'…The East retained the words of Jesus in John 15:26: 'Who proceeds from the Father.'"

11. This approach by Paul is sometimes called "Adamic Christology." Throughout Romans fifth chapter and First Corinthians fifteenth chapter, Paul compared the Adam of Genesis with Jesus Christ, referring to Adam as the 'figure' of him who was to come. Concerning Christ, Paul calls Him "the last Adam" (1st Cor. 15:43-45) who fixed what the first Adam destroyed.

For Adamic Christology, see: Steven Gill, *The Last Man: Reclaiming Father & Son Language in the Oneness Pentecostal Movement*, (Steven Gill, 2023), 68-69.

12. Smith, Brandon D. "Eternal Generation According to Athanasius." The Center for Baptist Renewal. Last modified September 21, 2021. https://www.centerforbaptistrenewal.com/blog/2021/9/20/eternal-generation-according-to-athanasius.

While Paul acknowledged that Judaism was largely represented by factions that either abused, misused, or misunderstood the Law of Moses (Phil.3:3-9; Gal. 3:1-7) he often characterized faith in Christ as neither foreign or inconsistent with all that he and his fellow Jews had been taught. Even when criticizing those who would try to misuse the Law as a means of justification, Paul qualified his criticisms carefully, as seen in (1 Tim. 1:6-9; Gal. 3:24-25). Furthermore, Paul did not believe that gentile participation in the plan of God should be a novel concept to the Jews who were familiar with scriptures: "...for we say that faith was reckoned to Abraham for righteousness. How was it then reckoned? when he was in circumcision, or in uncircumcision? Not in circumcision, but in uncircumcision" (Rom. 4:9-10 KJV). Thus, as much of the orthodox Jewish community acknowledges today, the first Jew was, in fact, a convert himself.[13]

All of this suggests a Paul who prioritized harmony between Christian faith and the teachings of the Hebrew scriptures. In light of Paul's complicated relationship with Judaism in the first century, it is unsurprising to discover that Christianity was not initially viewed as an independent religion that began in the Judaean province, but as an extension or sect within the Jewish community itself.[14] This notion appears supported by the early church's teaching about the oneness of the godhead, a fact which a great deal of Paul's writing was devoted to.[15] Thus, harmony between the Hebrew scriptures and the teaching of the first-century church was not an inconsistency to be worked out by Paul over many epistles in varying iterations, but a primary feature on which all of his doctrine hung.

---

13. Joseph Telushkin, *Jewish Literacy: The Most Important Things to Know About the Jewish Religion, Its People, and Its History*, (William Morrow and Company, Inc., 1991) 626. Here, Telushkin cites Tanhuma B concerning Lekh Lekha 24, which reminds the hearer that, lest they believe they are too old to convert, Abraham was ninety-nine years old when he himself converted.

14. Eric Myers, "Jewish Culture in Greco-Roman Palestine," in *Cultures of the Jews: A New History*, ed. David Biale, (Schocken Books, 2002), 168-169. Myers refers to the Tannaitic Period in which written and oral disputation between Jewish Christians and non-Christian Jews was common.

15. In First Timothy 3:16, Paul wrote to his traveling companion and son in the gospel: "And without controversy great is the mystery of godliness: God was manifest in the flesh, justified in the Spirit, seen of angels, preached unto the Gentiles, believed on in the world, received up into glory." This description of the story of the incarnation neatly summarizes nearly all that Paul taught about Jesus in his epistles to the churches.

20

Paul and the Identity of Jesus

Andrew Herbst

INTRODUCTION

There are particular Pauline texts that, in the same verse, speak of the glory or power of both Jesus Christ and God the Father (cf. 1 Cor. 8:6 and Phil. 2:11).[1] Trinitarians admit that New Testament (NT) authors identify Jesus with the one God of the Old Testament (OT), but interpret these passages to mean that Jesus was included in the divine identity. Indeed, Paul grounds his theology upon the OT and applies OT language regarding the Lord (YHWH) to Jesus, but it is not sufficient to claim that the apostle merely "included" Jesus into divine status. This paper will analyze 1 Corinthians 8 and its OT foundation to conclude that Jesus was believed to be YHWH (God of the OT) in the flesh, not simply identified alongside YHWH.

FIRST CORINTHIANS 8

The context of 1 Corinthians 8 focuses on Christian liberty, which is illustrated by the example of eating meat offered to idols. Paul asserts that idols are not actually gods and have no power, and that there is "none other God but one" (1 Cor. 8:4). Many pagan cultures of the first century worshipped many gods and lords (1 Cor. 8:5), "But to us *there is but* one God, the Father, of whom are all things, and we in him; and one Lord Jesus Christ, by whom are all things, and we by him" (1 Cor. 8:6). There is only one God and one Lord, thus, there is no power in the meat, the offering, or the idol. Paul concludes, by instructing those with this understanding, that they should not be a stumbling block to those with an unsettled conscience (1 Cor. 8:9).

1. Unless otherwise noted, all biblical passages referenced are in the *King James Version*.

THE FOUNDATION OF THE OT

Paul's comments regarding the one true God echo back to the Shema (Deut. 6:4-5). The NT authors consistently tied their comprehension of who Jesus was back to the OT. Richard Bauckham, although arguing with a pre-existent Son in mind, articulates that the NT authors recognized Jesus as belonging "to the unique identity of God" and thus revealing the divine identity to humanity.[2] Furthermore, Bauckham states that this line of belief is "fully consistent and continuous with OT understanding of God."[3] This is why John wrote that the Logos was made flesh (John 1:14), because Jesus is the full revelation of who God is.[4] Therefore, the NT authors tied OT passages, which spoke of YHWH, and applied those same concepts to Jesus.

FIRST CORINTHIANS 8:6

The Apostle Paul applied the sacred Jewish confession of the Shema and the one Lord to Jesus. David Capes contends that Paul's revision of the "Shema links Christ with God's oneness and his name ('Lord'/*kyrios*/YHWH)."[5] While Capes interprets this text as showing Jesus as distinct and subordinate to the Father, he does admit that Paul associated Jesus with the divine name from the OT.[6] Bauckham explains that Paul's concern here is strictly monotheistic, and he maintains his "Jewish monotheistic concern" by emphasizing that "loyalty to the only true God entails loyalty to the Lord Jesus Christ."[7] If Paul was adding or attempting to focus on Jesus as distinct, then Paul's Jewish monotheistic foundation would fall apart, and this text would be "outright ditheism."[8]

Bauckham states that Paul "reproduced all the words of the statement about YHWH in the *Shema*" (The LORD our God is one LORD) and produced "an affirmation of both one God, the Father, and one Lord, Jesus Christ."[9] Therefore, the apostle sees Jesus as the one Lord of whom the Shema declares to be one. James D. G. Dunn observes that "Paul attributes the lordship of the

---

2. Richard Bauckham, *God Crucified*, (Grand Rapids, MI: Eerdmans Publishing, 1999), viii.
3. Bauckham, *God Crucified*, viii.
4. See this author's essay on John 1 in the God's Kingship in the Gospels chapter.
5. David Capes, *The Divine Christ*, (Grand Rapids, MI: Baker Academic, 2018), 11.
6. Capes, Divine Christ, 11.
7. Bauckham, *God Crucified*, 37.
8. Bauckham, *God Crucified*, 38.
9. Bauckham, *God Crucified*, 38.

one God to Jesus Christ," but without breaking his original statement regarding God as one.[10] In addition, it seems that Christ's Lordship was not considered an intrusion or overthrow of God's authority, but His Lordship was considered the clearest evidence of God's authority (cf Phil. 2:10-11).[11]

The impact of this passage moves from who Jesus is to what He has accomplished, "by whom are all things, and we by him" (1 Cor. 8:6). Dunn explains that Jesus is shown to act as the mediator, reconciling God to humanity and humanity back to God.[12] Christ's actions fulfilled God's plan of creation and redemption; thus, God is revealed and made "known in and through Jesus."[13]

THE IMPLICATIONS OF I CORINTHIANS 8:6

The three aforementioned scholars convey crucial insight on this passage; however, they present some conclusions that are unsatisfactory. For instance, Capes wonders how early Jewish Christians could accept the worship of Jesus and retain their monotheism, and then he presents Jesus as merely the agent of creation and redemption as a possible solution.[14] Dunn asserts that Jesus did not usurp God's glory but was included to share God's glory.[15] Bauckham claims that Paul reconstructed Jewish monotheism into Christian monotheism, and achieved this aim by the inclusion of Jesus with the divine image.[16]

Most of these statements are made upon the foundation of Jesus as distinct from the Father. If the emphasis of distinction was on His humanity, then this would be understandable, but according to these authors, He is divine yet distinct. These arguments need more clarity and working out. By maintaining that Jesus was "included" within the divine identity, and thus shares in God's glory, the arguments presented by these writers goes against what God said He would never do (cf. Isa. 42:8 and 48:11). Jesus was not included in God's glory, but He was the full revelation of it (John 1:14). If distinction language focuses

---

10. James D. G. Dunn, *The Theology of the Apostle Paul,* (Grand Rapids, MI: Eerdmans Publishing, 1998), 253.

11. Dunn, *Theology of the Apostle Paul,* 253.

12. James D. G. Dunn, *Did the First Christians Worship Jesus?,* (Louisville, KY: Westminster John Knox Press, 2010), 110.

13. Dunn, *Did the First Christians Worship Jesus?,* 110-112.

14. Capes, *Divine Christ,* 159-66.

15. Dunn, *Theology of the Apostle Paul,* 254.

16. Bauckham, *God Crucified,* 38.

too heavily on His deity, and not His humanity, then inclusion language runs the risk of polytheism. If the supposed remedy is then to claim Jesus held divine status since the OT era, then the difficulty becomes the absence of OT language to affirm a second person in the Godhead, as well as the necessary implication that the apostles reinterpreted and potentially altered the understanding of OT texts to fit this view.[17] This situation differs from the claim that the NT authors built their positions solely upon an OT foundation. They did not need to adjust texts, but rather saw the revelation of God's plan as He became flesh to fulfill what was prophesied in the OT.

CONCLUSION

In conclusion, it has been argued that trinitarian scholarship has contributed helpful and thoughtful insight into Paul's view of Jesus as divine. However, their positions pause and appear not to continue to assert that Jesus is more than a divine inclusion. If the OT YHWH texts are truly applied to Jesus, then the conclusion should be that Jesus is YHWH incarnate. However, it is probable that trinitarian tradition will not fully allow for this interpretation.

17. This statement should not be read in isolation but in light of the arguments developed throughout this book.

21

Jesus, the Spirit, and YHWH—Jesus as the Revelation of God's Glory

Jeremias D. Zuniga

INTRODUCTION

The impact of the Apostle Paul's ministry cannot be understated when exploring the spread of early Christianity. As early as c. 45, Paul begins traveling to preach (Acts 13:1-5). Paul, Barnabas, and John's first preaching point was the synagogue where Jewish believers gathered. Coming from a Pharisaic background (Phil. 3:5), the reader should anticipate that Paul has some knowledge of the Old Testament texts, and his preaching and letters reflect the theology that emerged from his encounter with the risen Lord.[1] Crucially, the way that Paul quotes from the Old Testament not only demonstrates some knowledge, but an extensive engagement with the language of the Bible.[2] Peter Balla, commenting on 2 Corinthians notes, "The ways in which Paul uses the OT is of great significance for the hermeneutics of Christians today."[3]

---

1. H. H. Drake Williams III, "*From the Perspective of the Writer or the Perspective of the Reader: Coming to Grips with a Starting Point for Analyzing the Use of Scripture in 1 Corinthians,*" Essay, in Paul and Scripture (Brill, 2019), 153–157. Drake notes, "The normal, first-century, Jewish experience would have meant exposure to Scripture and its contemporary interpretation at home and in the synagogue as evidenced by statements in Philo and Josephus as well as in the Mishnah. The goal of this instruction would have been accurate knowledge of Scripture. There is no reason to expect that Paul's upbringing was any different than this. From his own testimony in Phil 3:4b–6, Paul clearly implies that his family upheld distinctive Jewish characteristics: circumcised on the eighth day, a member of the people of Israel, and of the tribe of Benjamin, a Hebrew born of Hebrews (cf. 2 Cor 11:22)."

2. For a contemporary discussion reviewing the debates surrounding Paul's "Jewishness", see Michael Bird, "*An Introduction to the Paul within Judaism Debate,*" essay, in *Paul within Judaism: Perspectives on Paul and Jewish Identity* (Mohr Siebeck, 2023), 1–28.

3. Peter Balla, "2 Corinthians," essay, in *Commentary on the New Testament Use of The Old Testament* (Baker Academic, 2007), 753.

In agreement with Balla's point, I want to focus my efforts in this essay on Paul's identification of Jesus in 2 Corinthians 3:16-18. Here, I will contend that Paul identifies Jesus as the same God who covenanted with the mixed multitude that left Egypt in the Exodus and gave freedom to them in the power of His Spirit. While it is possible to engage with this essay on its own, the reader will benefit from reading this essay in conversation with my essays on Genesis, Exodus, and John.

MOSES AND THE LORD

Throughout the Old Testament, translators are often careful to communicate to the reader the distinction between two Hebrew words, "א-ד-ו-ן" (*'āḏôn*) and "י-ה-ו-ה" (YHWH). This carefulness is typically captured by rendering the two words in this way, "*'āḏôn*" as Lord or lord (Exod. 32:22), and "*YHWH*" as LORD (Exod. 32:5). These distinctions are important because in some cases, the biblical authors are using the divine name, and in other cases they are not.

Without Moses' conjuring or coaxing an occurrence, the LORD revealed Himself through the burning bush and spoke through His angel saying, "but by my name, *YHWH,* I had not made myself known to them" (Exod. 6:3).[4] It was by this name that the LORD brought covenant and established a nation, those people would bear His name and be His representatives in the earth (Exod. 19:5-6, 20:7a; 2 Chron. 7:14). Additionally, as Israel represented God's Creator-covenant name, their responsibility was to demonstrate to surrounding nations God's glory. However, when God spoke to them at Sinai, they cowered and asked Moses to stand between them and God out of fear that they would perish (Exod. 20:18-21).[5] Because of this, Israel would later feel the distance between them and the LORD, whereas Moses communed with God (Exod. 34).

---

4. See my essays, "*Who will be your God,*" and "*Does God Body.*" Included in this volume. In the former, I argue that the focus of God revealing His name in Exodus relates to the closing statement from Joseph in Genesis, "but you all, you thought evil upon me, but God thought it for good" (Gen. 50:20a). And in the latter essay, I argue that theophanic language should be carefully considered and not so widely used. In this way, God is unconjured and throughout the Old Testament, appears for the purpose of communion. To this end, He is "unbodied," though spoken of in anthropomorphic terms.

5. For more on the testing of Israel, see Victor P. Hamilton, *Exodus: An Exegetical Commentary* (Grand Rapids, MI: Baker Academic, a division of Baker Publishing Group, 2023), 354-357.

WHO IS THIS LORD?

From the New Testament, I want to highlight that Paul recalls this account to the Corinthians. He begins the chapter by emphasizing the new covenant, a covenant that has been written in their hearts by the Spirit (compare 2 Cor. 3:1-3 with Ezek. 36:25-27; Jer. 31:31-33).[6] In this way, Paul has begun to claim that the Spirit has accomplished the fulfillment of establishing the new covenant people. Importantly, Paul continues to allude to the moment when Moses originally wrote the Table of Covenant from Exodus 34, finally referencing a text that directly addresses Moses' experience with the LORD. As Moses concluded speaking with the LORD, he was veiled, but when he went in again, the veil was removed, changing Moses' face to shine from the LORD's glory (Exod. 34:33-35). This text of Exodus refers to *YHWH*, the name of the One God of the Old Testament.

Paul progresses from alluding to these Old Testament texts, claiming that this veil is "abolished in Christ" (2 Cor. 3:14), and continues speaking of Christ when he says, "But when it turns to the Lord," (2 Cor. 3:16). In this text, Paul has identified Christ as *YHWH*:

> "The clear declaration of Jesus Christ as 'Lord' is not only the content of Paul's gospel—a gospel veiled to those perishing—but it can and ought to inform the previous statement: 'When one turns to the Lord, the veil is removed." When taken together [with 2 Cor. 4:5], these contextual factors suggest that Paul applies the YHWH text in 2 Cor. 3:16 to Christ."[7]

Further, the allusion to repentance and conversion is critical; unless the reader turns to Christ, they will remain outside of the new covenant people that are called by the LORD's name. This allusion to conversion and identification of Jesus as the Old Testament *YHWH* is not merely an effort to describe Christ as sharing the divinity of *YHWH*, because the text synonymizes Christ with *YHWH*.[8] This point is driven as Paul continues in 2 Corinthians 3:17, when he writes "Now the Lord is that Spirit":

> "establish[ing] the closest relationship between 'the Lord' and 'the Spirit' that

---

6. Balla, "*2 Corinthians*," 755-762.
7. David B. Capes, *The Divine Christ: Paul, the Lord Jesus, and the Scriptures of Israel* (Grand Rapids, MI: Baker Academic, 2018), 143-146.
8. Contra Capes, *The Divine Christ*, 12.

language can express. Robertson, Grammar, 768, noted: 'When the article occurs with the subject and predicate, both are definite, treated as identical, one and the same, interchangeable.'"[9]

CONCLUSION

Taking 2 Corinthians 3:16 with 3:17, Paul has discussed Christ and Spirit in interchangeable ways with *YHWH*. This identification is crucial, as I conclude. 2 Corinthians makes the final point that I will highlight here. When Paul writes that we are seeing "the glory of the Lord" (2 Cor. 3:18), he is invoking the identification described above. It was in the work as the man Jesus that *YHWH* established His new covenant, redeeming those foreigners to the promise of God. In this way, Paul is claiming that Jesus is not just any person; He is the revelation of God's glory in human form, YHWH became salvation.[10] To put this in the language of Scripture, "To wit, that God was in Christ, reconciling the world unto himself," (2 Cor. 5:19 KJV).

9. David B. Capes, *Old Testament Yahweh Texts in Paul's Christology* (Waco, TX: Baylor University Press, 2017), 156n320.

10. "Certainly this pattern of speech finds significant parallels in Paul's letters, where the apostle regularly speaks of how Jesus "appeared" (ὁράω) to him, and identifies Jesus as the revelation of "the glory of the Lord / God" (ἡ δόξα κυρίου / θεοῦ)." See Murray J Smith, "*The Theophany of the Resurrected Messiah: The 'Jewish' Christology of Paul's Speeches in Acts*," essay, in *Paul within Judaism: Perspectives on Paul and Jewish Identity* (Mohr Siebeck, 2023), 235–264, especially 256.

WEEK EIGHT

Hebrews and the Godhead—Priesthood, Kingship, and the Better Covenant

22

Hebrews—A Son Over His Own House

Steven Gill

The book of Hebrews stands unique in the New Testament epistles as perhaps the quintessential examination of Jesus-as-Christ in the most proper sense. While often lauded for his homiletical structure[1] and thoroughgoing use of the Old Testament,[2] the book of Hebrews also deserves praise for its invaluable insight into first-century perspectives on Jesus of Nazareth. If He is the Christ, how exactly could believers know this to be so? In what way is He the Son of God? How much of the Christian understanding of God's promised anointed one is informed by the Old Testament? The steady focus of Hebrews touches all these questions in some way, but much of the central material of the book may likely be summed up in (3:6 KJV): "But Christ as a son over his own house; whose house are we, if we hold fast the confidence and the rejoicing of the hope firm unto the end." For the purposes of this paper, the aforementioned verse may be divided into three distinct parts: The continued disclosure

1. William Lane, "Hebrews" in *Dictionary of the Later New Testament and its Developments*, ed. Ralph P. Martin, Peter H. Davids, (IVP Academic, 1997), 450. Here, Lane states, "The writer confirms the sermonic genre when he describes the discourse as a 'word of exhortation' (Heb 13:22), an idiomatic expression for a sermon in Hellenistic-Jewish and early Christian circles, where the public reading of Scripture was followed by preaching (cf. Acts 13:15 with Acts 13:16-41)." This style suggested by Lane may serve as rationale for the missing autograph which often appears in other epistles.

2. There are no less than seven Old Testament quotations in the first chapter of Hebrews alone (1:5/Ps. 2:7; 1:5/2 Sam. 7:14; 1:6/Ps. 97:7; 1:7/Ps. 104:4; 1:8-9/Ps. 45:6-7; 1:10-12/Ps. 102:25-27; 1:13/110:1). The writer's dependance upon the Old Testament to inform his statements continues throughout the epistle, but it is not the Old Testament alone that is echoed in Hebrews. Dominant themes of the New Testament, particularly Pauline epistles, are frequently found within the book. This is perhaps most evident in Hebrews chapter two, in which there are found many themes unique to Paul's writings. In some cases, the subject of the chapter may be characterized as exclusively Pauline (eg. 2:5-8/1 Cor.6:1-3 [subjection of the angels to human dominion/judging of the world] 2:10/1 Cor. 8:6/Col. 1:16-17 [of whom are all things/by whom are all things] 2:17/Rom. 5:17 [things pertaining to God] 2:17/Rom. 5:10/Eph. 2:16/Col. 1:20 [reconciliation]).

of Christ's superiority, the church's place in relation to Christ as sons, and the conditionality of assurance.

Throughout the book of Hebrews, Christ's continued Sonship is often discussed in the context of mediation, but this mediation should also be understood in light of all else that is said about Jesus in the opening three chapters of Hebrews. He is both heir of all things and maker of the worlds (1:2), better than the angels yet made a little lower than the angels (1:4;2:9), and the express image of God, yet the brother of the sanctified (1:3;11). This is not different from the portrait of Christ throughout much of the New Testament, which variously refers to Jesus as God with us (Matt. 1:23) the last Adam (1 Cor. 15:45) The exalted servant (Phil. 2:7-9) and God manifest in the flesh (1 Tim. 3:16). Taken together, these passages could create tension for those of a trinitarian persuasion, provided their view of Sonship is especially divine rather than royal; is Jesus eternally God the Son, or is the Son of God truly the image of the invisible God (Col. 1:15) as Paul wrote?[3] The question of what, precisely, is meant by 'Sonship' was asked by the early church as well. Drane writes,

> Application of the title 'Son of God' to Jesus underwent considerable change in early Christianity. In the earliest Christian communities, it was primarily a functional expression, taking an image from the extant OT and Jewish thought and applying it in a generally imprecise way to articulate the meaning of the Christ event. In combination with insights drawn from other images (notably of the divine logos), "Son of God" was gradually invested with more metaphysical understandings until it eventually became the church's preferred Christological title...In the past, this development engendered heated debate...The generic term "son of God" had a wide currency in ancient culture...It did not, however, denote a divine figure descending from

3. John Drane, "Son of God" in *Dictionary of the Later New Testament & Its Developments* ed. Ralph P. Martin, Peter H. Davids (IVP Academic, 1997), 1111-1112. There is some sorting out that should be done here as to Drane's overarching point. In his entry, he does not suggest that the terminology "Son of God" was a wholly foreign concept to the scriptures and therefore should never have been adopted by the church. Rather, he stresses that the defining boundaries of the phrase shifted over centuries, perhaps alienating the term from its original application. Of the book of Hebrews, he writes, "...'Sonship' can be almost synonymous with perfection and totality of salvation (Heb 4:14 – 5:9; 6:6; 7:3, 28; 8 – 9), rooted in the assumption that Jesus achieved this status through suffering and resurrection (Heb 5:8; 6:6; 10:29) and with the language of divine begetting (Ps 2) providing the frame of reference."

heaven as the bearer of salvation, except insofar as angels were messengers or agents of God..."

If Jesus is the image of the invisible God, does the image reveal the eternal Son, or is the image a man who discloses God in His fullness? Drane's observation that how, precisely, the term 'son of God' was received in the ears of the original hearers of the New Testament epistles may, perhaps, be distanced from the way that it is understood by many believers today should give us pause. For the audience of Hebrews, the Son of God was a messianic term used to disclose the coming king who would reestablish the throne of his father David and usher in everlasting dominion over the world.[4] That the king-to-come is also 'God with us' is a primary theme of the New Testament, but for the audience of Hebrews, it would have likely possessed special significance with regard to His humanity as well. "For this *man* [emphasis added] was counted worthy of more glory than Moses, inasmuch as he who hath builded the house hath more honour than the house. For every house is builded by some man; but he that built all things is God" (Heb. 3:4). Here, the writer of Hebrews makes Christ analogous, not to Moses, but to a man that is better. Christ is worthy of more glory than Moses – often considered the greatest leader of Jewish antiquity – in much the same way that the builder of a house is greater than the house.[5] Even the priesthood of Christ – which many rightly identify as a dominant theme

4. Beale notes, "The overt eschatological nature of Heb. 1:1-6 (indeed of the whole book) is introduced by 1:2, where it says that God has revealed these things through Christ 'in these last days.'...the exact form of this phrase...occurs four times in the OT, all of which are translations of the Hebrew 'in the latter days'...from Num. 24:14; Jer. 23:20; 25:19 (49:39 MT); Dan. 10:14. It appears that the Num. 24 messianic passage may be uppermost in mind, since the wording at the end of Heb. 1:2...is an allusion to Ps. 2:7-8 concerning the messianic 'son' who will 'inherit' the nations and the 'ends of the earth.' Both Num. 24:14-20 and Ps. 2:8-9 use 'scepter' (*šēḇeṭ* [Num. 24:17; Ps. 2:9]) as an image for the Messiah, who will 'crush" the "nations' (Num. 24:17; Ps.2:9), 'rule' over them, and receive them as an 'inheritance' (Num. 24:18; Ps. 2:8)."

G.K. Beale, *A New Testament Biblical Theology: The Unfolding of the Old Testament in the New*, (Baker Academic, 2011), 464.

5. David Peterson, "Hebrews: An Introduction and Commentary" in *Tyndale New Testament Commentaries*, ed. Eckhard Schnabel, Nicholas Perinn (IVP Academic, 2020), 105. Of this passage, Peterson writes "Here also, Christ is faithful as the Son over God's house (compare 10:21, 'a great priest over the house of God')." While perhaps nuanced, it is important here to grasp that Christ's Sonship over the house of God (whose house we are) can only be rightly understood in view of the sonship of the other sons of God (Heb. 2:10). Thus, the sons of God become heirs within the household of God, not because they are innately like Him, but because they become like Him (1 John 3:2).

of the book of Hebrews – cannot be understood without an especially human view of the Christ that is sometimes avoided out of fear of offending His deity. Nevertheless, Hurst writes,

> Hebrews has been justly called the epistle of the priesthood. Nowhere else in the NT is Christ's work set forth against the background of the OT priesthood. He is our great high priest (Heb 4:14) who is able to "sympathize with our weaknesses" and who was "tempted in every point as we are" (Heb 4:15)...Aaron's priesthood relates to Christ's as shadow to substance (Heb 8:5; 10:1)...The author is interested in the Levitical service in which the priest is chosen from among men and appointed by God (Heb 5:1; 8:3) to serve in the earthly sanctuary...and he is particularly interested in the ritual of the Day of Atonement, wherein the animal was killed and its blood brought into the holy of holies by the high priest (Heb 9:7) so that the people might have access to God (Heb 4:16; 7:18-28; 10:1, 19, 22).[6]

To 'sympathize with our weaknesses' and be tempted as we are tempted, the High Priest must be comprehensively understood as a man, as James reminded his readers that God cannot be tempted/tried in this way (Jam. 1:13). Of course, this insistence extends to the death of Christ as well, as God is a Spirit (John 4:24) and cannot be said to have died in any rational sense (cf. 1 Timothy 1:17). This portrait of the Christ harmonizes well with all that Paul says of Him in his epistles, namely Romans. In Romans, Paul wrote that 'we joy in God because we have received the atonement by Christ' (5:11) and that this atonement came 'by one man' (5:15). The atonement that comes through a man who is approved by God (Matt. 3:17) is particularly priestly language that discloses the Son in the truest sense. Hebrews image of Christ as the Son over the house of God is, therefore, not a picture of a divine second person, but the revelation of the man in whom the fulness of God dwelled (Col. 1:19; 2:9). This man, better than Moses or the angels, is the Son in whom God was well pleased to reconcile to Himself (2 Cor. 5:19) the sons in whom He was not well pleased.[7] For

6. Lincoln Hurst, "Priest, High Priest" in *Dictionary of the Later New Testament & Its Developments*, ed. Ralph P. Martin, Peter H. Davids, (IVP Academic, 1997), 964-966.

7. Steven Gill, *The Last Man: Reclaiming Father & Son Language in the Oneness Pentecostal Movement*, (Steven Gill, 2023), 81. The emphasis here is placed on sorting out Luke's inclusion of the genealogy of Jesus Christ. In Matthew's gospel, the ancestry of Christ appears at the

this reason, He may rightly be called the mediator of the New Testament who grants His followers access to an inheritance once denied them by means of His death (Heb. 9:15; Rom. 5:2). In this way, the quality, work, and promise of the Son are identifiable within the first three chapters of the book of Hebrews, and neatly address our subject concerning the continued disclosure of Christ's superiority, our role as sons of God, and the conditionality of assurance. The reader discovers the remarkable *quality* of this man who is the propitiation for the sins of the whole world (1 John 2:2) as early as the opening verses: "God…hath in these last days spoken unto us by his Son, whom he hath appointed heir of all things, by whom also he made the worlds" (Heb. 1:1-2 KJV). The work of the Son becomes clearer in view of the quality of the man, summarized in Hebrews 2:10 (KJV): "For it became him, for whom are all things, and by whom are all things, in bringing many sons unto glory, to make the captain of their salvation perfect through sufferings." Finally, the summary focus of this disclosure – rightly framed - is revealed in the promise of the Son, found in the subject of our central verse (3:6 KJV): "But Christ as a son over his own house; whose house are we, if we hold fast the confidence and the rejoicing of the hope firm unto the end."

---

introduction of the book, and, beginning with Abraham, it works its way down chronologically to the birth of Christ. By contrast, Luke begins with Christ and takes the ancestry backwards, not to Abraham, but to Adam. Furthermore, in Luke, the ancestry of Christ is detailed immediately after Christ's baptism – a decision by the writer that may appear curious unless the reader is familiar with larger picture of Sonship throughout the Old and New Testaments. Luke tells the story of Christ's approval in the eyes of God as the redeeming Son of God (Luke 3:22) by placing the event in contrast to Adam – the first son of God who was not pleasing to the Father (Luke 3:38).

23

After the Order of Melchizedek

Andrew Herbst

INTRODUCTION

Melchizedek appears in Genesis, Psalms, and Hebrews. He appears in only five chapters of Scripture, and the limited information provided about Melchizedek gives his background an element of obscurity. This study will examine the Old Testament (OT) and New Testament (NT) passages regarding Melchizedek and establish his identity as a human priest in service to the true God.

MELCHIZEDEK IN THE OT

In Genesis 13, Lot had moved towards Sodom and eventually dwelled inside the city (Gen. 14:12). Around this time, Sodom joined a coalition and rebelled against the kings that the coalition had paid tribute to. The enemy kings came down to regain control and pillaged the region, taking Lot captive in the process. Abraham came to his nephew's aid, rescued Lot, and returned the stolen plunder to the King of Sodom.

Upon his return, Abraham was met by Melchizedek, the King of Salem and "priest of the most high God" (Gen. 14:18b).[1] Melchizedek blessed Abraham and also blessed the most high God for granting victory to Abraham. Before leaving, Abraham gave a tithe to the priest-king. These three verses contain the entire historical account of Melchizedek in Scripture (Gen. 14:18-20). All other passages look back to this record.

In the NT, Psalm 110 is one of the most frequently cited OT passages. Psalm 110 was authored by David and is a prophetic look at the Messiah (Acts 2:33-34). The focus of this study highlights the middle verse of the passage,

1. Unless otherwise noted, all biblical passages referenced are in the *King James Version.*

David wrote, "The LORD hath sworn, and will not repent, Thou art a priest for ever after the order of Melchizedek" (Ps. 110:4). This messianic figure would be powerful and rule God's enemies, but he would also be an eternal priest. The Messiah would be both king and priest, following after the "order" or function of Melchizedek. As the Son of David, He would rule forever (2 Sam. 7:13), and serving as a priest-king like Melchizedek, He would serve as the mediator forever.

MELCHIZEDEK IN THE NT

The Book of Hebrews references Melchizedek (Melchisedec) nine times within Hebrews 5-7. Hebrews 5 depicts the man Jesus as the Son and high priest. Just as Psalm 110 connected the Messiah's kingdom and priesthood together, so too does Hebrews 5, drawing attention to Jesus as the Son (Heb. 5:5 and Ps. 2:7) and His priestly order (Heb. 5:6, 10 and Ps. 110:4).

Hebrews looks back to Melchizedek to build numerous arguments to defend Christ's high priesthood. One of the primary hindrances to accepting Jesus as priest was that the Law of Moses demanded that the priesthood must come from the Tribe of Levi. Jesus was from the Tribe of Judah and was, therefore, not eligible to hold a Levitical office. However, Hebrews reminds the Jews that David wrote that the Messiah-king would be a priest "after the order of Melchizedek" (Ps. 110:4). Furthermore, Abraham gave a tithe to Melchizedek, thus Levi paid tithes through his ancestor (Heb. 5:9-10). This indicates the Melchizedek priestly line to be older and not inferior to the Levitical line. And, finally, the Levitical priests sacrificed and died year after year, but Christ offered one sacrifice and is sat down as an eternal priest. All of these facts provide valid reasoning for acknowledging Jesus as high priest, even though He was not a Levite.

IDENTIFYING MELCHIZEDEK

Therefore, Melchizedek plays a crucial role in the NT for understanding and accepting Jesus' ministry. However, identifying Melchizedek is another task. There have been attempts to label Melchizedek as a theophany, or manifestation of God, in the OT.[2] Upon careful consideration of Genesis and Hebrews, it can

2. See Jeremias Zuniga's essay on Theophanies.

be determined that Melchizedek is not a proper candidate for an OT theophany.

Regarding Genesis 14, there is simply nothing in the passage to indicate the deity of Melchizedek. Merely receiving tithes from Abraham is not sufficient to define his status as deity, for he could have received them on God's behalf just as the Levites did under Mosaic law. Hebrews recalls Abraham giving the tithe but calls Melchizedek a man (Heb. 7:4).

In Hebrews, when Jesus is said to be "after the order" of Melchizedek (Heb. 5:6, 5:10, 6:20, 7:17, and 7:21), the focus appears to be placed on the priesthood and the type of office.[3] Of course, the duration of the office is eternal, which the author attributes to Melchizedek being "Without father, without mother, without descent, having neither beginning of days, nor end of life;" (Heb. 7:3a).[4] Therefore, he was "made like unto the Son of God; abideth a priest continually" (Heb. 7:3b). However, the next verse begins by calling Melchizedek a man (Heb. 7:4). The comments regarding Melchizedek's lack of parental record, age, and death seem to refer to the fact that none of these details were recorded in Genesis.[5] In addition, archaeology may assist in unfolding this situation.

Amarna Tablet 287 preserves statements by a ruler from Jerusalem, the same city that Melchizedek ruled over several centuries earlier. 'Abdi-Heba wrote to Egypt, "It was not my father and not my mother but the arm of the mighty king that placed me in the house of my father."[6] Joseph Holden and Norman Geisler argue that this phrase means that the ruler did not receive his office from his father or lineage, but that it was appointed unto him. This aligns with Jesus being appointed after Melchizedek's order, for Jesus did not receive His office from a Levitical lineage. The same could be said for Melchizedek's position and parenthood; he did not inherit his kingdom nor his priestly status from his father (Heb. 7:3).

---

3. "Similitude" is also used in 7:15.

4. For more insight, see Dana Harris in Gregory K. Beale et al., eds., *Dictionary of the New Testament Use of the Old Testament*, (Grand Rapids, MI: Baker Academic; Baker Academic, 2023), 629.

5. See George Guthrie in Gregory K. Beale and Donald A. Carson, eds., *Commentary on the New Testament Use of the Old Testament*, (Grand Rapids, MI: Baker Academic; Baker Academic, 2007), 967.

6. Joseph M. Holden and Norman Geisler, *The Popular Handbook of Archaeology of the Bible*, (Eugene, OR: Harvest House Publishers, 2013), 241.

CONCLUSION

There may be small pieces of evidence to suggest Melchizedek was more than a man, but placing all relevant texts together reveals that he was a human. Examples like the Passover lamb, a prophet like Moses, or a king like David are OT elements that look forward to the work of Jesus. In this light, it is possible to see Melchizedek and his life also looking forward to Jesus, as he is the example of the royal-priestly order and function that Jesus followed.[7] However, that is not enough to label Melchizedek as more than human.

---

7. We also see kings Saul, David, and Solomon acting as king-priests. (In 1 Sam. 13:9-13, Saul was not chastised for sacrificing, but for sacrificing at the wrong time. See 2 Sam. 6:14, 17 for David wearing a priestly ephod and sacrificing, and 1 Kings 8 for Solomon giving a priestly prayer and sacrificing). Scripture shows that Jesus would unite the king and priest positions in a more official way.

24

The Footstool of a King—Reading Hebrews and Psalm 110 in Context

Jeremias D. Zuniga

INTRODUCTION

While exploring Peter's sermon in Acts 2, I remarked that Psalm 16 does not include language of the throne, although that motif "is implicit in the favorite New Testament Psalm, Psalm 110 and appears to be understood in Peter's statement" found in Acts 2:30.[1] In Peter's sermon, he progresses from Psalm 16 (Acts 2:25-28) into Psalm 110 (Acts 2:35), and expresses that Jesus, unlike David, has ascended from the grave to sit on the throne of God in power (see Acts 2:30 & 34). As shown from Acts, Psalm 110 holds a crucial place throughout the theology of the New Testament. This is seen as the Psalm is found in all the Gospels and holds an important place in the Epistle to the Hebrews.[2] On the foundation of the Apostle Peter's sermon, I want to turn my reader's attention to Hebrews 10. My aim is to explore the language of verses 12-13 and show how the author of Hebrews describes Jesus in an expectation of a future return of triumph, establishing His earthly reign in totality. To support the reader's understanding of the textual focus, I invite you to read Hebrews 10:12-13 and Psalm 110.[3]

---

1. See my essay, "*The Promise of a King*," included in this volume.

2. Donald Alfred Hagner, *Encountering the Book of Hebrews: An Exposition* (Grand Rapids, Mich: Baker Academic, 2002), 44. Hagner highlights that references to Psalm 110 are found in the Gospels, Acts, Romans, 1 Corinthians, Ephesians, and Colossians.

3. For a helpful overview of the Melchizedekian nature of this text see T. Desmond Alexander, *Face to Face with God: A Biblical Theology of Christ as Priest and Mediator* (Downers Grove, IL: InterVarsity Press, 2022), 92-106.

THE LANGUAGE OF SITTING AT THE RIGHT HAND

Hebrews' author offers his audience engagement with Psalm 110 in twelve references, five of those references are to Psalm 110:1 and seven are to Psalm 110:4.[4] As early as Hebrews 1:3, the author introduces this important text, making the point that the Son, who is the "express image of [Gods] person" took His seat "on the right hand of the Majesty on high." This language of sitting at the right hand is also found in 1 Kings 2:19, where Solomon positions his mother in an act that symbolically carries the weight of honor and authority. This position of honor and authority is likely why Solomon responds strongly to Bathsheba's request and condemns it as an affront and attempt to usurp his reign (1 Kings 2:19-24).[5] The notion of being at the right hand of Majesty is not disconnected from the symbolic positioning found in Kings, and in Psalm 110:1b it carries metaphorical implications. The point of that language is that the king will sit in the honor and authority of the LORD, which sits in anticipation of a future "footstooling" of this king's enemies.[6] Because the language of Psalm 110 is focused towards metaphorically acknowledging the status of the king, when the text expresses "Sit thou at my right hand, until I have set thine enemies as thy footstool," it is communicating that the king is honored and in authority despite the enemies remaining free from the humbling position of the footstool.[7]

---

4. The references to Psalm 110:1 are found in Hebrews 1:3, 1:13, 8:1, 10:12-13, 12:2; and the Psalm 110:4 in Hebrews 5:6, 5:10, 6:20, 7:11, 7:15, 7:17, 7:21. See "*Psalm 110 in Hebrews*," ESV Bible, accessed November 2025, https://www.esv.org/resources/esv-global-study-bible/chart-58-03/. Here I will focus most strictly on the language of Psalm 110:1.

5. Donald J Wiseman, *1 and 2 Kings*, vol. 9, of Tyndale Old Testament Commentaries (IVP Academic, 1993), 85.

6. For an excellent treatment of the concept of honor and shame in this text, I refer the reader to review the work of Lodewyk Sutton, "*A footstool of war, honour and shame?" Perspectives induced by Psalm 110:1*. Journal for Semitics, 22(1), 2016, 51-59. While Sutton is focused here on the footstool, his work highlights the military focus of this text. I propose that the language of military conquest, honor, and shame is expressed throughout the entirety of this first verse and follow the statement from Goldingay that "The only other OT reference to sitting at someone's right hand concerns Bethsheba, who could sit at Solomon's right hand because she was the king's mother (1 Kings 2:19. That is often a position of great power in the Middle East, and to sit at someone's right hand is to sit in a position of prestige and authority… It is difficult to imagine how the king could have literally sat at the Yhwh's right hand…and it is in any case unwise to infer some literal concrete event from a poetic colon in a prophetic oracle in a liturgical text, whose main point is metaphorical." See John Goldingay, *Psalms: Psalms 90-150*, vol. 3, of Baker Commentary on the Old Testament (Grand Rapids, MI: Baker Academic, 2008), 193-196.

7. I take from the example of the King James translators here in rendering the singular pronouns as "thou, thine, and thy" instead of "you and your." In many cases, contemporary

FOOTSTOOLS IN SCRIPTURE AND HISTORY

Throughout the Old Testament, there are a number of references and allusions to the footstool, a piece of furniture included in the throne. To the fact that this is war-focused language, 1 Kings 5:1 describes how Solomon sent informants to Hiram, letting him know why David was unable to build a temple to the LORD. Solomon reports that David had been engaged in too many wars, but there is an expression of conquest "until the LORD set them beneath the soles of his feet" (1 Kgs 5:3b), which should be taken as the moments of rest found in 2 Samuel 7:1, when David is finally able to sit and reign because his enemies have been subdued.[8]

The position of the king in the Psalm establishes the promise of honor and authority, whereas the promise of the footstool anticipates conquest and vindication. Thus, when the Hebrews proclaim that after the man [Jesus] offered the sacrifice [His crucifixion], He sat at God's right hand [was elevated to His throne in honor and authority]. And continuing, the text does not anticipate the throne to remain distant forever but expects Jesus' future return to shame His enemies by making them His footstool. To this end, Hebrews 10:22-25 can instruct the readers to "draw near," "hold fast," and "consider" as the day approaches. The message of Hebrews 10:22-25 includes a baptismal note and claims a future day of judgment by that coming and conquering king (see Rev. 19:11-20:15).[9]

CONCLUSION

Considering Peter's Pentecost sermon alongside Hebrews' use of Psalm 110:1, I conclude that there are two explicit expectations that the Biblical authors

translations muddy what the text communicates by generically translating the language using the ambiguous "you," which may connote or denote singularity or plurality in texts where only one is in focus.

8. Wiseman, *1 and 2 Kings*, 107. Wiseman notes, "To Put *enemies under* the *feet* (v.3, LXX/ Kethib 'his (the LORD's) feet'; Qerē 'my feet', i.e. Solomon) was the symbolic act marking conquest ('made them subject to him', REB; Josh. 10:24; Ps. 8:6; cf. Rom. 16:20; 1 Cor. 15:25, 27; Eph. 1:22).In contemporary art enemies were often depicted as a footstool (as Ps. 110:1)." For an overview of the Egyptian (c. 1400-1300) uses of the phrase see Joel M LeMon, "*Egypt and the Egyptians," essay, in The World around the Old Testament: The People and Places of the Ancient near East* (Grand Rapids, MI: Baker Academic, 2016), 169–96, Specifically 189-195. For an accessible exploration more focused on the wider context that includes Egypt, Persia, Babylonia, Assyria, Ugarit, Greece, and Rome see Sutton, *A footstool of war, honour and shame?*, 57-65.

9. Importantly, Revelation 19:11-20:15 is a text of war, and with the witness of the New Testament presents to us an unfulfilled Millennial reign that can be expected in the Eschaton.

communicated to their readers. It is these two points that I wish to drive here. First, Peter recognized that Jesus had not simply ascended to the spatial position of "the right hand" of the invisible God, but that He ascended to sit on His throne. Notice the contrast to 1 Kings 2:19, where Bathsheba did not sit on her own throne, as the text clearly indicates another seat was made so she could have her own place that was distinguished from Solomon's throne. That language of distinction is absent from the Psalm, Acts, and Hebrews. Secondly, the texts expect Christ's ascension to His heavenly throne to remain until a future time, when His enemies are conquered, shamed, His reign is realized, and rest is found. It is because of the undistinguished language of the Biblical authors and the anticipatory language that I pose to the reader, we should not read the language of the right hand as indicating distinction of Christ sitting positionally on the arm of the throne where God is seated, but that we should read the text eschatologically. That is to say, we should read our focus texts as describing Jesus' power, authority, and honor as He awaits His return to conquer all and establish His reign in the Millennium.

WEEK NINE

The General Epistles and the Godhead: Fellowship, Priesthood, and the Faith That Works

25

The Godhead—In the General Epistles

Steven Gill

Where the New Testament is concerned, if there exists a consistent undertone in my contributions to this volume it is likely to be found in this emphasis: There is, and must be, harmony between the Old and New Testament portraits of the Godhead. This emphasis continues in examinations surrounding the general epistles, namely the writings of James, Peter, John, and Jude.[1]

In James, the reader is offered a glimpse into the first-century church's attitude toward the godhead in a way that calls the reader back to the Old Testament. "Thou believest that there is one God; thou doest well: the devils also believe, and tremble. But wilt thou know, O vain man, that faith without works is dead?" (James 2:19-20 KJV). Keener writes,

> The oneness of God was the basic confession of Judaism, recited daily in the Shema…Thus by "faith" James means monotheism, as much of Judaism used the term (*'emunah*). He thus says, "You acknowledge correct basic doctrine – so what? That is meaningless by itself."…Jewish teachers would have agreed with James that the oneness of God must be declared with a genuine heart; his oneness implied that he was to be the

---

1. While an oft neglected perspective, it is likely fair to assume that that 'Jude the brother of James' (Jude 1:1) was also the brother of Jesus. Like James, readers are made to understand that this Jude would not have been a disciple during the earthly ministry of Christ, but he became a believer later. Webb writes, "Most scholars identify the author as the brother of Jesus (cf. Mt 13:55 par. Mk 6:3; Eusebius *Hist.* Ecc. 3.19.1 – 20.1; eg., Bauckham 1983, 21-25) on the strength of the author's self-designation, 'brother of James' (Jude 1)…like his brother, James, he became a member of the early Christian movement after the resurrection of Jesus. The strength of this view is that it explains the evidence in Jude's letter in the simplest way."

For Webb: Robert Webb, "Jude," in *Dictionary of the Later New Testament & Its Developments*, ed. Ralph P. Martin, Peter H. Davids, (IVP Academic, 1997), 616.

supreme object of human affection (Deut 6:4-5).[2]

For James, the acknowledgement of God's oneness was not only a fundamental aspect of faith upon which even devils could agree – it was also connected to the "faith" which, unaccompanied by works, was dead. Walls writes,

> It almost appears that James employs this statement to shock his readers into considering what they have been professing without possessing. To emphasize that faith alone is not sufficient to manifest salvation, he informs them that even the demons have faith. They acknowledge that there is one God.[3]

The question may rightly be asked, "How, precisely, does one practice good works according to such a faith?" Furthermore, it is apparent that James saw no incongruity with the basic confession of Judaism (God's oneness) and the opening remarks of his epistle: "James, a servant of God and of the Lord Jesus Christ, to the twelve tribes which are scattered abroad, greeting" (James 1:1). The conjunction "*and* the Lord Jesus Christ" was not dissonant with James' later statement, but it was a disclosure of a particular belief about the God of Israel that not all Jews of his time shared – that Jesus of Nazareth is the Christ of God. This form of self-identification was characteristic of Paul's greetings as well, perhaps signaling its importance when addressing communities where Jews would have been present.[4]

Other writers of the general epistles harmonized faith in Christ and the first-century Christian experience with the Old Testament in much more direct ways. In some cases, these writers demonstrated the consonance of the Spirit of the Messiah with the God of the Old Testament in ways that appear

---

2. Craig Keener, *The IVP Bible Background Commentary: New Testament*, (IVP Academic, 2014), 676-677.

3. Muncia Walls, *James: A Servant of God*, (Walls, 1997), 70.

4. See (Rom. 1:7; 1 Cor. 1:3; 2 Cor. 1:2; Gal. 1:3; Eph. 1:2; Phil. 1:2; Col. 1:2; 1 Thess. 1:1; 2 Thess. 2:2). While it is possible that these greetings were simply generic ways that the apostle chose to address the congregation, it is important to remember that had he begin his epistles thus: "Grace be unto you and peace from God our Father" with no additional clause disclosing faith in the Messiah, it would not have raised the attention of devout gatherers in the first century. Even synagogues which rejected Jesus of Nazareth would have gladly received such a greeting. The qualifier "and the Lord Jesus Christ" meant a great deal when disclosing one's authority/identity in the first century. In this way, it is probably better to think of the addendum as a disclosure of a particular kind of faith in the God of Israel (i.e., one that exists through faith in His Christ), rather than as an acknowledgement of two distinct powers in heaven.

indistinguishable from one another. For example:

> Of which salvation the prophets have enquired and searched diligently, who prophesied of the grace that should come unto you: Searching what, or what manner of time the Spirit of Christ which was in them did signify, when it testified beforehand the sufferings of Christ, and the glory that should follow. Unto whom it was revealed, that not unto themselves, but unto us they did minister the things, which are now reported unto you by them that have preached the gospel unto you with the Holy Ghost sent down from heaven; which things the angels desire to look into.[5]

The Spirit of the Christ, to whom Peter attributes the inspiration of the prophets, is introduced to the readers of the Old Testament as the 'word of the LORD (י-ה-ו-ה)' (Jer. 1:1-2), 'visions of God' (Ezek. 1:1), and 'the Spirit (רוח)' (Ezek. 2:2). In this way, the Spirit who dwells in the heart of the believer (Rom. 8:9-11) is not to be confused with anyone other than the God of the Old Testament who revealed Himself by His Word to His prophets. Thus, Jesus is truly "God with us" and not another partition, persona, or dispensation of Him that was with us in the past (Isa. 7:14; Matt. 1:22-23).[6] This distinction is important. The first-century writers saw their faith in Christ as a continuation of – not a dissolution of – their relationship with the God of their fathers (see *Reframing Paul* in week seven). This is also born out in Jude's writing, in which he states, "For there are certain men crept in unawares, who were before of old ordained to this condemnation, ungodly men, turning the grace of our God into lasciviousness, and denying the only Lord God, and our Lord Jesus Christ" (Jude 1:4). Much like John, Jude did not believe it was possible to claim to serve

---

5. 1 Peter 1:10-12 (KJV).

6. It has become increasingly popular to disassociate the prophecy of the child to be born in Isaiah with Christ in the New Testament. Many now claim that Isaiah simply spoke of his own son and the traditional reading is little more than Christians superimposing upon the text what is not there. Nevertheless, Christians are made to understand from Matthew that the birth of Christ was not merely a fulfillment of Isaiah's ninth chapter, but the seventh as well: Matthew 1:22-23: "Now all this was done, that it might be fulfilled which was spoken of the Lord by the prophet, saying, Behold, a virgin shall be with child, and shall bring forth a son, and they shall call his name Emmanuel, which being interpreted is, God with us." Furthermore, it is the name "Jesus" to which this fulfillment passage was associated. Thus, the salvation of God ('Ιησοῦς) is truly God ('Εμμανουήλ). It is the opinion of this writer that, whatever the sign of the prophecy may have been in the eighth century BC, it was certainly fulfilled in the first century AD.

the God of Abraham, Isaac, and Jacob, yet reject His Christ – a possibility that many unbelieving Jews clung to in the first century.[7] This title "Lord" which Jude attributes to Jesus is *kyrios* (κύριος) of which Cullman states:

> It is characteristic of the expression *Kyrios Jesus* that it refers to his post-Easter, present work fulfilled in the state of exaltation. The title thus naturally developed with the salvation event itself. The first Christians perceived this when they emphasized that God 'has *made* him both Lord and Christ' (Acts 2:36), that only after his obedience as the *ebed Yahweh* God 'more than exalted him' and bestowed upon him this *Kyrios* name, 'the name which is above every name' (Phil. 2:9).[8]

This post-resurrection emphasis to which Cullman refers is seen most evidently in John 20:28 (KJV): "And Thomas answered and said unto him, My Lord (*kyrios*) and my God." The authority of the Messiah by which He took His rightful place as king over mankind was delivered unto Him through His death, burial, and resurrection. That Jesus is called "Lord" in this way should give Christian readers who remain unpersuaded by the oneness of God pause. "There is one body, and one Spirit, even as ye are called in one hope of your calling; One Lord, one faith, one baptism, One God and Father of all, who is above all, and through all, and in you all" (Eph. 4:4-6 KJV). That Jesus is both "Lord" and "God" is, perhaps, the centerpiece of Christian theology. Far from setting himself at odds with the Apostle Paul, Jude's decision to use the phrase, "...the only Lord God, and our Lord Jesus Christ" offers important insight into how the Godhead was understood in the first century. In light of Ephesians' fourth chapter, Jude's statement should likely not be considered the disclosure of two different lords to which Christians pay homage, but of the only Lord who was disclosed in the earth by the man, Jesus Christ. In this way, John's statement is better understood: "Who is a liar but he that denieth that Jesus is the Christ? He

---

7. 1 John 2:22-23. In this passage, John states that 'those who deny the Son do not have the Father.' For modern Christians this sentence may appear redundant or nonsensical, but it had a very pointed effect in the first century. There were many Jews who, while claiming to serve the God of their fathers, rejected His Christ. John's point is very simple: You cannot claim to serve the God who is in heaven if you have rejected His messenger in the earth; we can also rest assured that if we have the Son, we have the Father also.

8. Oscar Cullman, *The Christology of the New Testament*, (The Westminster Press, 1963), 203-204.

is antichrist, that denieth the Father and the Son. Whosoever denieth the Son, the same hath not the Father: (but) he that acknowledgeth the Son hath the Father also" (1 John 2:22-23 KJV). Lest there be any confusion on the part of the reader, Paul offered a similar sentiment in his letter to the Colossians: "And whatsoever ye do in word or deed, do all in the name of the Lord Jesus, giving thanks to God and the Father by him [emphasis added]" (Col. 3:17 KJV). For the Jews of the first century, the point could not have been clearer: The one God – the God of their fathers – was honored and could only be honored in His Christ, in whom He dwelled.

26

And These Three Are One

Andrew Herbst

INTRODUCTION

First John 5:7 is the perpetual point of contention within Bible translation and textual issues. Labeled the Johannine Comma, some have questioned whether the longer sentence within verses 7-8 is authentic or not. In other words, the question centers on whether the Apostle John wrote these words in the original epistle or if they represent a later insertion. This paper will analyze the evidence and demonstrate that it is reasonable to accept the *Johannine Comma* as genuine.

> 1 John 5:7-8 KJV
> 7 For there are three that bear record in heaven, the Father, the Word, and the Holy Ghost: and these three are one.
> 8 And there are three that bear witness in earth, the Spirit, and the water, and the blood: and these three agree in one.

> 1 John 5:7-8 ESV (And other critical text translations)
> 7 For there are three that testify:
> 8 the Spirit and the water and the blood; and these three agree.

THE MANUSCRIPT EVIDENCE

A standard argument against the Comma is that it is absent in early Greek manuscripts (mss). Although it is acknowledged that the Johannine Comma has the least Greek mss support for a New Testament (NT) passage, which will be addressed in connection with the historical context below, the Comma can be found in approximately ten later Greek mss.[1] The passage is missing in nearly

1. For overview of mss evidence, see Jack Moorman, *When the KJV Departs from the "Majority" Text*, (Collingswood, NJ: Dean Burgon Society, 2010), 153, and Edward F. Hills, *The*

500 Greek mss.[2] At first glance, this evidence appears to work decisively against accepting the Comma, but modern translations thrive on minority texts.[3] While the Comma does not appear in early Greek mss, the passage has a strong witness amongst Latin mss. Nearly all Latin Vulgate mss have the passage, including an Old Latin ms from near AD 500.[4]

EARLY CHRISTIANITY

The lack of Greek mss attestation may be related to the historical context of early Christianity. Protecting Scripture from corruption was a concern to some, and certain Christian leaders instructed their churches to beware of forgeries and spurious writings.[5] Guarding genuine Scripture against false works eventually led leaders to establish lists of authoritative Biblical books. In this context, the issue of the Biblical canon emerges, not as a way for Christians to pick and choose what belonged in Scripture, but to preserve what was already acknowledged as Scripture and exclude known forgeries.[6]

Others were not so interested in safeguarding Scripture but attempted to use the Bible for their own advantage. Writing around A. D. 200, Origen complained about the many differences among the mss of the Gospels, which stemmed from scribal negligence or perverse intentions.[7]

Some scribes apparently did not check their work, or shortened or lengthened mss according to their agenda. Eusebius, writing near A. D. 300, recorded that some false teachers had fearlessly laid "their hands upon the holy Scriptures,

King James Version Defended, 162-165, Chapter 8 §3.

2. Also, for more comments on the mss, see Thomas Holland, *Crowned with Glory*, (Lincoln, NE: Writers Club Press, 2000), 164.

3. The rebuttal would likely argue that, even if a reading appears in only a minority of mss, it may still be accepted if it occurs early in the manuscript tradition. The tradition of the Comma is strong among Latin mss, and has early witnesses outside Biblical mss, as demonstrated below.

4. Moorman, *When the KJV Departs*, 155-56.

5. For example, see Serapion in Eusebius, *Ecclesiastical History*, Book 6.12., trans. by C. F. Cruse, (Peabody, MA: Hendrickson Publishers, 2018), 202-203.

6. For more on the Canon, see Michael Kruger, *Canon Revisted: Establishing the Origins and Authority of the New Testament Books*, (Wheaton, IL: Crossway, 2012).

7. "For we find a substantial difference between the copies, whether from the negligence of the scribes, or the rashness of some, or because of those who fail to emend the writings, or because of those who either add or remove what pleases them in their emendations." Origen, *The Commentary of Origin on the Gospel of St. Matthew*, vol. 2., trans. by Ronald E. Heine, (Oxford Press, 2018), 454-55.

saying that they have corrected them."[8] These false teachers and their followers had their own versions of the Bible, based on their own perceived corrections, and comparison with other mss would show the variants to be abundant.

This situation becomes more consequential, due to the fact that a majority of the mss corruptions appear to be Christological in nature, compounding the problem for later readers. Scribes and teachers sometimes altered Biblical texts in order to match what they believed about the identity of Jesus.[9] Such scribal alterations may be why so few Greek mss include the Comma. In addition to the testimonies of Origen and Eusebius, Jerome noted that 1 John was often altered in his day. Jerome lived around A. D. 400 and provides a specific report that the Comma was being omitted,

> Just as these (epistles) are properly understood and so translated faithfully by interpreters into Latin without leaving ambiguity for the readers nor [allowing] the variety of genres to conflict, especially in that text where we read the unity of the trinity is placed in the first letter of John, where much error has occurred at the hands of unfaithful translators contrary to the truth of faith, who have kept just the three words water, blood and spirit in this edition omitting mention of Father, Word and Spirit in which especially the catholic faith is strengthened and the unity of substance of Father, Son and Holy Spirit is attested.[10]

Jerome knew of Greek mss that included the Comma and understood that some scribes were removing the phrase. This statement provides evidence that the Comma was known and believed to be genuine near 400 A. D.

Further witness of tampering with 1 John comes from Socrates of Constantinople, writing around the same time as Jerome. Although not reporting about 1 John 5:7, Socrates documented a false teacher who mutilated

8. Eusebius, *Ecclesiastical History*, Book 5.28.13, trans. by C. F. Cruse, (Peabody, MA: Hendrickson Publishers, 2018), 188.

9. This is a key point in Bart Erhman, *The Orthodox Corruption of Scripture*, (New York, NY: Oxford University Press, 1993). Although I do not endorse many of Erhman's beliefs regarding inerrancy and preservation of Scripture, he lays out evidence showing the significance of these early Biblical alterations.

10. Jerome, in *The Prologue to the Canonical Epistles* in Codex Fuldensis, trans. by Thomas Caldwell, https://faithsaves.net/wp-content/uploads/2014/04/Prologue-Canonical-Epistles.pdf.

1 John 4, attempting to diminish the deity of Christ.[11] Thus, the point is again demonstrated that there existed scribal corruptions within John's first epistle in order to deny the deity of Jesus.

Jerome cited the Comma as evidence of the Trinity, as did other Christians throughout the centuries, as we shall observe below, but before Jerome, other Christians may have referenced the Comma to oppose the Trinity. Edward F. Hills makes the case that Sabellianism influenced the Greek-speaking east into rejecting the Comma.[12] Therefore, scribal corruptions and theological positions may have contributed to the rejection and exclusion of the Comma.

TESTIMONY FROM EARLY PREACHERS

The small amount of Greek mss testimony should not completely prevent the acceptance of the Comma. Early preachers over multiple centuries cited or alluded to the text, understanding it to be Scripture. If the passage was quoted as Scripture, then the preachers had to have retrieved it from somewhere. It seems historically plausible that Jerome was correct, that some scribes omitted the passage on purpose, but others knew of the Comma and referenced it. Tertullian and Origen alluded to it, Cyprian, Priscillian, Athanasius, Augustine, and many more either alluded to or quoted the passage.[13] These

---

11. Socrates, "*Historia Ecclesiastica*," Book VII:32, in *Nicene and Post-Nicene Fathers, Second Series: vol. 2*, eds. Philip Schaff and Henry Wace, (Christian Literature Publishing Company, 1890, reprinted by Hendrickson Publishers, Peabody, MA: 1995), 171.

12. "It is possible, therefore, that the Sabellian heresy brought the *Johannine comma* into disfavor with orthodox Christians. The statement, these three are one, no doubt seemed to them to teach the Sabellian view that the Father, the Son and the Holy Spirit were identical. And if during the course of the controversy manuscripts were discovered which had lost this reading in the accidental manner described above, it is easy to see how the orthodox party would consider these mutilated manuscripts to represent the true text and regard the *Johannine comma* as a heretical addition. In the Greek-speaking East especially the comma would be unanimously rejected, for here the struggle against Sabellianism was particularly severe. Thus it was not impossible that during the 3rd century amid the stress and strain of the Sabellian controversy, the *Johannine comma* lost its place in the Greek text, but was preserved in the Latin texts of Africa and Spain, where the influence of Sabellianism was probably not so great. In other words, it is not impossible that the *Johannine comma* was one of those few true readings of the Latin Vulgate not occurring in the Traditional Greek Text but incorporated into the Textus Receptus under the guiding providence of God. In these rare instances God called upon the usage of the Latin-speaking Church to correct the usage of the Greek-speaking Church." Edward F. Hills, *Believing Bible Study*, (Des Moine, IA: The Christian Research Press, 1991), 213-14.

13. For an outline of historical use see David Daniels, Answers to your Bible Version Questions, (Ontario, CA: Chick Publications, 2003), 111-15. Also see Hills, *Believing Bible Study*, 211.

particular preachers, from around A. D. 200 to 400, believed the passage to be genuine and quoted it as such.

THE GREEK CONSTRUCTION OF THE COMMA

Finally, attention must be given to the Greek syntax of 1 John 5.[14] Hills demonstrates that there are grammatical inconsistencies within 1 John 5:6-8 if the Comma is removed. In 1 John 5:6, the three words, *spirit*, *water*, and *blood* are neuter in gender but change to masculine in 5:8.[15] If 5:7 is removed, then this switch of gender endings is inconsistent within the grammar.[16]

CONCLUSION

There are difficulties with the Johannine Comma, but evidence is not completely lacking. Historical witnesses acknowledge known scribal corruptions, including specific alterations to 1 John and to the Comma itself, but it was not expunged completely. Even though many early Greek mss are missing the passage, the text can be observed in numerous citations and allusions from early preachers, as well as attestation within the Latin mss. Even as a single verse, 1 John 5:7 can be seen as a remarkable example of God preserving His Word amid textual challenges and efforts to undermine it.

---

14. See Thomas Holland, *Crowned with Glory*, (Lincoln, NE: Writers Club Press, 2000), 166.

15. "In the third place, the omission of the *Johannine comma* involves a grammatical difficulty. The words *spirit, water,* and *blood* are neuter in gender, but in 1 John 5:8 they are treated as masculine. If the Johannine comma is rejected, it is hard to explain this irregularity. It is usually said that in 1 John 5:8 *the spirit, the water, and the blood* are personalized and that this is the reason for the adoption of the masculine gender. But it is hard to see how such personalization would involve the change from the neuter to the masculine. For in verse 6 the word Spirit plainly refers to the Holy Spirit, the Third Person of the Trinity. Surely in this verse the word Spirit is "personalized," and yet the neuter gender is used. Therefore since personalization did not bring about a change of gender in verse 6, it cannot fairly be pleaded as the reason for such a change in verse 8. If, however, the *Johannine comma* is retained, a reason for placing the neuter nouns *spirit, water,* and *blood* in the masculine gender becomes readily apparent. It was due to the influence of the nouns *Father and Word*, which are masculine. Thus the hypothesis that the *Johannine comma* is an interpolation is full of difficulties." Hills, *Believing Bible Study*, 213.

16. The irregularity was known at least by the late 4th century A. D. See Gregory of Nazianzus, *Fifth Orientation: the Holy Spirit,* XIX.

27

The Visitation of the King—A Case Study in Reading and Rereading Your Bible

Jeremias D. Zuniga

INTRODUCTION

Reading the texts of the New Testament at times can be difficult without the proper training, that is not to say that the Spirit cannot guide through the process, but at times readers feel discouraged or unsure if they are reading properly. 2 Peter 1:20-21 informs us that we should not come away from Scripture with our own private interpretation, and that holy men were moved to do so by the Spirit. Because of the importance of reading Scripture properly, I aim to offer an example of the effort that it takes to engage with Scripture well by offering a few opportunities for my reader to pause and reflect throughout this paper, while also offering a structure and resources that will help both beginners and advanced readers of Scripture. To accomplish this, I want to read, re-read, and aid in interpreting 1 Peter 2:9-12.

Thus, it is vital to this paper's structure that I read and re-read the proposed text before briefly exploring the historical setting and offering interpretive points. Because this paper sets as its primary focus the question of interpretive method, I will begin by making a series of observations. Then, I will review the historical setting and the passage's date, finally concluding with the claim of kingship from this passage.

A CLOSE READING OF 1 PETER 2:9-12

When reading the Bible, selecting the boundaries of a passage for study can be difficult, but the decision must be made through repeated reading or by consulting a commentary that offers an outline that creates those boundaries for the student. In this paper, I am relying on a prior study that I completed and will guide the reader through the process of studying using the text of the KJV.[1] To this end, I encourage my reader to refrain from skipping over each section of reading the text, as each time I will offer orienting remarks.

OUR FIRST READING

> 9. But ye are a chosen generation, a royal priesthood, an holy nation, a peculiar people; that ye should **shew forth** the praises of him who hath **called you out** of darkness into his marvellous light: 10. Which in time past were not a people, but are now the people of God: which **had not obtained mercy,** but **now have obtained mercy.** 11. Dearly beloved, **I beseech** you as strangers and pilgrims, **abstain** from fleshly lusts, which **war** against the soul; 12. **Having** your conversation honest among the Gentiles: that, whereas **they speak against** you as evildoers, **they may** by your good works, which **they shall behold, glorify** God in the day of visitation.

Let's consider for a moment the action language of 1 Peter 2:9-12. The text offers twelve verbs, two in verse 9 "shew forth…Him who hath called," two in verse 10 "had not obtained mercy…now have obtained mercy," three in verse 11 "I beseech…abstain from…war," and five in verse 12 "Having…they speak against…they may…they shall behold…glorify." These verbs show an interesting development in Peter's address, especially when it is highlighted that the verbs toggle between addressing things they do and things done toward them. They are to show forth "The praises," this is their responsibility. Their responsibility comes because God has "Called you out of darkness into His marvelous light," and because of God's call, their status as being His people has changed, and they no longer identify as "not obtained" as they have "now obtained mercy." These verbs switch between what they should be doing based on what God has done, to providing clarity as to what was obtained. Peter interjects at this point and encourages his reader, "I beseech you," providing a challenge to "abstain" because there are things that "war" against them. Notice that the things that war against the soul can be abstained from, and that the reader should "have" their conversation honest among the Gentiles. Here, another "against" verb appears, the Gentiles around the recipients of this letter "speak" or slander them, but there is hope that

1. This essay differs from other essays written in this volume where I have primarily offered my own translations of every text that is engaged. The decision to select the most commonly used Bible is to reflect accessibility and reliability, instead of creating confusion on translation choices.

by the good works of Peter's audience, those slanderers will "behold" them and "glorify" God. The text establishes a series of privileges that the reader has; they are recipients of God's mercy, even though the Gentiles around them are accusatory. They are called out by God and accused by others, yet God will visit.

OUR SECOND READING

I want to now consider the text focused on the key nouns of the text:

> **9**. But ye are a **chosen generation,** a **royal priesthood,** an **holy nation, a peculiar people**; that ye should shew forth the praises of him who hath called you out of **darkness** into his **marvellous light: 10**. Which in time past were **not a people,** but are **now the people of God:** which had not obtained **mercy,** but now have obtained **mercy. 11. Dearly beloved,** I beseech you **as strangers and pilgrims,** abstain from **fleshly lusts,** which war against the **soul; 12**. Having your **conversation honest** among the Gentiles: that, whereas they speak against you as **evildoers,** they may by your **good works,** which they shall behold, glorify **God** in **the day of visitation.**

Importantly, the text offers four descriptors of Peter's audience, they are "a chosen generation, a royal priesthood, an holy nation, a peculiar people," and this fourfold description sets the text up to discuss what was obtained and what should be abstained. Additionally, these four descriptors parallel what is read in verse 17, however it is outside of this paper's purview to explore that further. These four descriptors state the status of the readers and are also found as a promise in Exodus 19:5-6. While the texts of Exodus promised Israel a covenant with the King who had delivered the Israelites from Egypt, Peter recognizes that the once wandering people he is writing to are now a part of God's inaugurated kingdom.[2] This status has made them citizens of a kingdom now, but also anticipates the future coming of the King in the day of His visitation. Because of these observations, the Household Code found in 1 Peter 2:13-17 becomes clearer. Peter's audience should demonstrate "abstinence" and "good works" because they are recipients of the mercy of the King and Judge of a superior Kingdom, and the slanderers around them will one day glorify God because they show His praises.[3]

---

2. See my essays included in this volume, "*Who will be your God*" and "*The Promise of a King*" for more on the Exodus of the Old and New Testaments.

3. As demonstrated above, these observations can be derived from sitting and annotating the text. However, once an initial observation is completed, the work of identifying the surrounding context described in my conclusion, and the historical information begins. One of the best

THE HISTORICAL CONTEXT

Our journey back begins with looking at the reception of the Epistle. It is purported that Peter was martyred in Rome during the reign of Nero, an Emperor who was not friendly to the Christian community.[4] The Epistle was likely written from Rome and addressed to scattered Christian communities facing forms of persecution that likely differed from what was experienced in Rome. If we consider these underpinnings of the Epistle, it is likely to have been authored in the 60s. This period boasted rampant persecution and would have offered the Epistle's author a genuine encounter with oppression, accusations (1 Pet. 2:12b), and ignorant claims (1 Pet. 2:15). It is important to note that scholars have offered dates later into the first and second centuries, although later dating assumes that Peter was not the author of the epistle which creates a disjunction to the aforementioned data from within the letter itself.[5]

CONCLUSION

The offering of my above observations and the historical points made mandate a final interpretive turn, understanding that the earthly ruler and his subjects were not favorable to Christians at this time. 1 Peter 2:9-12 is a part of a letter that takes a primary interest in encouraging scattered Christians to maintain good conduct and offers hope in alienation.[6] This promise aligns with the challenges these scattered Christians faced, and exploring the entirety of the epistle we find that Peter places a focus on the Father as ultimate judge (1 Pet. 1:17), Christ's ability to call strangers to Him (1 Pet. 1:2-5; 2:5 & 25), and a hope in suffering as Christ experienced (1 Pet. 1:2, 7, 11, 21; 2:23-24). Further, when

---

ways to complete this is to consult a semi-technical commentary, in this essay I recommend as a helpful tool on this specific passage Peter Davids, *The First Epistle of Peter,* of The New International Commentary on the New Testament (Grand Rapids, Mich: Eerdmans, 1990), 89-104.

4. Craig Keener, *The IVP Bible Background Commentary: New Testament* (Downers Grove, Ill: Academic, IVP, 1994), 705-707.

5. Michael J. Gorman, ed., *Scripture and Its Interpretation: A Global, Ecumenical Introduction to the Bible* (Grand Rapids, MI: Baker Academic, a division of Baker Publishing Group, 2017), 90. On the form and structure of ancient letters see page 82 in Gorman. Also see David E. Aune, *The New Testament in Its Literary Environment.* (Westminster Press, 1989), 160-162 & 189-197. Aune highlights Cicero, A. N. Sherwin-White, Pseudo-Demetrius, Pseudo-Libanius, and Stanley Stower's approach to identifying types of letters but ultimately offers three categories: Documentary letters, Official letters, and Literary letters but does not draw a hard line between these groupings.

6. Aune, *The New Testament in Its Literary Environment*, pp. 221-222.

Peter begins writing about the responsibility of the sojourners, he makes a clear indication that Christ has led them into covenant and will reappear (1 Pet. 1:7; 2:12). In this final appearance there will be judgment, as the King of the universe returns to vindicate those sojourners that were slandered for their faith (see Zech. 14:1-9).

WEEK TEN

Revelation and the Godhead—The Lamb, the Throne, and the End of all Things

28

The Godhead in the book of Revelation—Alpha and Omega

Steven Gill

While for centuries the book of Revelation has been dissected many times for its vivid portraits and symbolism by enthusiastic readers, where conversations surrounding the godhead abound, its general materials are often neglected. Many have tried to use the book of Revelation as a proof-text for their eschatological predictions to no avail; these predictions have existed for nearly two millennia with no end in sight.[1] But if the book of Revelation is valuable for its apocalyptic insights, its primary orientation appears fixed on

---

1. While sometimes thought of as a more recent development in Christian thought, end-time predictors have existed nearly as long as the church itself. These predictions often hang on beliefs surrounding 'Daniel's 70 weeks,' the rebuilding of the Jerusalem temple, jubilee years, and the like. Curiously, students of history will find that, often, the same passages of Scripture are used as proof-texts for assurances of competing conceptions of dating the apocalypse. Irshai writes, "Beginning in 350 C.E. the Christians entered what one might rightly define as the 'Hot Time Zone' of intensified Apocalyptic expectation, in which practically every major historical event especially when accompanied by supernatural portents and prodigies, was interpreted in Apocalyptic terms…a relatively unknown chronicler, Hydatius bishop of Aquae Flaviae voiced strong sentiments concerning the *Consumatio Mundi*. His chronicle, which is filled with portents, prodigies and pessimism, comes to an end in the year 468 announcing that Jesus' Second Coming – the *Parousia* – will occur on the twenty-seventh of May 482 C.E., nine jubilees after the Ascension." In the sixteenth century, Protestant reformer Michael Servetus wrote that his motive for composing *Restitutio* was his belief that "the end of time is now at hand," and that the battle of Armageddon would commence in 1585.

For Irshai: Oded Irshai, "Dating the Eschaton," in *Apocalyptic Time*, ed. Albert I. Baumgarten, (Brill, 2000), 149.

For Servetus: Michael Servetus, *The Restoration of Christianity.*

The quote above was omitted from the 1553 edition of Servetus' work, but was discovered in the Edinburgh Manuscript, heretofore untranslated until 2023, by Peter Zerner and Peter Hughes in their annotated translation of Servetus' work. Their translation is cited here (see selected bibliography).

something else entirely: the full disclosure of Jesus Christ and the culmination of His kingship.

A perhaps under-acknowledged pattern of Revelation is these repeated descriptions within a phrase that bookend the text: (1. Alpha and Omega) (2. beginning and end) (3. first and last).[2] The phrase appears in (1:8) and (22:13), the first and final chapters of the book, but is also scattered throughout the text with it and its variants appearing no less than eight times (1:8; 1:11; 1:17-18; 2:8; 4:8; 11:17; 21:6; 22:13). Each passage merits some sorting out, but the repeated emphasis of these adjectives: (1. Alpha/Omega) (2. beginning and end) (3. first and last) deserves special attention where our subject matter is concerned. Keener writes,

> Some Greco-Roman writers called the supreme deity the "first," but the Old Testament (Is 41:4) and Judaism…had already called Israel's God the "first and the last." This is the point of calling him by the first and last letters of the Greek alphabet, Alpha and Omega. (Some later Jewish teachers similarly came to call him the *'Alef* and the *Tav*, the first and last letters of the Hebrew alphabet…).[3]

Thus, it is worth noting that there exists in this three-fold invocation an expressed continuity with the Old Testament writers. "Who hath wrought and done it, calling the generations from the beginning? I the LORD, the first, and with the last; I am he" (Isaiah 41:4 KJV). Remarkably, these unique descriptors are used for God and His Christ interchangeably throughout the book of Revelation, perhaps signaling that the tidy divisions between persons and substance described by many trinitarian thinkers throughout history are not as simple as they might have us believe. In (1:8; 1:11; 1:17-18) the invocation is attributed to the Christ, while in (4:8; 11:17; 21:6) it is attributed to God. By the time the reader reaches the final chapter in (22:13) the attribution has once again returned to the Christ. When discussing Godhead theology, these passages may appear difficult to sort out from a strictly trinitarian perspective; either adjectives like "Almighty, Alpha, first, and beginning" have definable features

2. In some places, these descriptors are accompanied by the modifier, 'the Almighty' or some variation of it (1:8;11:17).

3. Craig Keener, *The IVP Bible Background Commentary: New Testament,* (IVP Academic, 2014), 729.

and meaning, or they don't. As not many Christian readers would be quick to suggest that there are two Almighties, two alphas, or two beginnings, readers are left to assume God and His Christ likely do not speak side by side, but that one is, perhaps, seen in the other. Kim writes,

> God, "who is and who was," "is to come" to earth in order to establish his rightful kingship, destroying the satanic forces. This is the main message of Revelation. John is sure of this because he saw in a vision the heavenly reality of God's triumph through Jesus Christ, which is to be unfolded on earth (Rev 5). In a real sense God has already come and triumphed in Jesus Christ. As the one who bears his names ("the First and the Last," "the Alpha and the Omega" and "the beginning and the End")...Christ is completely identified with God, so that God's future coming for salvation and judgement is none other than Christ's (Rev 22:12, 20).[4]

With this understanding in mind, debates about who, precisely is seated on the throne in (Rev. 4:2) or whose wrath is being poured out in (Rev. 6:17) become moot; the primary emphasis of the reading is that while the Christ in whom God dwells acts as His emissary in the earth, executing His judgement and authority, He is truly the revelation of the Almighty God who was, is, and is to come. The kingship that is attributed to God – the kind in which He dwells with his people and, "God himself shall be with them, and be their God" (Rev. 21:3 KJV) is not merely synonymous with the Christ – it is disclosed in the Christ. It is the opinion of this writer that much of the confusion surrounding the disposition of God has come down through the centuries to modern Christians by the improper adoption of the phrase, "God the Son," a nomenclature which was foreign to the first-century church.[5] This confusion, combined

4. Seyoon Kim, "Kingdom of God," in *Dictionary of the Later New Testament & its Developments*, ed. Ralph P. Martin, Peter H. Davids, (IVP Academic, 1997), 634-635.

5. While it is common to Christian vernacular today to speak of Jesus as "God the Son" Modern Christian readers may be surprised to discover that the phrase exists nowhere in the Bible. Jesus is never called, "God the Son" – He is always called the "Son of God." The difference between these two conceptions of the Christ is important to our discussion. Drane writes, "Application of the title 'Son of God' to Jesus underwent considerable change in early Christianity. In the earliest Christian communities it was primarily a functional expression, taking an image from extant OT and Jewish thought and applying it in a generally imprecise way to articulate the meaning of the Christ event...'Son of God' was gradually invested with more metaphysical understandings until it eventually became the church's preferred Christological

with certain misunderstandings surrounding the ministry and purpose of the Messiah has led many to conclude, incorrectly I think, that the imagery of the book of Revelation is intended to bifurcate the godhead.[6] In reality, this dual-disclosure is intended to confirm the promise of the prophets to Israel that one day there would be a true king from the house of David who would gather back together the people of God under one banner again.[7] Of the promised king from the seed of David it is said that he will "bear the glory" (Zech. 6:13) and his name will be called, "THE LORD (י-ה-ו-ה) OUR RIGHTEOUSNESS" (Jer. 23:6).[8] Far from attempting to bi-sect the Lamb upon the throne from the Ancient of days who also sits upon the throne (Rev. 5:1; 7:17), these appear to be two descriptions or disclosures of a single Authority. Furthermore, the restoration of the tribes of Israel is depicted in twelve gates appearing with the names of the twelve tribes of Israel in Ezekiel 48:30-35. The same portrait is revealed in Revelation 21:9-13, with one important modifier: The restored kingdom also has twelve foundations, upon which are written the names of the twelve apostles (Rev. 21:14). In this way, the repeated emphasis and interchangeable use of the

---

title. The generic term 'son of God' had a wide currency in ancient culture…It did not, however, denote a divine figure descending from heaven as the bearer of salvation, except insofar as angels were messengers or agents of God…On the contrary, when the status 'son of God' was conferred on someone it was a recognition of a particular achievement." As Drane points out, the title "son of God" was gradually modified over centuries until it became a divine modifier rather than earthly one. With the rise of certain heresies in the second century, the term, "God the Son of God" first comes to us through Justin Martyr (*First Apology*, CA AD 155-157) as a way of framing the Godhead as numerically distinct and divine persons rather than as the incarnation of the fullness of God in a man (cf. Col. 2:8-9).

For Drane: John Drane, "Son of God," in *Dictionary of the Later New Testament & its Developments,* ed. Ralph P. Martin, Peter H. Davids, (IVP Academic, 1997), 1111-1112.

For Justin Martyr: Justin Martyr, *First Apology,* (Ch. LXI).

6. I say "bifurcate" here as opposed to "trifurcate" as there are no meaningful discussions to be had in these passages about the manner by which the third person of the trinity might co-rule with the theoretical two in Revelation.

7. Firth writes, "A crucial element in the messianic understanding of the prophets focused on the continuation of the reign of David, and in particular on a representative of David's family who would provide a reign consistent with Yahweh's promise to David. Such a king's reign would be truly consistent with Yahweh's reign." I concur with Firth's framing. The portrait of the Messiah in the prophets teaches that the kingship of Jesus Christ is different both in quality and kind from that of Israel's previous kings: He is not the executor of His own will, or a co-will; He is the emissary and disclosure of the true God in the earth.

For Firth: David Firth, "Messiah," in Dictionary of the Old Testament Prophets, ed. Mark J. Boda, J. Gordon McConville, (IVP Academic, 2012), 539.

8. Firth, *Messiah*, 541.

phrases: (1. Alpha and Omega) (2. beginning and end) (3. first and last) for God and His Christ are not bugs to be worked out in the text in order to explain complex Christian theology. They are defining features of the text that, perhaps, demonstrate comprehensively what Paul wrote in brevity: "To wit, that God was in Christ, reconciling the world unto himself…" (2 Cor. 5:19 KJV).

29

There is One on the Throne

Andrew Herbst

INTRODUCTION

The Book of Revelation contains more Old Testament (OT) allusions and references than any other New Testament (NT) book.[1] Nearly every verse in Revelation includes OT imagery. Specific to this examination, it will be shown that Revelation 4-5 is rooted in OT theology and that the throne scenes must be understood in this light.

THE CONTEXT OF REVELATION 1-5

The Apocalypse (Revelation) opens with John's statements regarding the accomplishments, power, and soon coming of Jesus Christ. Jesus proclaims twice that He is "Alpha and Omega" (Rev. 1:8 and 1:11), and instructs John to write unto the seven churches in Asia.[2] The admonitions and corrections to the churches are found in Revelation 2-3. In Revelation 4, John saw the heavenly throne and "He" that sat on it, and surrounding the throne were the twenty-four elders and the four beasts (Rev. 4:2-3, 6). The Lamb enters in Revelation 5, and is viewed as a living-slain lamb (Rev. 5:6). Jesus, depicted as the Lamb, receives a book from the one on the throne, and through the opening of its seals, He enacts judgment upon the earth (cf. Rev. 6). After taking the book, the Lamb is worshipped and exalted by the angels, beasts, and elders, soon to be joined by "every creature which is in heaven, and on the earth, and under the earth, and such as are in the sea" (Rev. 5:8-14). The Lamb has been enthroned and is universally recognized as king and receives worship (cf. Phil. 2:10-11).

---

1. Gregory K. Beale and Donald A. Carson, eds., *Commentary on the New Testament Use of the Old Testament* (Grand Rapids, MI: Baker Academic, 2007), 1081.

2. Unless otherwise noted, all biblical passages referenced are in the *King James Version.*

REVELATION 5

If the Lamb can be viewed as a completely different figure from the one on the throne, and yet worshipped in a similar manner, that may lend to a polytheistic interpretation. Furthermore, there are seven Spirits of God mentioned as well (Rev. 3:1, 4:5, and 5:6). If one must conclude that all distinctive language, such as is displayed in these passages, must necessarily identify separate beings, then we are left to assume monotheism is truly broken.

However, polytheism need not invade the interpretation. Robert Mounce argues that Revelation 5 is not a literal depiction but a representation of how God will carry out the completion of His redemptive plan (cf. Rev. 5:7).[3] Jesus was not literally a dead standing animal, but He was certainly crucified and resurrected. John's visions were symbolic but pointed to real occurrences.

Some may argue that the Trinity is pictured as the Lamb came unto the one on the throne (Rev. 5:7). However, the symbolism displayed points more to the unity of God and the Lamb, not revealing the Trinity. Grant Osborne notes that the unity of God and the Lamb is significant in these chapters, clearly showing that "God and the Lamb are one," citing John 10:30 as further verification.[4] Osborne continues to assert that the Lamb was at the center of the throne and was God himself.[5] The full picture of Revelation 5 reveals that God's plan for redemption and humanity will be fulfilled by His own action. God became the Lamb and reconciled the world unto Himself (2 Cor. 5:19). Therefore, He is worthy to receive honor and worship, and rule the eternal kingdom.

THE OT BACKGROUND OF REVELATION 1-5

G. K. Beale and Sean McDonough demonstrate that Revelation 4-5 is rooted in images from Daniel 7.[6] In Daniel 7, the prophet describes the Ancient of Days, the opening of the books of judgment, and the coming of the Son of Man (Dan. 7:9-14). The Ancient of Days will give the Son of Man an eternal kingdom, dominion, and authority to judge. This is what is seen in Revelation

3. Robert Mounce, *The Book of Revelation*, (Grand Rapids, MI: Eerdmans Publishing Co., 1997), 133.
4. Grant Osborne, *Revelation*, (Grand Rapids, MI: Baker Academic, 2002), 245.
5. Osborne, *Revelation*, 245.
6. For a complete layout and outline of the fourteen correspond points, and addition of Ezekiel 1, see Gregory K. Beale and Donald A. Carson, eds., *Commentary on the New Testament Use of the Old Testament*, 1098.

4-5. However, the theme of the unity between God and the Lamb reappears, now expressed as the unity of the Ancient of Days and the Son of Man.

After Jesus had finished speaking in Revelation 1:11, John turned to see who had spoken and identified the speaker as the Son of Man (Rev. 1:12-13). Notably, the visual portrayal of the Son of Man in Revelation reflects the depiction of the Ancient of Days in Daniel 7 (Rev. 1:13-15 and Dan. 7:9). Jesus is the Son of Man, but visibly appears as the Ancient of Days. This concept, the oneness of the Father and the Son, is consistent with the rest of John's writings. As mentioned above, Jesus stated that He and His Father are one (John 10:30), and He told Philip that when one sees Jesus, they see the Father (John 14:9). The pinnacle comes at the close of the Bible, when John writes that there will be one throne in the New Jerusalem. John sees only one on that throne and proclaims that it is God and the Lamb. However, God and the Lamb has only one face, and His servants shall see "His face" (Rev. 22:4a). This is because in the face of Jesus, you see both God and the Lamb, God that became the plan of salvation Himself.

CONCLUSION

The Book is called *Revelation*, singular. There is only one revelation of who Jesus is. He is shown to be the Creator who became a man to die as the Lamb. Yet, His sacrifice and humility do not represent a weak God, for He will return and recover creation. The Revelation is not merely about the Lamb that has died, but also presents Him as a conquering king. Jesus' kingship will fulfill the Davidic Covenant, as He will be enthroned over an eternal kingdom that He earned through His sacrifice and the conquering of God's enemies. The oneness of the throne and the revealing of His face will offer to His servants that which had not been seen before (cf. Isa. 6:1 and Ezek. 1:27): a full view of the revelation of God and human servants surrounding His throne. Through the work of God and the Lamb, the plan of redemption has been completed.

30

Who's Speaking to the Church? The Speaker of John's Letters to the Church of Philadelphia

Jeremias D. Zuniga

INTRODUCTION

Approaching the Book of Revelation shows that a diversity of challenges with history have persisted, impacting the reader's interpretive method. These challenges typically cause commentators to include some form of a distinctive label, highlighting their theological location and signaling divergence from other methods of interpretation.[1] While this is the case, my focus will not be to identify with one of many overarching interpretive methods. Instead, out of a deep sense of appreciation for every word of Scripture, I will approach the text investigating what is present, asking two questions: what immediate historical situation would have required the admonition in the text, and how does the text demand its hearers to reflect on the identity and nature of God? While it is not my intention to avoid the conversations of hermeneutics surrounding the fulfillment of God's plans in the eschaton, it is my aim to demystify the language of the opening letters by examining John of Patmos's letter to Philadelphia (Rev. 3:7-13).[2]

---

1. Craig S. Keener, *Revelation* (Grand Rapids, MI: Zondervan, 2000), 29. Keener includes his interpretive method in footnote 23, after taking the time to discuss other methodologies, i.e., the idealist, historicist, preterist, futurist, and eclectic. Similarly, Koester and Ryrie also begin their commentaries with identifying their theological location though Koester gives more time exploring the history of interpretation and reception history than Ryrie and Keener, e.g., see Charles Caldwell Ryrie, *Revelation* (Chicago, IL: Moody Publishers, 1968), 8-10 & Craig R. Koester, *Revelation and the End of All Things* (Grand Rapids, MI: William B. Eerdmans Publishing Company, 2018), 2-42.

2. I must note that my comment does not preclude that these methods do not value or

My thesis is that the letter was intended to be read as a sermon that is distinctive from other apocalyptic texts insofar as it carries a prophetic framework, a framework that identifies Jesus as *YHWH* and the Spirit. This paper will have two movements aligning with the two questions mentioned above. First, there will be a brief introduction to the historical setting of the Philadelphian church. Lastly, by looking at the proposed genre of the letter, I will investigate what the Spirit seeks to communicate to this church through the lens of prophetic utterance, similar to the forth-telling and foretelling of Old Testament prophets.

HISTORICAL SETTING

Two primary concerns will occupy the historical setting of John's revelation, namely the history of Philadelphia and the citizenship that may have contributed to the purported challenges the church faced. Importantly, the disputes between early and later dates should be raised at this point as they relate to the absence of recognition of the Jerusalem temple or its destruction (4 Ezra 3:2; 2 Baruch 1:4; 4:1-5).[3] John of Patmos appears distinct from these apocalypses, writing "things which must shortly come to pass" (Rev. 1:1, 19) instead of *ex eventu* as found in the two apocalyptic works cited.[4] Considering the distance and what appears to be a singular reference to a temple (Rev. 11:1-2), it seems probable that the temple had been destroyed, and the relationship between the Jews and Christians had progressed to instability as a result. This consideration would lend favorability to the late first century, which is accepted alongside Domitian leadership (c. 90-96).[5]

---

prioritize every word of Scripture, but does communicate that they are more broad sweeping in intended focus whereas I will be highly focused on the minutia of Old Testament revelation seen in John's letter. Consequently, the research below will include the work of authors that differ in their approach to reading the revelation and the reader should be aware that citation does not equate general acceptance. While I hold a premillennialist view, I recognize that others cited do not (e.g., G. K Beale and Craig Koester).

3. Mitchell Glenn Reddish, *Apocalyptic Literature: A Reader* (Peabody, MA: Hendrickson Publishers, 2015), 61, 99-100. These 1st century apocalypses appear aware and utilize the temple destruction from historic perspective, prophecy *ex eventu*. John's revelation seems unconcerned with this event, perhaps related to the location of his audience or the struggles they faced with Jewish groups that may have viewed them as outsiders in hopes to maintain Roman favor. See Keener, *Revelation*, 38-39.

4. David Edward Aune, *The New Testament in Its Literary Environment*, First (Philadelphia, PA: Westminster Press, 1987), 226-46. While John does demonstrate some similarities with other apocalypses, it must be noted that the general genre does not holistically capture all that is reported in John's revelation as he appears in many ways distinctive (241).

5. Keener, *Revelation*, 35-39.

Additionally, the city of Philadelphia had a unique history and may have been perfect for fostering emperor worship. The city had been destroyed by an earthquake multiple times and owed its rebuilding to the emperor, which inevitably caused the name change to Philadelphia.[6] Given this history, some have speculated that this caused John to refer to the church as becoming pillars, the only objects suspected to remain intact after the earthquakes.[7] While this is possible, it is most important to note that the contributions of the emperors led to the Philadelphians worshiping them and the deities associated with them. Temples to Artemis, Helios, Zeus, Dionysus, and Aphrodite were present, and it is presumed that a Jewish synagogue was also there, given the later third-century inscription and the internal witness of John's letter.[8] The area was also known for its agriculture and wine, though we do not find explicit references.[9] John seems much more concerned about aligning with the OT prophetic tradition as a covenant preacher, instead of addressing the larger prevailing cultural dynamics of Philadelphia.[10]

ATTENTION TO THE TEXT

The letter to the Philadelphians opens with the following proclamation, "These are the sayings of the Holy, the True, the One holding the key of David" (Rev. 3:7b). Focusing on the most immediate statement, "These things saith," John makes a considerably rich theological point.[11] This is a prophetic formula and introduces the general genre of his address to Philadelphia. It notifies the reader that John is operating in continuation with the OT prophets, a group whose ministry consisted of calling Israel back to covenant from their dependence on other nations (Jer. 2:1ff). Indeed, John expects his audience to be familiar with Israel's Scripture while also utilizing similar themes found

---

6. Koester, *Revelation and the End of All Things*, 69-70.

7. Keener, *Revelation*, 151-52.

8. Craig S. Keener, *The IVP Bible Background Commentary: New Testament* (Downers Grove, IL: InterVarsity Press, 1993), 773.

9. Koester, *Revelation and the End of All Things*, 69.

10. Alan S Bandy, "*Patterns of Prophetic Lawsuits in the Oracles to the Seven Churches.*," Neotestamentica 45 (2): 178–205, 2011, https://search.ebscohost.com/login.aspx?direct=true&AuthType=sso&db=rfh&AN=ATLA0001882542&site=ehost-live&scope=site.

11. On the usage of the Τάδε λέγει Prophetic formula, see Bandy, *Patterns of Prophetic Lawsuits in the Oracles to the Seven Churches*, 188-191, 189n31.

in contemporary apocalyptic literature.[12] Thus, the genre of the letter to the Philadelphians resembles in part an apocalypse but centers its connection with Old Testament prophetic covenant lawsuits.[13] Interestingly, a case is to be made that the letter more closely resembles a synagogue homily, which may account for the structure introduced below.[14]

A). The *Philadelphian church* is listening to what is said by He that is holy and true.

B). An *open door* is laid before the faithful that have faced opposition and not denied His name.

C). *Satan's synagogue* and the liars present will worship at their feet.

D). *The world and earth* will face the "hour of temptation".

C). God will make the overcomers pillars in *His temple.*

B). *God's city, New Jerusalem from Heaven* is open to those that receive His new name.

A). Anyone with the ability to hear is to listen to what has been said to the *Churches* by the Spirit.

John highlights seven key locations in his letter to the church: the church in Philadelphia (3:7a), an open door (3:8b), Satan's synagogue (3:9a), the world and earth (3:10), God's temple (3:12a), God's city New Jerusalem from Heaven (3:12b), and the churches (3:13). The order of these locations in the passage is important and builds a crescendo, pointing towards a chiasmus. I highlight these locations as an observation of clear contrasts on each side of the letter, pointing to my conclusion of a chiasmus as noted above. Although my focus here will exclude a more robust treatment of sections C and D.

Within section A, we see the Philadelphian church is written to utilize the prophetic formula (3:7a), a formula that appears to have fallen out of use in the time John wrote and was in the Old Testament preserved for *YHWH*.[15] A similar

---

12. Keener, *Revelation*, 32-33.

13. Bandy, 201. Interestingly, both Bandy and Aune identify the connection to royal law and proclamation. See Aune, *The New Testament*, 232.

14. Aune, The New Testament, 202-214. Additionally, what follows below is the application of the principles found in Kenneth E Bailey, *Poet and Peasant and Through Peasants Eyes: A Literary-Cultural Approach to the Parables in Luke*, Combined (Grand Rapids, MI: Wm. B. Eerdmans Publishing Company, 1983).

15. G. K Beale notes "Jesus introduces himself with a stock formula that the OT prophets used to introduce prophetic sayings from God: τάδε λέγει κύριος παντοκράτωρ ("these things

formula is related to the Spirit instead of Christ (3:13; see Acts 21:11, the only other New Testament mention of the formula outside of Revelation). Further, the identity of the speaker is disclosed, it is the Holy One,[16] the True One (Isaiah 65:16), which anticipates John's reference to Isaiah 22. John purports Christ's identity as the key holder, similar to Eliakim (Isaiah 22:20-25), which may represent His access to the feeble church's provisional needs (Rev. 3:8b).

Additionally, on one side of section B, an open door is present based on Christ's ability as the key holder, and on the other, access to New Jerusalem (3:7b-8, 12:bc). This language reflects the kingly focus of the passage, the coming Kingdom is a promise to those willing to keep covenant, and Christ is the one that gives access to this kingdom. The motif of the door keeping Christ deposits a theology not fully expressed in the NT, the duty of porters in the wilderness tabernacle, and the promise that the section D holds will have to be revisited in another study. However, it is important to note that this proleptic promise of vindication would not necessitate the Philadelphians being alive to experience, another focus to be discussed elsewhere.

CONCLUSION

Importantly, the language described above identifies Christ as the speaker to the church in synonymous terms as *YHWH* of the Old Testament and further asserts this when section A clarifies that those able should hear, "what the Spirit saith to the churches" (Rev. 3:13). These observations demonstrate a synonymizing of the identity of the Christ with *YHWH* and the Spirit that

---

says the Lord Almighty"). This OT formula occurs 21 times in the Minor Prophets (about 12 times in Zechariah the phrase introduces a new literary unit, as here); likewise τάδε λέγει κύριος introduces sayings of the Lord and introduces new literary units in Ezekiel (at least 65 times), Jeremiah (about 30 times), and Amos (8 times). Consequently, the use of the formula here and to introduce the sayings of Christ in the letters emphasizes that Christ assumes the role of Yahweh. Such a role for Christ has already been shown in other respects in 1:12–18. Indeed, this formula demands that chs. 2–3 be seen as a group of prophetic messages rather than as mere letters." See Gregory K. Beale, *The Book of Revelation: A Commentary on the Greek Text* (Grand Rapids, Mich: Eerdmans, 2000), 2:1-7. Further, Bandy asserts "Aune (1990, 187) observes that τάδε (the accusative form of ὅδε) was obsolete in Koine Greek and would convey a sense of archaism. This usage, then, suggests an intentional archaic effect equivalent to the use of "thus saith" in English." (189n31).

16. Isaiah calls YHWH "the Holy One" some 30 times, (see Is. 1:4, 5:19, 24, 10:17, 20, 12:6, 17:7, 29:19, 23, 30:11-12, 15, 31:1, 37:23, 40:25, 41:14, 16, 20, 43:3, 14-15, 45:11, 47:4, 48:17, 49:7, 54:5, 55:5, 60:9, 14.

leaves no room for ontological distinction, proving a high Christology appropriate to John's use of Isaiah's strict monotheism. Finally, it must be noted of the church in Philadelphia, that regardless of the commendation they received, ceased to exist in the area at some point. However, Christ's promise reflects that there once existed there a group of believers living in covenant when John wrote, a group that contemporary churches may one day worship with in New Jerusalem.

WEEK ELEVEN

The Post-New Testament Church and the Godhead—Ignatius, Monarchians, and the Road to Nicea

31

The Godhead in Church History—Congruence in Christian Thought from the New Testament Writers to the Third Century

Steven Gill

When studying the ante-Nicene era of Christianity, it may be easy to assume that the apostles of the New Testament left behind creeds from which the post-New Testament church framed much of their doctrine, particularly with regard to the godhead. Nevertheless, if one were to make such an assumption, they would find the evidence to that effect disappointing. While many enthusiastic scholars have attempted to drum up creative interpretations from certain New Testament passages to draw out the appearance of early creed-like statements in the early church, it seems evident that no such statements exist.[1] Instead, what readers find are repeatedly emphasized doctrines, many from the Old Testament, which were frequently related to believers in such a way that they became, in many cases, the foundation upon which later ideas were developed.[2] It is these repeatedly emphasized doctrines to which we turn

1. David Wright, "Creeds, Confessional Forms," in *Dictionary of the Later New Testament & Its Developments*, ed. Ralph P. Martin, Peter H. Davids (IVP Academic, 1997), 256. Without question, the New Testament is filled with examples of fundamental doctrines taught by the early church such as continued emphasis on the oneness of God (Luke 4:8 Jam. 2:19; 1 Tim. 2:5) faith (Rom. 4:9-13; Eph. 2:8-9; Heb. 11:6) repentance (Mark 1:4;15; Acts 3:19; Rev. 2:5) water and Spirit baptism (Matt. 28:19; Acts 8:12-17; 10:44-48; 19:1-6) the resurrection of the dead and eternal judgement (Acts 24:15; 1 Cor. 15:12-28; 1 Thess. 4:16-17). In fact, many of these things are listed as principal doctrines in Hebrews' sixth chapter (6:1-3). Nevertheless, the catechismal creeds that later characterized much of the Christian world such as the Apostles' Creed, Athanasian Creed, or Nicene Creed were foreign to the early church.

2. This is not to suggest that the later creeds should therefore themselves be considered validated or effectual; the precise opposite may be the case. In many cases, the creeds bear only a passing resemblance to certain teachings of the early church, prioritizing polemical statements in

our attention in an effort to identify which writers and thinkers of the ante-Nicene era demonstrate the most congruence with the first-century church.

Where articulating the early church's position on the godhead is concerned, readers of this volume will be unsurprised to discover my unwillingness toward allowing anything described as "trinitarian" to be labeled "orthodox." On this point, I acknowledge this divergence may lead to conclusions about the ante-Nicene era that are not shared by other thinkers on the subject. Nevertheless, if one examines the first three centuries of Christianity carefully, they will discover that those ante-Nicene writers who resisted trinitarian conceptions are those who appear to have most nearly reflected the teachings of the early church on the subject. Tertullian wrote,

> The simple, indeed, (I will not call them unwise and unlearned,) who always constitute the majority of believers, are startled at the dispensation (of the Three in One), on the ground that their very rule of faith withdraws them from the world's plurality of gods to the one only true God; not understanding that, although He is the one only God, He must yet be believed in with His own οἰκονομία [*economy*]. The numerical order and distribution of the Trinity they assume to be a division of the Unity...[3].

Thus, it is from the father of the term itself that we learn many believers followed the early church in their aversion toward anything like a trinity. In

---

their clauses designed to champion one particular pattern of thought or to oppose one perceived heresy. For example, the Apostles' Creed states, "I believe in the Holy Spirit, the holy catholic Church, the communion of saints, the forgiveness of sins..." yet, there is, of course, nothing in the New Testament about a holy catholic Church. The Nicene Creed refers to Jesus as "God from God, Light from Light" yet this description of the Christ is not found within the scriptures either; it was created by the First Nicene council to combat Arianism. In perhaps the most egregious example, we find in the Athanasian Creed this statement: "...Now this is the catholic faith: that we worship one God in trinity and trinity in unity, neither blending their persons nor dividing their essence...their glory equal, their majesty co-eternal." Barring the incoherence of championing a necessary division (neither blending) while insisting upon no division (nor dividing) this statement has no parallel in the New Testament. There is nothing said of a plural glory (their) or a co-eternal majesty in the Bible. In fact, the New Testament writers seemed averse to such language (Col. 2:8-9; 2 Cor. 5:19; Eph. 4:4-6; Rom. 8:9-11). Nevertheless, many words, phrases, and principles within these creeds are saturated in biblical terminology. Without the scriptures, then, these creeds would have no standing-ground to begin with. They are, therefore, dependent on the teachings of the New Testament, even in cases where they represent a perversion of the scriptures.

3. Tertullian, *Against Praxeas*, ch. III.

Against Praxeas, Tertullian condemned the subject of his polemic for teaching a doctrine that, he believed, bore some resemblance toward the Jewish faith, "of which this [oneness] is the substance…".[4] Ironically, the apostles of the New Testament emphasized such resemblance as a feature of their doctrine rather than a problem to be sorted out.[5] Tertullian compared Praxeas to a group known as the Monarchians, whom he said believed, "Both of them [Father and Son] should be One, and One or the Other should be Both…".[6] Justin Martyr was critical of similar teachers, of whom he said,

> And that Christ being Lord, and God the Son of God, and appearing formerly in power as Man, and Angel, and in the glory of fire as at the bush, so also was manifested at the judgement executed on Sodom has been demonstrated…And do not suppose, sirs, that I am speaking superfluously when I repeat these words frequently: but it is because I know that some wish to anticipate these remarks, and to… maintain that this power is indivisible and inseparable from the Father…[but it] has been also amply demonstrated [this power] is not numbered [as different] in name only like the light of the sun[7] but is indeed something numerically distinct.[8]

It is possible that those whom Justin said would not accept his claim that there was 'numerical distinction' between the divine Father and Son were of similar persuasion as Praxeas, to whom Tertullian wrote, or the Monarchians, whom Tertullian criticized. Still, it is probably important to note that Tertullian characterized the anti-trinitarian persuasion as the one possessed by most

---

4. Tertullian, *Against Praxeas*, ch. XXXI.

5. This practice of harmonizing the teaching of the Hebrew scriptures with Christian doctrine began with John the Baptist and Christ, afterward extending itself into the teachings of the Apostles (John 1:23; Luke 24:27; Acts 2:14-36; 1 Cor. 10:1-12; Jude 1:5; Rom. 1:17; Rom. 11:13). In each of the cited passages, the early church drew upon the Hebrew scriptures and the teaching surrounding them to inform their understanding of Christian doctrine, demonstrating the lines between "Jewish" and "Christian" thought was much thinner than later thinkers might have had Christians to imagine.

6. Tertullian, *Against Praxeas*, ch. X.

7. This particular objection by Justin is interesting, as it put him at odds with the later Nicene Creed which called Jesus "Light from Light," leading one to wonder if Justin – a well-remembered father of the Catholic Church – would have attached his name to the creed they later came to embrace.

8. Justin Martyr, *Dialogue with Trypho*, ch. CXXVIII.

believers in the second century. Many oneness adherents in the twenty-first century have spent a great deal of time laboring to find anecdotal examples of a doctrine they have been led to believe was the exception to a rule in antiquity (i.e., oneness against the backdrop of trinitarianism). The reality of the situation may have been much more favorable to the oneness position than has been historically assumed.[9] It is also important to remember that, when examining groups or individuals that were labeled heretical by councils and creeds, many names may constitute one group or represent a single chain of thought. For example, the Sabellians of the third century were also sometimes referred to as the Monarchians. Writing in the seventeenth century, Christiano Wormio insisted that another name was attributed to these sorts of believers, most nearly translated to English, the "unionites" or "one-ites."[10]

> Sabellius states that there is only one person, [thereby] confusing the people of the Trinity...Sabellius taught a union between the substance and created confusion with respect to the three hypostasis of the Only Trinity, allowing the three substances of divinity to exist in one person...So, every time they [Sabellians] meet someone among the simplest or the most ignorant, who do not know exactly the Divine reality, they question him in this way: What

9. Peter Heather, chair of medieval history at King's College in London has engaged extensively with this misunderstanding. Concerning misapprehensions about the ubiquitous reception of the trinity, Heather writes, "As late as 300, at the time of Constantine's conversion Christianity possessed no central authority structure at all...Much remained in flux. Even such a fundamental Christian doctrine as that of the Holy Trinity only began to find a generally agreed formulation after Constantine's conversion, and many issues of theory and practice...remained unresolved for a long time." Concerning the issue of anathematizing sects that departed from the Catholic way, Heather goes on to say, "The third century saw continued disagreement about the nature of Christ, with a tendency for some theologies (often labeled Monarchian, from the Greek for 'single principle of authority') to stress the absolute divinity of Christ in such a way as to collapse most discernable differences between God the Father and God the Son. Both Sabellius in Rome (fl. c. 215) and Bishop Paul of Samosata (260-68) in the east were condemned for this." It is probably important to note that Heather offers two individuals as examples - one from the east, another from the west. This, perhaps, serves to underscore the point that opposition to the trinitarian persuasion was not as regional as has been sometimes supposed.

For Heather: Peter Heather, *Christendom: The Triumph of a Religion, AD 300-1300*, (Alfred A. Knopf, 2022), xiv; 27-30.

10. Christiano Wormio, *Sabellian History*, trans. Juan D. Pedraza, (Eugene Dominguez, 2023), 54. Here, Dominquez comments that this name "unionites" comes from a fifth century source named Prudentius. It is evident from many ancient sources that, far from being a settled doctrine with which minority teachings contested, the doctrine of the trinity received much criticism during its earliest formulation.

then, good man, say? Do we have a God or three?[11]

In addition to being labeled a Monarchian, Sabellius enjoyed criticism from a wide variety of sources, leading some scholars to the conclusion that he was a well-respected bishop of his time.[12] It is not enough to say that the first three centuries of Christian thought were characterized by non-trinitarian or anti-trinitarian sentiment; the ante-Nicene church was specifically concerned with preserving the oneness of God, which they believed to be a holy endeavor. Ironically, in the two factions of the era that have been discussed in this paper (oneness and trinitarian), there may be found thinkers who, drawing upon the scriptures, defended their position on the grounds that they were upholding the teachings of the scriptures, but only one demonstrated congruence with the attitude of the New Testament church. As attention toward these groups continues to grow among institutions of higher learning, it is becoming more evident that what is meant by "orthodoxy" is largely dependent upon what one believes about these critical early centuries of church history.

---

11. Wormio, *Sabellian History*, 56-60.
12. William Chalfant, *Ancient Champions of Oneness*, (Word Aflame Press, 1986), 96-97.

32

Irenaeus—An Early Witness

Andrew Herbst

INTRODUCTION

The age of the apostles ended with the completion of the Bible near A. D. 100. Even though Christians were persecuted by the Jews and Romans, the followers of Christ spread throughout the world, evangelizing and starting churches. However, false teachers also arose and spread ideas that did not completely originate from Scripture. Over the next few centuries, doctrines emerged and developed that many Christians today hold with firm conviction. This work will survey a few of these examples, specifically, inerrancy, cessationism, and Augustinian-Calvinism, and will observe relevant comments made by the early preacher, Irenaeus.[1] Within the traditions of Christianity, Irenaeus is held in high esteem. He lived shortly after the apostles and provides valuable insight into what an early respected Christian leader taught.

BIOGRAPHY

It is estimated that Irenaeus was born around A. D. 140 and possibly died near 200. He grew up in Smyrna listening to Polycarp, a disciple of the Apostle John.[2] Therefore, Irenaeus was only two chain links away from the teaching of an apostle. Irenaeus became the bishop of Lyon, in modern-day France, and served in that capacity for close to a quarter of a century.

Irenaeus is primarily known for his extensive work *Against Heresies*. These are five books in which he combats the growing heresies of his day. Many of these heretics are labeled as Gnostics, which is an umbrella term that encapsulates numerous false teachings.

---

1. Cessationism refers to the view that certain spiritual gifts, such as tongues, miracles, and prophecy, ceased with the completion of the Bible. Augustinian-Calvinism refers to *Reformed doctrine.*

2. Irenaeus, "*Against Heresies,*" Book III.3.4 in *The Ante-Nicene Fathers,* vol. 1, A. Cleveland Coxe, ed., (Peabody, MA: Hendrickson Publishers, 2004), 416.

INERRANCY

Inerrancy is a somewhat modern term within Christianity, but its concepts and implications are rooted in both the Old Testament (OT) and New Testament (NT). Inerrancy is tied to Biblical preservation and means "without error."[3] Irenaeus did not use the term *inerrancy*, as the word did not yet exist, but his writings portray a great care for the truth of Scripture. Throughout *Against Heresies*, Irenaeus articulates, analyzes, and critiques the doctrine of false teachers.[4] In his introduction, the bishop stated that "certain men have set the truth aside, and bring in lying words and vain genealogies," falsifying the words of God.[5] With these lying words, the heretics have taken many as captives; therefore, Irenaeus set out to write against them in order to "expose and counteract" their falsehoods.[6]

Heretics, such as Valentinus and Marcion, wrote many spurious books and forgeries, which Irenaeus contrasted with the truthfulness of Scripture.[7] Irenaeus maintained that Scripture was given by God through the Spirit, thus "perfect" and consistent.[8] These statements reflect Irenaeus' belief in inerrancy and align with apostolic teaching.[9]

Irenaeus can also shed light on a contemporary discussion of inerrancy. Mark 16:9-20 remains one of the most contested passages in debates regarding Biblical manuscripts and translations. Critical scholars assert that Mark did not write these last twelve verses, and that this final section was inserted into the Gospel at a much later date. Those who deny the authenticity of this passage claim that it is missing from the so-called best NT manuscripts available today.[10] These

---

3. See John Warwick Montgomery, ed., *God's Inerrant Word,* (Irvine, CA: 1517 Publishing, 2018).

4. History has revealed that Irenaeus was quite accurate in what he recorded about these heretical teachings. See Marvin Meyer, ed., The Nag Hammadi Scriptures: The Revised and Updated Translation of Sacred Gnostic Texts, (New York, NY: HarperOne, 2009), 6-7. Although these authors seem to disapprove of Irenaeus affirming only the four canonical Gospels, they show that Irenaeus is reliable in what he reported.

5. Irenaeus, *Against Heresies*, Book I preface, Coxe, 315.

6. Irenaeus, *Against Heresies*, Book I preface, Coxe, 315.

7. Irenaeus, *Against Heresies*, Book I.1.20, Coxe, 344.

8. Irenaeus, *Against Heresies*, Book II.28.2-3, Coxe, 399-400.

9. cf. 2 Tim. 3:16 and 2 Peter 1:20-21. Irenaeus also displays a care for proper hermeneutics and faithful interpretation of the Bible. See 1.1.3.

10. For further evidence and support of the authenticity of Mark 16, see David Otis Fuller, ed., *Counterfeit or Genuine*, (Grand Rapids, MI: International Publications, 1978).

NT documents date to near A. D. 350, and their lack of including the ending of Mark supposedly proves its status as a forgery. It is therefore surprising that Irenaeus cited the ending of Mark 16 over a century prior to A. D. 350. If the passage did not exist, then it is strange that Irenaeus quotes it, and even states, "towards the conclusion of his Gospel, Mark says..." and proceeds to cite Mark 16:19.[11] Thus, Irenaeus, in the second century, knew about the ending of Mark's Gospel, and even attributed its authorship to Mark himself.

CESSATIONISM

Later writers from the 400s, such as Augustine and John Chrysostom, claimed that tongues had ceased in their day.[12] However, Irenaeus, who lived two hundred years before these two preachers, wrote of saints in the Church who were empowered by the Spirit to speak in all languages.[13] Irenaeus clearly accepted that the Spirit was still filling believers with the evidence of speaking in tongues, and even labeled these individuals as "brethren in the Church," not as heretics to be corrected. If the gifts of the Spirit ceased when the Bible was completed, then either Irenaeus was lying in his report or gravely mistaken. As a highly esteemed Christian leader, traditional Christians should have a difficult time dismissing him without thought, for he is an early witness to the continuation of the gifts of the Spirit in the post-NT age.

THE ISSUE OF FREE WILL AND HUMAN NATURE

Today, Reformed Theology is connected to numerous denominations and has a wide range of beliefs. At the risk of oversimplifying and inadequate definitions, a primary question within Christianity is that of free will and human nature. Many in the Reformed tradition assert that humans can do nothing Godly unless God has elected them and transformed their wicked nature. Alternate

---

11. Irenaeus, *Against Heresies*, III.10.5, Coxe, 426. (There may also be an allusion to Mark 16:17-18 with a combination of Luke 10:19, see II.20.3.)

12. See Augustine, *Homily 6.10 on the First Epistle of John*, and John Chrysostom, *Homily 29.1 on 1 Corinthians*

13. "Terming those persons 'perfect' who have received the Spirit of God, and who through the Spirit of God do speak in all languages, as he used Himself also to speak. In like manner we do also hear many brethren in the Church, who possess prophetic gifts, and who through the Spirit speak all kinds of languages, and bring to light for the general benefit the hidden things of men, and declare the mysteries of God, whom also the apostle terms 'spiritual,' they being spiritual because they partake of the Spirit..." Irenaeus, *Against Heresies*, Book V.6.1, Coxe, 531.

views claim that humans are born into a sinful world but that God has provided the opportunity for them to choose or reject Him. Neither position diminishes God's sovereignty nor attributes salvation to the work of humanity.[14]

Irenaeus is an early example of a Christian leader who taught that man's ultimate destination was based on his obedience or disobedience to God. Book 4 of *Against Heresies* contains multiple chapters focused on human choices, nature, and eternal destinations. This situation is relevant since there were Gnostic doctrines that were deterministic, and Irenaeus sought to critique and correct these positions.[15] The bishop states that "because God made man a free [agent] from the beginning, possessing his own power, even as he does his own soul, to obey the behests (*ad utendum sententia*) of God voluntarily, and not by compulsion of God."[16] Irenaeus argued that humans will receive what they deserve based on their choices, and that this is just because humanity has received the knowledge of good and evil, having the mental capacity from God to choose.[17] God calls mankind to salvation, but many reject His call, not because He is weak but because of their willful blindness.[18] Based on his quotations, it would be safe to argue that Irenaeus would not accept basic Reformed doctrines if he were alive today.

CONCLUSION

Studying Christian history is important because it demonstrates the beliefs of Christians over the centuries, and how those beliefs may or may not be rooted in Scripture. Irenaeus is a helpful example of someone closely situated near apostolic teaching and taught many doctrines that align with Scripture. The further Christianity moved away from the apostles, the more that unbiblical doctrines crept into mainstream tradition. Irenaeus reveals that many NT doctrines were still held in his day, but later historical testimonies show a decrease in belief over time.

---

14. For clear examples of Reformed thought regarding freewill and election, see The Westminster Confession of Faith, chapters 9-10.

15. See Book IV of "*Against Heresies*" in Coxe, 518-525.

16. Irenaeus, *Against Heresies*, Book IV.37.1, Coxe, 518.

17. Irenaeus, *Against Heresies*, Book IV.37.1-39.1, Coxe, 518-22.

18. "...those who are [thus] blinded are involved in darkness through their own fault. The light does never enslave any one by necessity; nor, again, does God exercise compulsion upon any one unwilling to accept the exercise of His skill.Those persons, therefore, who have apostatized from the light given by the Father, and transgressed the law of liberty, have done so through their own fault, since they have been created free agents, and possessed of power over themselves." Irenaeus, Against Heresies, Book IV.39.3, Coxe, 523.

33

The God of the Earliest Followers—A Brief Introduction to Examining Historical Theology

Jeremias D. Zuniga

INTRODUCTION

While studying Church history and historical theology in graduate school, I was privileged to engage with primary sources from the Patristic era (c. 30-800). During this study, I discovered a variety of genres these early writers utilized to communicate and came to realize that the polemics they wrote against opponents were at times discussed in contemporary works in ways that did not always recognize the complexity of exploring the historical record. While history is not entirely lost to the contemporary reader, it is incumbent upon the historian to accurately express the reality of what is recorded versus what has been reconstructed, relying on theological aims.

Because of this, I will represent an early heretic and heresiologist. My aim is not to claim theological adherence to either, but to demonstrate that what is known about both figures demands reading about each as reconstructive work instead of assuming that what appears in generalized popular works is by necessity accurate. It is my intention to offer the reader a tool in reading historical theology, a way of distinguishing between reality and reconstruction.

WHO WROTE WHAT?!

Writing in the pre-Nicene (c. 100-325) period surrounding the historical figure known as Sabellius regularly speaks condemningly of him, perhaps correctly, possibly incorrectly.[1] In his book, "Why Church History Matters,"

1. Clarity to ambiguity introduced here will be offered below.

Robert F. Rea writes of Sabellius on three occasions, two of which are disparaging.[2] Additionally, Earle E. Cairns claims:

> "[Sabellius] taught a trinity of manifestation of forms rather than of essence. God was manifested in Old Testament times, later as the Son to redeem man, and as the Holy Spirit after the resurrection of Christ. Thus there were not three persons in the Godhead but three manifestations. This view may be illustrated by the relationships that a man may have. In one relationship he is son; in another, brother; and in a third, father. In all these relationships there is but one real personality. This view denied separate personality to Christ."[3]

Interestingly, in the very carefully edited volume *The Church from Age to Age*, there is no mention of Sabellius. When engaging the Monarchians' Christology, the authors transition from Praxeas to Paul of Samosata, remaining focused on the growing influence of Tertullian and Origen, who are described as:

> "Neither the position of Tertullian nor that of Origen was popular in their day. They were accused of being too philosophical in their analysis of Scripture. Both were accused of tritheism by their opponents in the Church. But it is ultimately their formulations that form the basis for the settlement of the problem in the fourth century—our Nicene Creed."[4]

I must note that while Rea and Cairns describe Sabellius' heresy in condemning terms and Engelbrecht does not, it is not indicative of the latter's attempt to ignore Sabellius. However, the lack of address in the edited work and very limited addresses in Rea and Cairn should cause the reader to recognize

---

2. Robert F. Rea, *Why Church History Matters: An Invitation to Love and Learn from Our Past* (Downers Grove, IL: InterVarsity Press, 2014), 116. "Understanding Sabellianism readies [students] to face today's modalists, who think that Father, Son, and Spirit are the same person" (102), "[Jim] had never heard of Sabellians...If Jim or his pastor had known the historic understanding of Scripture in the Christian tradition, they might have avoided a dangerous heresy" (107), and third is descriptive "A number of key characters converged to determine the church's position on Arianism...the emperor Constantine, the emperor's chaplain Hosius, Arius and other Arians, Eusebius of Caesarea and other semi-Arians, Sabellians..." (116).

3. Earle E. Cairns, *Christianity through the Centuries: A History of the Christian Church* (Grand Rapids, MI: Zondervan, 1996), 101. Cairns also includes a note about Sabellius on page 127, "One essence in three modes" and contrasts this with Tertullian in Against Praxeas.

4. Edward Engelbrecht, ed., *The Church from Age to Age: A History from Galilee to Global Christianity* (St. Louis, MO: Concordia Pub. House, 2011), 44-46.

that either Sabellius is not so well attested or that there is difficulty in reconstructing his supposed beliefs. Below, I will focus on Hippolytus, an early figure who engaged with Sabellius, to show that the complication is related to those who report his supposed beliefs.

EVIDENCE-BASED BELIEF

Hippolytus is a figure supposed to have lived c. 170-236 and engaged heavily in disputes against Calixtus, a man elected bishop in Rome in 217.[5] The challenge present with Hippolytus is the uncertainty of whether there is one figure referred to when Eusebius speaks of Hippolytus or three, and the distinctive focuses of the *Refutatio* and textual commentaries attributed to this figure.[6] Regardless of the attribution of what is named "The Refutation of all Heresies," it is important now that we introduce what Hippolytus expresses concerning Sabellius.

After introducing a figure known as Noetus, Hippolytus mounts his assault against Calixtus and his association with a man named Zephyrinus. He draws parallels between Noetus' view of God with the claims made by a Greek philosopher named Heraclitus, claiming "Did not (Heraclitus) the Obscure anticipate *Noetus* in framing a system of philosophy, according to identical modes of expression?"[7] Allegedly, Noetus did not distinguish the Father from the Son as ontologically distinct persons or substances, instead he is accused of believing that "Father and Son, so called, are one and the same (substance), not one individual produced from a different one, but Himself from Himself."[8] Thus,

---

5. Ulrich Volp, *Hippolytus*. The Expository Times, 120(11), 522. https://doi.org/10.1177/0014524609106838 (Original work published 2009)

6. Volp, Hippolytus, 523-528. For a positive argument see "*Introductory Notice to Hippolytus*" in Alexander Roberts and James Donaldson, eds., *Ante-Nicene Fathers: The Writings of the Fathers down to A.D. 325*, vol. 5 (Peabody: Hendrickson, 1995), 3-7. Although Volp's assertion that, "Whatever the answer may be: the Hippolytus question is still open and the question whether we are dealing with a single – eastern, western, or perambulating – author or two or even more authors, remains unsolved" (524), should not be overlooked.

7. Hippolytus in Roberts and Donaldson, *The Refutation of all Heresies*, 125-127.

8. Hippolytus in Roberts and Donaldson, *The Refutation of all Heresies*, 128. It should be noted, even if Noetus viewed Father and Son as distinct person sharing the same substance, the claim made by Hippolytus would remain. Additionally, the reason the charge would not differ is because in this day these early figures had not yet developed the language to discuss what would be called orthodoxy in the 4th century. Harnack notes of Hippolytus in this regard, "Against these there appeared, in the Roman Church, especially the presbyter Hippolytus, who sought to prove that the doctrine promulgated by them was a revolutionary error. But the sympathies of the vast majority of the Roman Christians, so far as they could take any part in the dispute,

Hippolytus' attack on Calixtus was that he had adopted Noetus' view that the Son and the Father were one and excommunicated Sabellius to "obliterate the charges *against him* among the churches, as if he did not entertain strange opinions."[9] In the earliest writings about Sabellius, albeit not the only ones, the information is hardly definitive. It is passed to the historian *vis-à-vis* an adversary who was taking aim at another person, Calixtus.

CONCLUSION

I want my reader to recognize that throughout this essay, I have not directly cited Sabellius himself, nor have any of the authors listed above. This absence of referential material is due to the fact that we have no material from Sabellius, all data that can be shared comes to the historian through the record of others. Others, who like Hippolytus, are writing polemically and, in most cases, passingly address the figure whose name became synonymous with the term "Modalistic Monarchianism." Because of this, the reader should recognize that when no primary sources are available and when the comments from the secondary sources are only shots in passing, making a claim so definitive as calling Sabellius dangerous places undue weight on the interpreter's reconstruction of Sabellius' belief, not the reality that we simply do not know. Perhaps this is why the church historian Adolf Von Harnack, who coined the term Modalism stated:

> "The scantiness of our sources for the history of Monarchianism in Rome, — not to speak of other cities — in spite of the discovery of the Philosophumena,

---

were on the side of the Monarchians, and even among the clergy only a minority supported Hippolytus" see Adolf von Harnack, *History of Dogma*, trans. Neil Buchanan, vol. 3 (Boston: Roberts Brothers, 1897), 57. This affirms the earlier point raised about Tertullian and Origen in the volume edited by Engelbrecht, the Monarchians are presumed to hold the dominant Christological adherents.

9. Hippolytus in Roberts and Donaldson, *The Refutation of all Heresies*, 130. Interestingly, Hippolytus accuses Sabellius of being unable to see that Calixtus was using him for personal benefit just prior to this account of Sabellius' excommunication. "And, at one time, to those who entertained true opinions, he would in private allege that they held similar doctrines (with himself), and thus make them his dupes; while at another time *he would act similarly towards* those (those embraced) the tenets of Sabellius. But *Callistus* perverted *Sabellius* himself, and this, too, though he had the ability of rectifying *this heretic's error*. For (at any time) during our admonition Sabellius did not evince obduracy; but as long as he continued alone with Callistus, he was wrought upon to relapse into the system of Cleomenes by this very *Callistus*, who alleges that he entertains similar opinions *to Cleomenes. Sabellius*, however, did not then perceive the knavery of *Callistus*; but he afterwards came to be aware of it, as I shall narrate presently" (128).

> is shown most clearly by the circumstance that Tertullian has not mentioned the names of Noëtus, Epigonus, Cleomenes, or Callistus; on the other hand, he has introduced a Roman Monarchian, Praxeas, whose name is not mentioned by Hippolytus in any of his numerous controversial writings."[10]

Because there are some things history has not handed to us.

10. Harnack, *History of Dogma,* 59.

WEEK TWELVE

Early Departures—Justin Martyr, Tertullian, and the Shift from Scripture to Philosophy

34

The Godhead in Church History—Early Departures from the Teachings of the Early Church

Steven Gill

Sorting out what, precisely, constitutes a departure from the teachings of the early church might be the fundamental question for all Protestant denominations around the world.[1] As many readers of the Bible today – Christian or otherwise – are prone toward reading back into the text of the New Testament certain doctrines, theological claims, and creeds, that were, perhaps, developed long after the New Testament, when studying history, we must be careful to remember that other men in centuries gone by have often been guilty of the same practice.[2] In some cases, these practices extended into embracing

1. I refrain from including Catholic Christians in this statement, not as a disparagement, but as an acknowledgement that the canonical hermeneutics that have characterized the Catholic Church for centuries do not demand strict adherence to the first-century church's teachings; the ecumenical councils, creeds, and papal issuances that have emanated from Catholic authorities in every age are characterized by their movement as legitimate teachings, whether or not they depart from the practice of the early church.

2. This sort of practice may be found as early as the writing of *Epistle of Barnabas*, of which Swartley says, "Barnabas cites the older story [of the OT] repeatedly to show it was intended spiritually for our (Christians') sake and was misunderstood by Jews in literally observing the laws and grasping the stories. Most famous are Barnabas's claim that the covenant is not 'both theirs and ours. It is ours' (*Barn.* 4.9; K. Lake trans.) and equating Abraham's 318 circumcised men (Barn. 8.8), via gemmatria [sic] play, with Jesus Christ and the cross (of the 18, 10 = I; 8 = H and IH are the first two letters for Jesus in Greek and T (Tau), the cross, = 300)." The writer's insistence on certain esoteric Christological readings of the OT, replacement theology, and gematria were not interpretive practices embraced by the NT writers but became more popular by the fourth century.

For Swartley: Willard Swartley, "Intertextuality in Early Christian Literature," in *Dictionary of the Later New Testament & Its Developments*, ed. Ralph P. Martin, Peter H. Davids, (IVP Academic, 1997), 540.

certain teachings that the New Testament writers explicitly forbade;[3] in other cases, their departures may appear more subtle, even if no less significant.

In the second century, many Christian heretical sects arose that were greatly influenced by the local traditions of their region. Why, precisely, this happened is perhaps the subject of another paper – but if one can imagine a Christian world in which its teachers and leaders were no longer drawn primarily from the synagogues of Jerusalem and Judaea,[4] but the grammarian schools of Rome, they have likely taken the first step in understanding how to sort out many of the second-century Christian controversies. After the destruction of the temple in AD 70 and the Bar-Kokhba Revolt in the second century, Christianity lost much of the Judaic influence that had characterized it for nearly a century.[5]

---

3. Explicit participation in heresies that were warned against by NT writers appears evident in the earliest ecumenical councils of the Catholic Church, especially with regards to their perspective on the Jews. Quoting Constantine I the Great, Eusebius writes, "And first of all, it appeared an unworthy thing that in the celebration of this most holy feast [Passover] we should follow the practice of the Jews, who have impiously defiled their hands with enormous sin, and are therefore deservedly afflicted with blindness of soul. For we have it in our power, if we abandon their custom, to prolong the due observance of this ordinance to future ages, by a truer order, which we have preserved from the very day of the passion until present time. Let us then have nothing in common with the detestable Jewish crowd; for we have received from our Saviour a different way...Beloved brethren, let us with one consent adopt this course, and withdraw ourselves from all participation in their baseness...For how should they be capable of forming sound judgement, who, since their parricidal guilt in slaying their Lord, have been subject to the direction, not of reason, but of ungoverned passion, and are swayed by every impulse of the mad spirit that is in them...". While commonly found in fourth-century Christian writing, such anti-Jewish sentiment was warned against by the Apostle Paul in Romans' eleventh chapter and was not characteristic of the first-century church.

For Constantine: Eusebius Pamphilus, *The Life Of The Blessed Emperor Constantine*, Book III, (Ch. XVIII).

4. In Acts, readers are made to understand that a Jew named Apollos was "an eloquent man, and mighty in the scriptures...This man was instructed in the way of the Lord...and he began to speak boldly in the synagogue..." who greatly influenced the early church. Because of his preaching in the synagogue, he was discovered by Priscilla and Aquila who showed Apollos "the way of God more perfectly." It may surprise some Christians to learn that this Apollos who was so fervent in spirit was described in this manner by Luke before he received the revelation of salvation in Jesus Christ (Acts 18:24-25). Thus, two things are demonstrated by this passage: The first, that early Christianity was made up of many Jews who were zealous for the preaching of John the Baptist. The second, that prominent leaders of the early church came from and were trained in the synagogues.

5. The influence of Jewish synagogues on early Christianity has been, and remains, under-appreciated in examinations of early Christian doctrine. Far from being a fringe piece of Christianity in which influence was isolated to Jewish converts, synagogues were often the founding locale of the earliest Christian churches. Chilton writes, "...James in fact cites the

Between the second and fourth centuries, interpretive practices of many popular Christian thinkers much more closely resembled those of the philosophers than the apostles. This is, perhaps, seen most evidently first in Justin Martyr, who wrote in his *Dialogue with Trypho*:

> "I will tell you," said I, "What seems to me; for philosophy is, in fact, the greatest possession, and most honourable before God, to whom it leads us and alone commends us; and these are truly holy men who have bestowed attention on philosophy...[6].

Justin went on to name the schools of philosophy to which he devoted so much of his time: The Stoics, Peripatetics, Pythagoreans, and Platonists are all mentioned by Justin as schools which greatly influenced his understanding of things immaterial. Justin characterized Christianity as the "highest philosophy"[7] and saw coherence between its basic tenets and the teachings of the schools in which he had been trained. This is important, because it is Justin who offered the first, if not most peculiar, example of a second-century departure from the teachings of the first century regarding water baptism.

> For in the name of God, the Father and Lord of the universe, and of our Saviour Jesus Christ, and of the Holy Spirit, they then receive the washing with water...in order that we may not remain the children of necessity and of ignorance, but may become the children of choice and knowledge...he who leads to the laver the person that is to be washed calling him by this name alone. For no one can utter the name of the ineffable God; and if any one dare to say that there is a name, he raves with a hopeless madness...[8].

---

preaching of Moses [.i.e., books of the Law] in synagogues as a reason for non-Jewish believers to maintain a rudimentary purity (Acts 15:19-21)...Acts assumes that Paul is received into synagogues and that he is permitted to preach (Acts 13:13-43). The repeated opportunity permits Paul to reach non-Jewish hearers in synagogues, which provokes jealously among 'the Jews' (Acts 13:44-52)...The link between the synagogue and wider civic debate was forged particularly by those known as 'God fearers,' those who acknowledged the God of Israel without accepting circumcision." For more on this subject see Reframing Paul in this volume.

For Chilton: Bruce Chilton, "Synagogue," in *Dictionary of the Later New Testament & Its Developments*, ed. Ralph P. Martin, Peter H. Davids, (IVP Academic, 1997), 1144.

6. Justin Martyr, *Dialogue with Trypho* (Ch. II).
7. Justin Martyr, *Dialogue with Trypho* (Ch. VIII).
8. Justin Martyr, *First Apology*, (Ch. LXI).

Justin's insistence that adherents to Christianity be baptized according to this formula cannot be characterized as a catechismal quotation of Matthew 28:19; it is neither identical in form to Matthew's phrase, nor consistent with the practice of the New Testament church.[9] Particularly curious is Justin's insistence that there is no name by which the Almighty God of the Old Testament was truly disclosed to believers. If there may be said to be one belief that remains congruent across the Gospels, Acts, and Epistles of the New Testament, it is that full deity of God is disclosed in the person and the name of Jesus Christ.[10] "Neither is there salvation in any other: for there is none other name under heaven given among men, whereby we must be saved" (Acts 4:12 KJV). While it is commonly accepted by Christians today that Jesus Christ is the true revelation of ה-ו-ה-י in the earth, for Justin, the Christ was a subordinate figure who should not be considered consubstantial or co-equal with God the Father.[11] This view of subordination was shared by later church writers such as Tertullian of Carthage, who asserted in his tract *Against Praxeas*,

> Do you then, (you ask,) grant that the Word is a certain substance, constructed by the Spirit and the communication of Wisdom? Certainly I do. But you will not allow Him to be a really substantive being, by having a substance of His own; in such a way that He may be regarded as an objective thing and a person, and so be able (as being constituted second to God the Father,) to make two, the Father and the Son, God and the Word...How could He who is empty have made things which are solid, and He who is void have made things which are full, and He who is incorporeal have made things which have body?...For who will deny that God is a body...and while I recognize the Son, I assert His distinction as second to the Father.[12]

---

9. In every anecdotal example of water baptism to be found within the New Testament, it was performed ubiquitously in the name of the Lord Jesus Christ (cf. Luke 24:47; Acts 2:38; 8:16; 10:48; 19:5; Rom. 6:3; Gal. 3:27).

10. Jesus said, "I am come in my Father's name..." (John 5:43) and Paul gave his readers assurance that in Christ dwells "all the fulness of the Godhead bodily" (Col. 2:9). These statements disclosing the nature of Christ's divinity are repeated in (John 1:1; 10:30; 14:9; 20:28; 2 Cor. 5:19; Col. 1:19; Rom. 8:9-11; Eph. 4:4-6; 4:9-10).

11. Justin Martyr, *Dialogue with Trypho* (Ch. CXXVIII). Here, Justin emphasizes the 'numerical' distinction between Father and Son, a view not shared by many Christians in the world today.

12. Tertullian, *Against Praxeas*, (Ch. VII).

In addition to Tertullian's insistence upon subordination between the Father and Son, there are other philosophical themes that stand out in the quote above. Although the scriptures are consistent in their teaching that "God is a Spirit..." (John 4:24 KJV) Tertullian resisted this idea on the grounds that he could not believe that 'He who is empty has made things which are solid, He who is void has made things which are full, and He who is without a body has made things which have bodies.'[13] This was not a concept that the first-century church struggled with, but it was consistent with the philosophical training that Tertullian received in the school of North Africa in the second century.[14] Thus, two of the most received Christian teachers of the ante-Nicene era by modern Christian academics are, in part, responsible for some of the most controversial beliefs that later came to characterize Christianity the world over, the doctrine of the trinity perhaps chief among them.

It is important to note that initial departures from the early church in matters of teaching and doctrine occurred within the context of an ideologically disparate and much less centralized movement than has been sometimes assumed.[15] The notion that there was a one governing body of church authority that issued statements of doctrine broadly applicable to all Christians in the ante-Nicene era is misguided. Teaching that was consistent with the perspectives of the New Testament remained widely dispersed and received broad acceptance in this era. For more on these topics, see *The Godhead in Church History: Congruence in Christian Thought from the New Testament Writers to the Third Century* in this volume.

---

13. Tertullian's idea is to be contrasted with Paul in Colossians' first chapter, which says, "For by him were all things created, that are in heaven, and that are in earth, visible and invisible, whether they be thrones, or dominions, or principalities, or powers: all things were created by him, and for him: And he is before all things, and by him all things consist" (Col. 1:16-17 KJV).

14. Otto Heick, *A History of Christian Thought.* Vol. 1. (Fortress Press, 1965), 124.

15. Far from a Roman centralized movement, Arnold identifies no less than six geographical centers from which the earliest Christian authority was passed down (Jerusalem, Antioch, Ephesus, Corinth, Alexandria, and Rome).

For Arnold: Clinton Arnold, "Centers of Christianity," in *Dictionary of the Later New Testament & Its Developments*, ed. Ralph P. Martin, Peter H. Davids, (IVP Academic, 1997), 144-150.

35

The Second Century and the Development of the Trinity

Andrew Herbst

INTRODUCTION

After the apostles passed away, it did not take long for factions to grow within Christianity. During the second century, only a few decades after Revelation was written, various teachers advanced their interpretations of Scripture. Some were deemed as heretical, such as Valentinus, but others appear to have been much closer to what the apostles believed.[1] This paper will survey different beliefs that contributed to the development of the Trinity, with the goal of demonstrating that there was not a single uniform doctrine of the Trinity at the second century. When comparing today's trinitarianism and the trinitarianism of the second and third centuries, they would look noticeably different from one another.

GNOSTICISM

Irenaeus's Against Heresies (c. 180 A. D.) aimed at analyzing and critiquing the growing factions of Gnosticism. A definition of Gnosticism is difficult to produce, as the term describes multiple groups with diverse beliefs. In a general sense, Earle E. Cairns classified Gnosticism as a mixture of Christianity and various Greek philosophies.[2] Gnosticism can be called one of the first great heresies in Christian history. The roots of the system, at times called pre-Gnosticism, may have been a central issue of import in books such as Colossians and 1 John. Some Gnostics claimed that matter was evil, and knowledge, from Greek gnosis, was most

1. See this author's paper on Irenaeus.
2. Earle E. Cairns, *Christianity Through the Centuries: A History of the Christian Church*, (Grand Rapids, MI: Zondervan, 1996), 96.

important. Their goal was teaching a higher knowledge hidden within Scripture that only the true intellects and spiritually enlightened could uncover. Gnostics reached their highest point of popularity in the second century, and, although considering themselves Christians, were in constant dispute with other Christians over theology. Because the Gnostics sounded Christian, they gained a substantial following. This is why Irenaeus took it upon himself to write *Against Heresies*.

VALENTINUS

In *Against Heresies*, Irenaeus identified Valentinus and his school of thought as one of the primary Gnostic branches. Valentinus taught in the second century and died around A.D. 160. Only fragments of his works have survived, but Kurt Rudolph notes that there is one theological title that is credited to Valentinus, *On the Three Natures.*[3]

On the Three Natures is of the utmost importance in understanding trinitarian development. Rudolph explains that in this volume, Valentinus "pondered, as the first to do so, on three *hypostases* (substances) and three persons (Father, Son, and Holy Spirit)."[4] First, Valentinus is described as the first theologian to consider the Christian God as a division of three substances, significant considering that he lived a century after the Apostle Paul. Second, as a Gnostic, Valentinus was in some ways under the umbrella of Christianity, but he was not a Christian. It is possible that Valentinus considered himself Christian, but he was opposed by celebrated men such as Irenæus and also labeled heretical by later Christian preachers. Nevertheless, his language of *hypostases* (substances) regarding God would be used by future church councils, contributing to the language used to describe the Trinity.

TERTULLIAN OF CARTHAGE

The mid-second century saw the birth of Tertullian of Carthage, the father of Latin theology. After his conversion to Christianity in his mid-adult years, he became a bishop and an avid writer.[5] The bishop was instrumental to the

---

3. Kurt Rudolph, *Gnosis: The Nature & History of Gnosticism*, (San Francisco, CA: Harper & Row, 1987), 319.

4. Rudolph, *Gnosis*, 319.

5. Tertullian asked the question, "what has Athens to do with Jerusalem?" in an attempt to indicate his rejection of philosophy, but Everett Ferguson argues that his theology proves the opposite to be true. See Tim Downley, ed., *Eerdman's Handbook to the History of the Christian*

development of Trinity, one major contribution being his creation of the term "Trinity" itself.[6] However, Charles Ryrie admits that Tertullian "did not have a full and accurate understanding of the Trinity."[7] As mentioned above, early trinitarianism looks different when compared with modern trinitarianism. Tertullian exemplifies this concept, as the man who coined the term Trinity, would be considered a heretic by today's standards. Ryrie's admission stems from Tertullian's instruction on subordination, and an investigation into Tertullian's volumes will confirm that he placed the Father in preeminence above the Son and Spirit.[8]

Tertullian demonstrates that there was not a single uniform doctrine of the Trinity by A. D. 200, nor did everyone accept the trinitarian doctrine. The bishop complained that the majority of Christians were "startled" at what he taught, and that they rejected the concept of the Trinity because it sounded like polytheism.[9] Interestingly enough, Tertullian's opponents offered the same objections to the doctrine that non-trinitarians still raise today, namely, that Trinitarians are accused of believing in two or three gods. This frustrated Tertullian, and he resorted to labeling those who misunderstood him as "uneducated" and "perversely disposed."[10]

CONCLUSION

Peter Heather states that it was not until after Emperor Constantine's conversion, around one hundred years after Tertullian, that the doctrine of the Trinity

---

Church, (Grand Rapids, MI: Eerdmans, 1977), 111. Many studies have explored how Tertullian integrated philosophy into his theology, for more on this topic, see Steven Gill, *The History & Development of the Doctrine of the Trinity,* (BHAO, 2022), chapter VIII.

6. "Unity into a Trinity, placing in their order the three *Persons*— the Father, the Son, and the Holy Ghost: three, however, not in condition, but in degree..." See Tertullian, "*Against Praxeas*", in *The Ante-Nicene Fathers,* vol. 3, A. Cleveland Coxe, ed., (Peabody, MA: Hendrickson Publishers, 2004), 598.

7. Charles Ryrie, *Basic Theology,* (Wheaton, IL: Victor, 1986), 56.

8. See Tertullian, *Against Praxeas,* Coxe, ed., 602-604.

9. "The simple, indeed, (I will not call them unwise and unlearned,) who always constitute the majority of believers, are startled at the dispensation (of the Three in One), on the ground that their very rule of faith withdraws them from the world's plurality of gods to the one only true God; not understanding that, although He is the one only God, He must yet be believed in with His own *oikonomia.* The numerical order and distribution of the Trinity they assume to be a division of the Unity; whereas the Unity which derives the Trinity out of its own self is so far from being destroyed, that it is actually supported by it. They are constantly throwing out against us that we are preachers of two gods and three gods, while they take to themselves pre-eminently the credit of being worshippers of the One God." Tertullian, *Against Praxeas,* Coxe, ed., 598-99.

10. Tertullian, *Against Praxeas,* Coxe, ed., 603.

began to find general agreement.[11] This claim is strengthened by our examination of trinitarianism's relationship to Gnosticism, a virtually undisputed heresy, and advanced further by later preachers and councils who used Gnostic language to describe God. Tertullian, a subordinationist, gave the trinitarian doctrine its name and bears witness that most Christians were not trinitarians in his era. Because many doctrines evolve over the course of time, it is important to examine the roots of a doctrine in order to determine its true nature. The Trinity developed outside of Scripture and kept evolving until its origin faded into obscurity. Facts such as these should hinder trinitarians from asserting that all non-trinitarians are unorthodox, for there has not always been a single orthodox Trinity.

11. Peter Heather, Christendom: The Triumph of a Religion, (New York, NY: Alfred A. Knopf, 2022), xiv. Heather is the Chair of Medieval History in the Department of History at King's College London.

36

Descendants, Derivations, and Deviations—Answering the Question of Historical Continuity

Jeremias D. Zuniga

INTRODUCTION

The notion of hermeneutics, a term meaning "the art and principles of interpretation," is important when contemporary believers begin to read Scripture.[1] Hermeneutics is important because when done thoughtfully, it can allow for a more faithful way of reading and engaging with Biblical texts. However, there is a critical point to raise concerning hermeneutics related to authority and autonomy.[2] In an effort to protect Christian readers from holding private interpretations (2 Pet. 1:20), contemporary historians may encourage alignment with the supposed history of Christian interpretation as seen succinctly in the creeds that emerged from the ecumenical councils.[3] The concern in aligning without critical exploration is that it may grant authority to

---

1. I owe this simple definition to the work done in Michael J. Gorman, ed., *Scripture and Its Interpretation: A Global, Ecumenical Introduction to the Bible* (Grand Rapids, MI: Baker Academic, a division of Baker Publishing Group, 2017), 411. While there are a variety of competing approaches introduced in this book, I find it helpful as an introductory catalogue of diverse and divergent interpretive methods. These methods at times demand different conclusions concerning biblical texts and theological positions. For an introductory approach that prioritizes the biblical text, I recommend engagement with Henry A. Virkler and Karelynne Gerber Ayayo, *Hermeneutics: Principles and Processes of Biblical Interpretation,* 2nd ed. (Grand Rapids, Mich: Baker Academic, 2007) in conversation with D. A. Carson, *Exegetical Fallacies,* 2nd ed. (Grand Rapids, Mich: Baker Academic, 1996).

2. For the point of autonomy and identifying with the broader history of Christianity see Robert F. Rea, *Why Church History Matters: An Invitation to Love and Learn from Our Past* (Downers Grove, IL: InterVarsity Press, 2014), 59-129.

3. Rea, *Why Church History Matters*, 36-41, 116-119.

readings of Scripture that diverge from what Scripture itself communicates, on the grounds that it has historically been accepted; this will be discussed below.

In a previous essay, I underscored the point that the Christological beliefs of Tertullian were not commonplace during his lifetime. While theological popularity does not guarantee continuity with the earliest Christians, neither does an unfamiliar or an unfavorable position. Because of this, it is important that all Christian history is read with criteria to aid in distinguishing writers who were aligned with the earliest Christians, as well as identifying those who departed through intentional and unintentional methods. To this end, I pose three categories: Descendants, Derivations, and Deviations. Because of the current limitations of this work, I will briefly introduce the three categories before offering a cursory reading and cataloguing of Tertullian's use of Scripture when discussing God. I propose that Tertullian's "trinity" is best catalogued as a derived theology, and to this extent, Tertullian should be considered as having departed from Scripture.

CATEGORIZATION FOR CONSIDERATION

Above, I identified three categories for situating early Christian writers: Descendants, Derivations, and Deviations. In addition to the work of this essay, it is important that the reader consults the primary works of these early figures, as well as some of the major secondary works that have caused for a rather monolithic assumption of what is orthodox.[4] The first category is the

4. Some of the works that the reader may find beneficial in understanding how heresiology has become prominent today I refer to the following work as a primary source for understanding the tone of polemics; see Irenaeus of Lyons, "*Against Heresies*," https://www.newadvent.org/fathers/0103.htm. Also see my essay in this volume, "The God of the Earliest Followers," for recommendations on reading the polemical works. Additionally, the church historian Adolf von Harnack, *History of Dogma*, trans. Neil Buchanan, (Boston: Roberts Brothers, 1897) demonstrates the condemnation and categorization of many heresies and is very influential within the enterprise of Historical Theology. I must note that Harnack objects to the doctrine of the Trinity as being an imposition of Greek philosophy. For an attempted defense against Harnack's claim see Michael A. G. Haykin, "*Biblical Exegesis in Fourth-Century Trinitarian Debates: Context, Contours, & Ressourcement*," Reformed Faith & Practice, June 1, 2017, https://journal.rts.edu/article/biblical-exegesis-fourth-century-trinitarian-debates-context-contours-ressourcement/. However, it must be noted that I find Haykin's attempt to faulter. While he does demonstrate other influences alongside Greek philosophy, he does not demonstrate that the trinitarian doctrine does not derive from Greek philosophical thought, only that its development also considered Scripture.

Descended theologies, and captures theologies that remain in continuity with the expressions and practices of the New Testament authors. The second category is the ***Derived theologies***, consisting of theologies that express an intention to remain faithful to Scripture while syncretically melding external philosophies or practices into those of the biblical witness.[5] Finally, the category of ***Deviated theologies*** focuses on groups that intentionally subvert or misuse the Scriptures to accomplish personal or sectarian goals.[6]

TESTING THE CATEGORIZATION—DESCRIBING TERTULLIAN'S THEOLOGY OF GOD

While writing his Prescription against Heretics, Tertullian is noted as declaring against worldly philosophies:

> "What indeed has Athens to do with Jerusalem? What concord is there between the Academy and the Church? What between heretics and Christians? Our instruction comes from the porch of Solomon, who had himself taught that the Lord should be sought in simplicity of heart. Wisdom 1:1 Away with all attempts to produce a mottled Christianity of Stoic, Platonic, and dialectic composition! We want no curious disputation after possessing Christ Jesus, no inquisition after enjoying the gospel! With our faith, we desire no further belief. For this is our palmary faith, that there is nothing which we ought to believe besides."[7]

---

5. Crucially, there are Pauline quotations from the pagan poets (see Acts 17:28; Titus 1:12). To the point that Paul is distinct from the Stoics see Craig Keener, *The IVP Bible Background Commentary: New Testament* (Downers Grove, Ill: Academic, IVP, 1994), 376-378. Interestingly, the scholarship surrounding Paul's distance from Stoic ideas is growing, thought Tertullian appears highly influenced by this system of thought. For a treatment of Paul's proposed address against Stoic infiltration see Timothy A. Brookins, *Rediscovering the Wisdom of the Corinthians: Paul, Stoicism, and Spiritual Hierarchy* (Grand Rapids, MI: William B. Eerdmans Publishing Company, 2025). And to the extent that Tertullian was influenced and knowledgeable of the Stoics see Everett Ferguson, *Tertullian*. The Expository Times, 120(7), 313-321. https://doi.org/10.1177/0014524609103464 (Original work published 2009).

6. This category is reflected in the efforts of the opponents of the Colossian church that held what has been called the "Colossian Heresy." For a survey of who those figures might have been, see the more accessible Grant R. Osborne, "*Unpacking the Colossian Heresy. (Backdrops).*" Bible Study Magazine 8, no. 6 (2016): 24–25. EBSCOhost. For a reader wanting to dive deeper, see F. F. Bruce, "*Colossian Problems, Pt 3: The Colossian Heresy.*" Bibliotheca Sacra 141, no. 563 (1984): 195–208. EBSCOhost.

7. Tertullian, *"Prescription against Heretics," CHURCH FATHERS: The Prescription Against Heretics (Tertullian)*, https://www.newadvent.org/fathers/0311.htm, 7.

While the statement appears to demand strict use of Scripture, Tertullian was not adverse from making use of the thought system of the Stoics.[8] This connection to the use of Stoic notions appears when exploring his writing against Praxeas, when Tertullian expresses that his opponent is in error:

> "In thinking that one cannot believe in One Only God in any other way than by saying that the Father, the Son, and the Holy Ghost are the very selfsame Person. As if in this way also one were not All, in that All are of One, by unity (that is) of *substance*; while the mystery of the dispensation is still guarded, which distributes the Unity into a Trinity, placing in their order the three *Persons*— the Father, the Son, and the Holy Ghost: three, however, not in condition, but in degree; not in substance, but in form; not in power, but in aspect; yet of one *substance*, and of one condition, and of one power, inasmuch as He is one God, from whom these degrees and forms and aspects are reckoned, under the name of the Father, and of the Son, and of the Holy Ghost."[9]

Although he aimed to oust the heretics who had holistically bought into the philosophies of the Greeks, Tertullian integrated the language of the same philosophers in his rhetorical effort to dispel his opponents.[10]

---

8. Ferguson, *Tertullian*, 315-316.

9. Tertullian, *"Against Praxeas," CHURCH FATHERS: Against Praxeas (Tertullian)*, https://www.newadvent.org/fathers/0317.htm, 2. I offer emphasis in the above quote to identify the words Tertullian has adopted from Greek philosophy not merely in kind, but also in similar use foreign to the authors of the New Testament. For an accessible introduction to the philosophy of the Stoics on Ontology see Marion Durand, Simon Shogry, and Dirk Baltzly, *"Stoicism," Stanford Encyclopedia of Philosophy*, January 20, 2023, https://plato.stanford.edu/entries/stoicism/#BodiInco, 2.6. Insomuch as this language of Substance and Persons participates in the larger growing influence of Aristotle, compare the review of his work in the following Howard Robinson and Ralph Weir, *"Substance," Stanford Encyclopedia of Philosophy*, May 6, 2024, https://plato.stanford.edu/entries/substance/#Cate, 2.2.

10. Ferguson notes, "Making the first use of *trinitas* as a technical term, Tertullian affirms that monotheism is consistent with an internal trinity. The one God within himself is three – one in quality, substance and power, but distinct in sequence, aspect and manifestation (*Praxeas* 2.4). This trinity does not destroy the divine unity but administers it. Tertullian introduces the words 'substance' (*substantia* – the Stoic word for the 'stuff' or constitutive material of something) for the divine unity and 'person' (persona) for the individual entities of Father, Son and Holy Spirit... In describing this union Tertullian had access to Aristotelian and Stoic analyses of different kinds of union of physical things." (see Ferguson, *Tertullian*, 316).

CONCLUSION

I want my reader to notice in the brief review above, that it is not simply a pedantic use of the Stoics that Tertullian raises their terms. In using these terms, Tertullian intended to carry the associated notion of ontological categorization, or more simply said, Tertullian aimed to express that what it means to exist can be separated into categories, and God's being should be separated in a way that distinguished the Christians from the Jewish theology from which it emerged.[11] The point of my categorization of Tertullian emerges here as I conclude, in his effort to dispel heresy, Tertullian accomplished an unmooring of the Christian faith from its Old Testament theological roots. Because of this, he showed a willingness to adopt philosophy to accomplish his aims. In this way, he derived a theology from the New Testament that syncretized Stoicism, baptizing elements of it to create a way of discussing God that was not outlined in Scripture and creating a historical discontinuity between himself, the New Testament authors, and the Old Testament believers.[12]

---

11. To this end, Tertullian concludes his polemic with "But, (this doctrine of yours bears a likeness) to the Jewish faith, of which this is the substance — so to believe in One God as to refuse to reckon the Son besides Him, and after the Son the Spirit." (Tertullian, *Against Praxeas*, 31).

12. Whether this is a positive or negative accomplishment was not the focus of this paper. However, I must note that any effort that does not take seriously the Jewish origins of the Christian faith is an effort that neglects the Old Testament description of God's being in strict terms. To this end, I posit that Tertullian, though he appears sincere in his aims to preserve the Christians from persecution and heresy, fell into the same error of creating room for persecution of Christians that differed from his expression and adopted the heresy of the philosophers he expressed contempt with.

WEEK THIRTEEN

The Ecumenical Councils and the Godhead—From Nicea to Icons

37

The Godhead—Two Ecumenical Councils in View

Steven Gill

It would be impossible to offer a comprehensive examination of the impact of all the ecumenical councils on the Christian conception of the godhead in this volume. Instead, my entry will focus upon two councils which, when examined together, perhaps offer the reader a sense of the effect of the whole. When examining these councils, it is important to remember that Christianity was far less centralized in the fourth and fifth centuries than has, at times, been supposed.[1] As research continues to develop, those who study this era are more frequently concluding that what constituted "settled" Christianity in the traditional sense of the term was not so settled at all. Therefore, these two councils should not be considered a grand-sweeping generalization of what all believers globally believed or taught. Instead, they offer a glimpse into one movement and how the early church approached the issues addressed in these meetings. The two councils of our subject are the First Council of Nicaea in AD 325 and the Council of Ephesus in AD 431.

---

1. Peter Heather, chair of medieval history at King's College in London, cites decentralization before Nicaea I as one of the driving forces behind the diversity of judgements surrounding the doctrine of the trinity. He writes, "Not only did more than half the Empire's cities not yet have a bishop at all by the early fourth century…but even in those that did, episcopal leadership was still more consensual than authoritarian…Before Constantine, bishops were chosen by and from their local congregations, not imposed from outside or from above by other bishops or archbishops…This slow emergence of even limited episcopal authority provides a further reason – beyond the inherent theological complexities – why a recognizable Christian orthodoxy could not develop before the fourth century. Up to that point, the religion did not possess authority structures of sufficient strength through which a monolithic solution to the complexities of the Trinity could be identified or enforced."

For Heather: Peter Heather, *Christendom: The Triumph of a Religion, AD 300-1300* (Alfred A. Knopf, 2022), 39.

Much has been written about the First Council of Nicaea, as it represented the first time that a non-Christian Roman emperor was given plenary power to execute judgment over controversial issues in matters of church doctrine.[2] While sometimes thought of as a council that united Christianity in judgment surrounding the teaching on the godhead, when examined more closely, precisely the opposite appears to have been the case. In addition to debates surrounding the proper dates for Easter,[3] the first Nicene council convened to address the issue of Arianism – a heresy which is itself worthy of a lengthier address. Arius, from whom the teaching received its name, was a student of Lucian who apparently taught that Jesus was less than God but more than man. In his tract *Against Arius*, Athanasius wrote:

> ' 'For God,' he says, 'was alone, and the Word as yet was not, nor the Wisdom. Then, wishing to form us, thereupon He made a certain one, and named Him Word and Wisdom and Son, that He might form us by means of Him.' Accordingly, he says that there are two wisdoms, first, the attribute co-existent with God, and next, that in this wisdom the Son was originated, and was only named Wisdom and Word as partaking of it...Moreover he has dared to say, that 'the Word is not the very God;' 'though He is called God, yet He

---

2. While sometimes thought of as a Christian leader who upon his ascension to the throne loosed Christianity from the bands of persecution, the truth of Constantine's life is much more complicated. Constantine continued to have a public relationship with paganism long after his supposed conversion to Christianity. Constantine's Arch in Rome paid homage to the Roman pantheon after his victory over Maxentius at the Milvian Bridge in AD 312. Coins minted by Constantine in AD 326 – one year after the First Council of Nicaea – continued to honor *Sol Invictus* as the patron God of the emperor. Even the supposed vision in Gaul during which Constantine saw a light superimposed upon the sun should be examined with scrutiny, as Gaul was home to the cult of Apollo, a Roman god to whom Constantine was a devotee. It is to Apollo that Constantine attributed his military victories, often making sacrifices to the god in the very same place where Eusebius claims the vision occurred.

For Constantine's Arch and coins minted: Steven Gill, *The History & Development of the Doctrine of the Trinity*, (Biblical Hebrew Academy Online, 2022), 263-264.

For attribution of Constantine's victories to Apollo: Heather, *Christendom*, 5.

3. Eusebius wrote extensively on this issue that vexed the church. One party of bishops was content to preserve celebration of Passover according to the 354-day lunar calendar while another party wanted a fixed date based upon the 365-day solar calendar. In an effort to distance Christianity from the Jews, (his exact words were, "have nothing in common with the detestable Jewish crowd") Constantine issued a statement at the council demanding adherence to the latter format. For more on this, see:

Eusebius Pamphilus, *The Life Of The Blessed Emperor Constantine*, Book III, (Ch. XVIII).

> is not very God,' but 'by participation of grace, He, as others, is God only in name.' And, whereas all beings are foreign and different from God in essence, so too is 'the Word alien and unlike in all things to the Father's essence and propriety,' but belongs to things originated and created, and is one of these. Afterwards, as though he had succeeded to the devil's recklessness, he has stated in his Thalia, that 'even to the Son the Father is invisible,' and 'the Word cannot perfectly and exactly either see or know His own Father.'[4]

While there is much to sort out in *Against Arius*, key takeaways of the text relevant to our subject are Arius' apparent claims that 'the Word is not the very God' and that the Word is 'alien and unlike in all things to the Father's essence and propriety.' Because of Arius' subordination of Christ in such a way that He should not be thought of as God with us, but as another lesser power, contemporary thinkers were motivated to address the issue at the First Council of Nicaea. Concluding Arius to be in error, the council proclaimed that,

> We believe in one God, the Father almighty, maker of heaven and earth, of all things visible and invisible; And in one Lord, Jesus Christ, the only begotten Son of God, begotten from the Father before all ages, light from light, true God from true God, begotten not made, of one substance with the Father...[5].

While any criticism of the First Nicene Creed should be balanced against the issues it was attempting to address, it is important to note a few phrases from the creed that became the catalyst for later conceptions of the trinitarian persuasion. "Light from light, true God from true God..." are adjectives attributed to Christ that are not found in the New Testament. Jesus is not called the 'light who was from light,' but He is called "The light of the world."[6] The New Testament writers did not refer to Jesus as "God from true God," but as "My Lord and my God."[7] Far from being called "God from God with us" at His

---

4. Athanasius, *Against Arius*, ch. II. It is important to remember that our primary sources for Arius' teaching are his opponents. While it certainly appears that much of what Arius taught would not be cohesive with most modern Christian teaching, polemics such as Against Arius were often written as disparagements designed to galvanize support around or against one particular view of an issue. Thus, keeping all things in balance, we can only know what we know.

5. *First Nicene Creed*, AD 325 (amended AD 381).

6. John 8:12 (KJV).

7. John 20:28 (KJV).

birth, Jesus was called "God with us."[8] While some may argue as to whether or not the First Nicene Creed departed from the teaching of the New Testament in such a way that it constituted heresy, what no reader can argue against is that the inaugural ecumenical creed disrupted the *simplicity* of the New Testament portrait of Christ. While nearly all Christians today agree that Jesus should be worshipped as truly God, the manner by which His godhead is explained has become quite complex, unnecessarily so in the opinion of this writer. Much of this confusion may be attributed to the extra-biblical phrases found within the First Nicene Creed, which were later amended into their present form.[9] A little over one century after the First Council of Nicaea, another council convened in Ephesus, which condemned another group to heresy: the Nestorians. It is to this council that we turn our attention toward next.

> The holy and great Synod therefore says, that the only begotten Son, born according to nature of God the Father, very God of very God, Light of Light, by whom the Father made all things, came down, and was incarnate, and was made man, suffered, and rose again the third day, and ascended into heaven...but even in taking to himself flesh remaining what he was. This the declaration of the correct faith proclaims everywhere. This was the sentiment of the holy Fathers; therefore they ventured to call the Holy Virgin, the Mother of God, not as if the nature of the Word or his divinity had its beginning from the Holy Virgin, but because of her was born that holy body with a rational soul, to which the Word being personally united is said to be born according to the flesh...But we do not call the Word of God the Father, the God nor the Lord of Christ, lest we openly cut in two the one Christ, the Son and Lord, and fall under the charge of blasphemy, making him the God and Lord of himself.[10]

At the Ephesian council, Cyril of Alexandria charged Nestorius with heresy on the grounds that he insisted Mary, the mother of Jesus, be referred to as "the mother of Christ" rather than embracing the Catholic doctrine which stated

8. Matthew 1:23 (KJV).

9. The final iteration of the Nicene Creed was not issued until AD 381 at the First Council of Constantinople.

10. "Council of Ephesus (A.D. 431)." New Advent. Accessed November 8, 2025. https://www.newadvent.org/fathers/3810.htm.

that she was the "mother of God." While the differences between these two sentiments may appear semantical to modern readers, their significance in the fifth century cannot be overstated. In fact, if modern readers can grasp why theotokos vs. Christotokos was controversial at all, they have likely taken the first step in grasping the downstream effects of the first codified doctrine of the Trinity. For Nestorius, it was irrational to refer to Mary as the mother of God, as God has no beginning nor may any part of Him be said to have begun. In calling Mary the mother of Christ, Nestorius believed he was preserving the early church's understanding of the incarnation; God was manifest in the flesh as Jesus of Nazareth, who is indeed the Messiah – the son of God promised in the Law and the Prophets. Inasmuch as He is a man, He surely may be said to have been born and have a mother. In this way, it is proper to conceive of Mary as the mother of the promised Messiah, but she may not be said (from Nestorius' view) to be the mother of God. Important to our discussion here is Cyril's primary claim, that Jesus Christ is the incarnation of the Son of God – the co-equal second person, 'God of God and light of light' – rather than the incarnation of God. On this issue hangs all of what became known as the "Nestorian controversy" – is Jesus 'God with us,' or is He 'God the Son with us?' Is there any difference between these two labels? When one says, "Son of God," what is meant, precisely, by "son?" Because Cyril and many Catholics believed that Jesus Christ is God the Son, the second person in the triune godhead in the earth, they found no issue in calling Mary the mother of God. In this way, she is the mother of God the Son, not God the Father. For Nestorius, the whole issue was much simpler; Mary gave birth to a man and called His name Jesus. He is truly the Christ, and therefore it is proper to say that Mary is the mother of Christ. Far from dismissing the divinity of the Christ, Nestorius simply chose to stress one key aspect of Christian doctrine that nearly all denominations embrace today: Jesus is truly man and truly God; Mary gave birth to the man in whom God dwelled. This understanding is much closer to Paul's portrait of the Christ than anything resembling Cyril's heady and confusing explanations of the God who is both one and divided (Rom. 5:10-19; 1 Cor. 15:20-28). The controversy over Mary's role in the church continues to divide many Catholics even today.[11]

---

11. Doctrinal Note on Marian titles: Mother of the faithful, not Co-redemptrix." Vatican News. Last modified November 4, 2025. https://www.vaticannews.va/en/vatican-city/news/2025-11/doctrinal-note-mother-of-the-faithful-not-co-redemptrix.html. In 2025, Pope

The judgments of the Ephesian council rested entirely upon the conclusions reached at the First Nicene Council. When the Council of Ephesus convened in AD 431 to discuss the Nestorian issue, Cyril shored up his argument by citing the Nicene Creed as a proof-text for his chief claims. By introducing Christianity to the notion that there was a co-equal, consubstantial, and co-eternal God the Son who co-existed co-equally with God the Father in the beginning (God from God), these trinitarian thinkers, wittingly or not, created a contradiction in terms that unsettled Nestorius and many thinkers like him. Their disagreement is reflected in the doctrinal disputes between oneness and trinitarian thinkers today.

Leo XIV brought attention to the subject of Marian veneration when he insisted that Mary no longer be referred to within the dioceses as 'co-redeemer' with Christ, but only as the 'mother of the faithful.' This issuance brought backlash from some Catholics who resisted the doctrinal note. Mary's contemporaneous status with Christ (and historically with the trinity, as Vatican II stressed Mary's role in the 'economy of salvation, as Queen of the universe, and as mother of God.') has long been an issue of great controversy between non-Catholic and Catholic Christians.

38

The Supposed Victory of Orthodoxy

Andrew Herbst

INTRODUCTION

As noted previously, the doctrine of the Trinity was not a single unified doctrine in the second century.[1] Peter Heather states that it was not until after Emperor Constantine's conversion, in the early 300s, that the doctrine of the Trinity began to find general agreement.[2] Millard Erickson claims that Biblical evidence leads to monotheistic belief, but then asks why the church "moved beyond this evidence?"[3] Erickson states that the Trinity is not "expressly asserted" within the Bible, but due to Biblical implications, he deems it understandable why the later church "formulated the doctrine."[4] This paper will survey the early Christian councils to demonstrate that the Trinity was not universally accepted by the fourth century, but developed over time so that A.D. 381 marks the earliest date for a definitive statement of the doctrine.

THE EARLY COUNCILS

The councils of Nicaea (A. D. 325) and Constantinople (A. D. 381) are considered the first orthodox councils. Many Christians across Protestantism, Catholicism, and Eastern Orthodoxy view both councils as authoritative. Both assemblies met to address different aspects of the Godhead, with the hopes of answering challenges and building consensus. Tertullian reminds us that in his era, most Christians denied the doctrine of the Trinity.[5] The doctrine of the

---

1. See this author's paper in the Early Departures chapter.
2. Peter Heather, *Christendom: The Triumph of a Religion*, (New York, NY: Alfred A. Knopf, 2022), xiv.
3. Millard J. Erickson, *Introducing Christian Doctrine*, (Grand Rapids, MI: Baker Book House, 1992), 98-100.
4. Erickson, *Introducing Christian Doctrine*, 98-100.
5. "The simple, indeed, (I will not call them unwise and unlearned,) who always constitute

Godhead developed over the next couple hundred years, so much so that the original trinitarian thinkers would be recognized as heretics today. R. P. C. Hanson states that there was no "theologian in the Eastern or the Western Church before the outbreak of the Arian Controversy, who does not in some sense regard the Son as subordinate to the Father."[6] Subordinationism, the belief that the Son is in some form inferior to the Father, is what ultimately led to the First Council of Nicaea.

NICAEA

The controversy originated in Alexandria, Egypt, where the priest Arius pushed earlier subordinationist theology to its next logical step. Theologians, such as Tertullian and Justin Martyr, taught that Jesus was subordinate to the Father yet divine, but Arius taught that Jesus was created at some point. Arian theology accepted the divinity of Christ but on a lower level than God the Father.[7]

There was a desire to bring uniformity to Christianity across the empire, so at the summons of the Roman emperor, Constantine the Great, church leaders were called to resolve the issue of the Son's divinity and relationship to the Father. This assembly has come to be known as the First Council of Nicaea, taking place in A. D. 325. At times, it has been inaccurately regarded as the first appearance of a generally accepted Trinity. However, the council's focus was not on defining the entire Trinity; instead, it was the Son who received primary attention. Furthermore, the historical context following Nicaea reveals that the council's outcome was not a complete triumph.

Earle Cairns evaluates the achievements of Nicaea and attributes the

---

the majority of believers, are startled at the dispensation (of the Three in One), on the ground that their very rule of faith withdraws them from the world's plurality of gods to the one only true God; not understanding that, although He is the one only God, He must yet be believed in with His own *oikonomia*. The numerical order and distribution of the Trinity they assume to be a division of the Unity; whereas the Unity which derives the Trinity out of its own self is so far from being destroyed, that it is actually supported by it. They are constantly throwing out against us that we are preachers of two gods and three gods, while they take to themselves pre-eminently the credit of being worshippers of the One God." Tertullian, *Against Praxeas*, in *The Ante-Nicene Fathers*, vol. 3, A. Cleveland Coxe, ed., (Peabody, MA: Hendrickson Publishers, 2004), 598-99.

6. R. C. P. Hanson, *The Search for the Christian Doctrine of God*, (Edinburgh, Scotland: T&T Clark, 1988), 64.

7. Peter Heather, *Christendom*, 26-27.

temporary success of the council to Eusebius of Caesarea. Eusebius led the largest party, and his "dislike of controversy led him to propose a view that he hoped would be an acceptable compromise."[8] The compromise eventually led to the Nicene Creed.[9] Within the Creed, the Father is only the main subject in line one, in which His deity is affirmed. Any other reference that is made of the Father is with the Son in focus, to assert the Son's divinity. The Holy Spirit is mentioned in passing with just one line, "And [we believe] in the Holy Ghost." The Spirit receives no declaration of deity or identity. Following Nicaea, attacks sparked against the Spirit's divinity and caused further theological unrest. Thus, Cairns declares that Nicaea gained only a "temporary victory" in 325.[10]

THE UNORTHODOX COUNCILS

Nicaea not only failed to properly address the Spirit, but it also did not bring total satisfactory conclusions to explaining the Son. Heather reports that "The key term chosen at Nicaea to define the relationship of the Father to the Son - 'of one substance,' *homoousios* - was a complete novelty."[11] This term was used in Greek literature but does not appear in Scripture.[12] *Homoousios* was deemed problematic because it had no Biblical support, but also because it reminded some Christians of Sabellius and the Monarchians. Many questioned the implications of the word, for if God the Father and God the Son shared the same essence or substance, then they could not be distinct.[13]

The conflict of definitions and implications led to four different factions after Nicaea, and eventually brought about the next three councils.[14] These three councils, Seleucia (A. D. 359), Rimini (A. D. 359), and Constantinople (A. D. 360) are not listed as official orthodox ecumenical councils. The assemblies are considered unorthodox because they overturned the decisions of Nicaea for a generation or two, only to adopt theological positions that were themselves later

---

8. Earle E. Cairns, *Christianity Through the Centuries: A History of the Christian Church*, (Grand Rapids, MI: Zondervan, 1996), 128.

9. This is the original Nicene Creed, not the revised Nicene Creed from the Council of Constantinople. For the original Creed, see Eusebius, *Letter to the people of Caesarea*.

10. Cairns, *Through the Centuries*, 128.

11. Heather, *Christendom*, 32.

12. See this author's comments on Valentinus in the Early Departures chapter.

13. Heather, *Christendom*, 32.

14. For an overview of the different groups, see Heather, *Christendom*, 33.

overturned. Specifically, they replaced *homoousios* (one substance) with *homoios*, asserting that the Son was of 'like' substance with the Father.[15]

THE ORTHODOX COUNCIL OF CONSTANTINOPLE

The decades after Nicaea saw ongoing debates concerning the Son, and shortly thereafter the Spirit was subjected to similar controversies. In A.D. 381, Emperor Theodosius called 150 bishops together to restore unity to the church. Erickson confirms that at Constantinople, "there emerged a definitive statement" of the Trinity.[16] The council achieved its goal and set forth an authoritative doctrine of a co-equal and co-eternal Trinity.

The creed that came out of Constantinople is today called the Nicene Creed, as it revised the older creed of A.D. 325. The greatest theological change was the additional statements of the Spirit. However, compared to the Spirit, the section concerning the Son received approximately the same number of newly inserted words. Nevertheless, the Niceno-Constantinopolitan Creed of A.D. 381 is considered an orthodox victory. Although additional questions arose regarding the Trinity in future years, the Creed has remained the authority for trinitarian doctrine. Primary tension came about in A.D. 589, when the Western Church inserted "and the Son" after "that proceedeth from the Father" in respect to the Spirit's relationship to the other two persons (the Spirit proceedeth from the Father and the Son).[17]

CONCLUSION

Speaking of orthodox beliefs, Vincent of Lérins stated, "Moreover, in the Catholic Church itself, all possible care must be taken, that we hold that faith which has been believed everywhere, always, by all."[18] Supposedly, orthodoxy was orthodoxy because it was "believed everywhere, always, by all." If this is correct, then Christian history demonstrates that the Trinity cannot fall under the orthodox category, for it has had a shaky and evolutionary history. The councils may be deemed as orthodox victories, but it appears that orthodoxy itself can change depending on who the voters are. Therefore, our standard for doctrine should not be councils and creeds, but Scripture alone. Scripture cannot change; therefore, it is a safer foundation upon which to stand.

---

15. Heather, *Christendom*, 33-34.
16. Erickson, *Introducing Christian Doctrine*, 102.
17. This is called the Filioque Clause, for more see Jeremias Zuniga's paper in this chapter.
18. Vincent of Lérins, *A Commonitory*, chapter II.6.

39

The Filioque Clause—Exploring Its Development and Impact

Jeremias D. Zuniga

INTRODUCTION

Today, the presence of the two "Churches," often called Roman Catholic and Eastern Orthodox, is not always discussed or widely understood within the Pentecostal movement.[1] While the two exist, many contemporary believers are unsure of why they exist separately from one another or if there are any tangible differences between the two. Because of the unawareness regarding the division of these two Churches, I will spend a considerable portion of this essay introducing the historical situation that culminated in what is commonly called The Great Schism. To accomplish this task, I will begin by offering a brief survey of the rise of sees (a seat of authority) just prior to the Schism. Then, I will turn my attention to reviewing the development of the Nicene Creed from its inception up to the Schism, ultimately highlighting the two Trinities described in the variant versions of the Creed. I must note that it is not my intended purpose to offer an exposition that explores the philosophical errors of the *filioque* (phonetically pronounced philly-oak-way) clause, only to highlight that it speaks of two distinct expressions of "the Trinity."

---

1. For more on the designations of Catholicism and Greek Orthodoxy as the "Churches," see Douglas G. Jacobsen, *Global Gospel: An Introduction to Christianity on Five Continents* (Grand Rapids, MI: Baker Academic, 2015), 14-26, especially figure 2.4. It must be noted, Jacobsen's characterization of the Pentecostal movement as having fuzzy boundaries and being relatively new is objectionable. However, the rapid growth experienced by Pentecostals today is unique in its documentation, e.g., Talmadge L. French, *Early Inter-Racial Oneness Pentecostalism: G.T. Haywood and the Pentecostal Assemblies of the World (1901-1931)* (Cambridge: James Clarke, 2014).

THE FIGHT FOR POWER

Not long after the death of the Apostles, Christianity spread quickly throughout the Roman empire, and following this expanse, it proceeded to infiltrate Africa, Asia, and Europe.[2] By the 400s, Christianity had many churches throughout these regions, and among these churches, bishops often represented their locale as they engaged with other groups of churches and other regions. Naturally, some churches emerged with more influence than others:

> "In the Roman Empire, these were the sees of its four largest cities: Rome in the West, Antioch of Syria, Alexandria of Egypt, and eventually Constantinople in the East. Since Constantinople was the new capital of the empire, it came to rank immediately after Rome because it was 'the new Rome.'"[3]

It was not uncommon in this period for bishops to discuss or even dispute the practices of other regions. This dialoguing would eventually lead to the Roman bishops claiming that they held authority over all regions because they were the successors to Peter, supposing that he had established the bishopric in Rome.[4] The rise of the Roman bishops over the patriarchs of the five sees is crucial, and tensions never appear to completely subside.

THE CREED AND ITS DEVELOPMENT

In its initial draft, the Nicene Creed was not the expanded statement that is known of today, as the statement from 325 read:

> "We believe in one God, the father almighty, Maker of heaven and earth, and of all things visible and invisible.
>
> And in one Lord Jesus Christ, the Son of God, begotten of the Father, Light of light, very God of very God, begotten, not made, being of one substance

2. For a brief introduction of the first 900 years of Christianity's growth, see Jacobsen, *Global Gospel*, 1-6.

3. Edward Engelbrecht, ed., *The Church from Age to Age: A History from Galilee to Global Christianity* (St. Louis, MO: Concordia Pub. House, 2011), 162. For awareness, I note that Jerusalem also rose to become influential in the fifth century.

4. On the fact that this claim may have been in response to the claim that Roman bishops had its primacy because they lived in the previous capitol see Engelbrecht, ed., *The Church from Age to Age*, 163-165, 355.

with the Father; by whom all things were made ; who for us men, and for our salvation, came down and was incarnate and was made man ; he suffered, and the third day he rose again, ascended into heaven ; from thence he shall come to judge the quick and the dead.

And in the Holy Ghost."[5]

Notably, the Spirit receives only a passing mention. However, it would receive additional focus in 381 at Constantinople when the following was added:

"And in the Holy Ghost, the Lord and Giver of life, who proceedeth from the Father [***and the Son***], who with the Father and the Son together is worshiped and glorified, who spake by the prophets. In one holy catholic and apostolic Church ; we acknowledge one baptism for the remission of sins ; we look for the resurrection of the dead, and the life of the world to come. Amen."[6]

In 589, the Nicene Creed would undergo another development. The development of the creed is known as the "*filioque* clause," a Latin word meaning "and the Son." I have included this clause in brackets above.

This development came because of the Third Council of Toledo's aim to combat Arianism.[7] Notably, this decision was made by the churches in the West, without consulting the churches in the East. The tension that had already existed would grow over the next 400 years until it exploded in 1054 when a series of accusations against the West was published, which included the *filioque* as an error in expressing the doctrine of God. As the East and West fought for authority, the divide grew, and the expression of the supposed Trinity took two divergent shapes.[8] One postulated that the Spirit proceeded from the Father alone, the other, that the Spirit proceeded from Father and Son. From 325, 381, and 589, we see three developments in trinitarian language about the nature of God. Each moment where development occurred it is no coincidence that they

5. This quotation comes from Philip Schaff, *Creeds of Christendom: A History and Critical Notes*, 4th ed., vol. 1 (New York, N.Y: Harper & Brothers, 1905), 28-29. For the issue of discussing the substance of God see my essay, "*Descendants, Derivations, and Deviations*," included in this volume.

6. Schaff, *Creeds of Christendom*, 29.

7. Engelbrecht, ed., *The Church from Age to Age*, 145n14. Also see Andrew Herbst's essay covering Arianism in this volume.

8. Engelbrecht, ed., *The Church from Age to Age*, 355-359. Also see Jacobsen, *Global Gospel*, 26-28.

emerged during struggles for authority between bishops from different regions. These moments of power struggle culminated in 1054, creating what is called today, The Great Schism.

CONCLUSION

What today might be described as the doctrine of the Trinity is not always the same conceptual Trinity expressed in the creeds described above. Additionally, within those creeds we find two distinct forms that are adhered to today. The Eastern Orthodox does not permit the *filioque*, whereas the Roman Catholics accept the clause. The distinction was important enough to cause the two to part ways and is likely related to the diminishment of the Spirit while creating two progenitors within the Godhead. Pentecostal readers should be careful to observe that the appropriation of philosophical notions foreign to the texts of Scripture will always pose challenges in expressing the doctrine of God, and the words of Scripture itself should not simply be preferred, but prioritized in expressing the mighty God in Jesus Christ (see Col. 2:8-9).

WEEK FOURTEEN

Theophanies and the Godhead—Appearances, Misdefinitions, and the Revelation of One God

40

Does God Body? Defining a Theophany and Theophanic Language

Jeremias D. Zuniga

INTRODUCTION

Throughout the Old Testament, God is described through various terms and by highlighting certain characteristics about His nature. Among these are the idea that God is not only present, but that God is personal and personally committed to the redemption of people that have covenanted with Him.[1] It is on this foundation that God calls Abraham out of Ur, He aims to create covenant, and Abraham willingly responds to God's call. This Creator-God's personal nature distinguishes Him from the gods that permeated the social environment of the ancient Near East (ANE), as it is clear from the texts of other cultures that gods created for their own relief and were present to humanity through conjuring.[2] For ancient Israel and Judah, there was a *milieu interieur* that identified their God, the LORD, as uniquely uncreated and unconfined to the talisman, ritual artifacts, and other material conceptions that may have tethered the gods of other cultures to the earth.[3] To this end, God is

1. The hiddenness and presence of God are both critical in recognizing the nature of God. YHWH is effectively a God who saves, caring for His people and about His glory. For more see Jeffrey Jay Niehaus, *God at Sinai: Covenant & Theophany in the Bible and Ancient near East* (Grand Rapids, MI: Zondervan Publishing House, 1995), 17-20. Also see my essay, "*The Name of our Divine King*," in this volume.

2. I owe the point about the creator-gods of the ANE to the following primary sources, Jiménez, E. and Rozzi, G. (2024). *Story of the Flood (Atraḫasīs) Chapter Old Babylonian I.* With contributions by A. C. Heinrich and F. Müller. Translated by Benjamin R. Foster. electronic Babylonian Library. https://www.ebl.lmu.de/corpus/L/1/1/OB/I A. C. Heinrich, *Poem of Creation* (*Enūma eliš*) Chapter VI. With contributions by Z. J. Földi and E. Jiménez. Translated by Anmar A. Fadhil and Benjamin R. Foster. electronic Babylonian Library, especially Tablet VI.1-8. https://doi.org/10.5282/ebl/l/1/2.

3. This point is well elucidated in John N. Oswalt, *The Bible among the Myths: Unique Revela-*

described in the following way:

> לא איש אל ויכזב ובן־אדם ויתנחם ההוא
> God is not a man to tell a lie, or a son of man to be repenting (Num. 23:19).

This statement should be considered carefully, especially inasmuch as it informs the reader of the nature of God's ability to keep His word to His people.

This recognition raises the question of theophany: Does God ever appear in the Old Testament as a human? While there has been substantial work completed on this front, I want to introduce a few cautions against over-reading ANE texts into Scripture, which presents a *milieu interieur* that is often contra the cultural conceptualizations. I raise that as interpreters of Scripture, our goal and aim should be to come to an emic understanding that prioritizes the texts of Scripture, rather than an etic knowledge that relies too heavily on external comparative assumptions. To this end, I will offer a definition of the term theophany, relating it to the anthropomorphic underpinnings that are throughout the Bible. Since definitions will be the focus, it will be outside of my purview to offer exegesis to every supposed theophanic text. However, for readers aiming to more thoroughly understand the current literature on this discussion, I refer you to explore both Andrew Herbst's essay covering Melchizedek included in this volume, and the footnote below.[4]

---

tion or Just Ancient Literature? (Grand Rapids, MI: Zondervan, 2009), 99-104. Oswalt is correct in noting that Enuma Elish is not about creation at all. Additionally, Oswalt insightfully offers the term "continuity," as an outgrowth of Kaufmann's "correspondence," see Oswalt, *The Bible among the Myths*, 43-62 in contrast to Walton's statement, "The gods did not 'intervene' because that would assume that there was a world of events outside of them... The Israelites, along with everyone else in the ancient world, believed... every event was... an act of God" see John H. Walton, *The Lost World of Genesis One: Ancient Cosmology and the Origins Debate* (Downers Grove, IL: IVP Academic, 2009), 18. Additionally, the supposed dependance presented in Victor H. Matthews, *A Brief History of Ancient Israel* (Louisville, KY: Westminster John Knox, 2002), 2-3. Also see W. Robertson Smith, *Religion of the Semites* (London: Routledge, Taylor & Francis Group, 2002), 114-116.

4. While recommend engaging these works to survey the landscape of scholarship on the topic, the conclusions that the various authors come to are not endorsed. For exposure to the concept of theophanies, I recommend Niehaus, God at Sinai. For an example of reading Genesis 18 as YHWH appearing in a body to Abraham see Esther J. Hamori, *When Gods Were Men: The Embodied God in Biblical and near Eastern Literature* (Berlin: Walter De Gruyter, 2008). For a more advanced study presented with robust engagement with the literature see Mark S. Smith, *Where the Gods Are: Spatial Dimensions of Anthropomorphism in the Biblical World* (New Haven: Yale University Press, 2016). I want too note that I differ substantially from the methods of

WHAT IS A THEOPHANY?

Building on the above point that God is personal, it is through this personal nature that I want to turn our attention to defining the term theophany. For a contemporary reader, this term can invoke different ideas, and while the various ideas may be present, it has appeared to me that a theophany is commonly perceived as God physically appearing to humans.[5] The danger of imposing physicality as a first order in the Old Testament is best recognized in the following question: does materiality impact the claim that God is a spirit (see Jn. 4:24a)? The authors of the New Testament, alongside the Old Testament, claim that God is a spiritual being, and unlike man prior to His incarnation. To this end, exegetes are careful to denote Old Testament appearances of God as describing His "willingness to identify with us…his desire for relationship, and points forward, ultimately to the incarnation."[6] Presenting theophanies first as "physical," creates the dilemma of God being confined, even if momentarily, to bodily representation on earth and ultimately unjustly requires texts like Genesis 3:8 to be read as God's body rustling through His garden in similar ways to ANE kings.[7]

The error in this point is not simply reading ANE texts into Scripture but claiming that God has taken a body in a real way.[8] Thus, I opine that it is more

---

each of the above listed sources in various places. An example is found in Niehaus' engagement with Genesis 3 and what I would define as overreading the language as Sinaitic (Niehaus, *God at Sinai*, 142-180), Hamori's identification of the 'îš Theophany, and Smith's engagement with ANE parallel literature (Smith, *Where the gods are*, 13-44).

5. In contrast to Hamori, the caution represented in the following podcast is important "*Theophanies, Chariots, and Wheels within Wheels (Ezekiel 1)*," Apple Podcasts, October 15, 2024, https://podcasts.apple.com/us/podcast/theophanies-chariots-and-wheels-within-wheels-ezekiel-1/id1504944937?i=1000673220794, 6:37-6:46. While the host initiates conversation using the language of "physical forms," the respondent navigates toward anthropomorphic terms. I also want to raise the point that both the host and guest ultimately recognize in their discussion about the Angel of the LORD that "it leads to a faulty Christology, actually, if we start having the incarnation like Jesus has to appear as humans in previous settings…do they look like Jesus or something like that? I think its creating a false Christology that's not extremely helpful, that we can be more precise about" 15:16-15:43.

6. Robin Routledge, *Old Testament Theology: A Thematic Approach* (Westmont: InterVarsity Press, 2008), 102-103.

7. For this point of contention, see Smith, *Where the gods are*, 14-18.

8. For God to appear and eat would not only imply that His physical body was a reality, but that it was physical in the way other humans exist in the earth. To this end, I question whether that body died, was abandoned, or ceased to exist when God was manifested in the incarnation and was literally born as an infant (see Matt. 1:16-2:11; Lk. 1:26-56; Jn. 1:1-18; and 1 Tim. 3:16).

feasible to posit that in the Old Testament God appears for the purpose of relationship through visible encounters that can only be described anthropomorphically. To this end, my claim does not diminish the real encounter with God's presence but connotes that these encounters are best described in terms that were relatable, as God is seen through His relationship with the material world. Because of this relational aspect of God's nature, theophanic language like *kābod* may be expressed as physical light; however, the definition above does not allow for reading into potentially ambiguous texts a body where the language does not exist.[9] Thus, God does appear to His people, at times it is through the light of His glory and all of creation responds (Exod. 19:18-25), and at other times a messenger appears on His behalf yet the encounter can only be described as "face-to-face" (Gen. 32:30; Exod. 33:11).[10]

CONCLUSION

While at times texts like Genesis 18 have been described as God physically appearing in bodily form to Abraham, I conclude that these texts should be reexamined to allow for the total biblical witness to attest to God's nature in the Old Testament. While the people of the Old Testament really encountered God in tangible ways, I propose that we should be careful in reading into these capacities that were not expressed in the text, and even more, catching the anthropomorphisms that have at other times caused readers to confuse what a theophany might truly be; the appearance of God to those that He is covenanting with. To this end, I refrain from language of condescension, and preserve from the later platonic notion that the deity could not become a human.

---

9. This definition aligns with the primary "Sinaitic" focus found in Niehaus' *God at Sinai*, and with the second-body focus of Smith's *Where the gods are.*

10. In Exodus, the LORD presence of the LORD is described as a cloud of glory. Yet it is God speaking to Moses as a man would speak to his friend. The idiomatic expression "face to face" does not infer a literal face in this case, but the nature in which they have communed, as close friends able to address real issues which is why Exodus 33:23 explains that God's face would not be seen. For the confrontational nature of this exchange see Victor P. Hamilton, *Exodus: An Exegetical Commentary* (Grand Rapids, MI: Baker Academic, a division of Baker Publishing Group, 2011), 560-571.

WEEK FIFTEEN

Father and Son Language in the New Testament—Sonship, Submission, and the Last Adam

41

The Godhead—Father & Son Language in the New Testament

Steven Gill

Questions surrounding what is meant, precisely, by "Father" and "Son" in the New Testament largely stem from this oft-neglected question: Is Jesus Christ to be understood as 'God the Son,' or is He 'the Son of God?' How one answers this question will likely determine how Father and Son language informs their understanding of the Godhead in the New Testament. To address the distinction between these two terms in a succinct way, I will refrain from leading this essay into extended conversations on the way the term "son of God" is used throughout the Old Testament. For more on that subject, the reader may refer to my essay entitled, *Hebrews: A Son Over His Own House* located in this volume. In this essay, I intend to compress the conversation into an examination of a few key passages from the New Testament that, perhaps, shed light on this subject for the reader.

Many readers of this entry will quickly identify the answer to the question posed in paragraph one: In the New Testament, Jesus is called the Son of God. In fact, the term "God the Son" or "God the Son of God" appears nowhere in the Bible.[1] Far from semantical, the distinction between these two terms is quite significant. Still, the latter title finds popularity in many Christian denominations today. In some ways, the reason for this term's popularity may stem from a misunderstanding, not of the Sonship of Jesus Christ, but of our own. "Beloved, now are we the sons of God, and it doth not yet appear what we shall be: but we know that, when he shall appear, we shall be like him; for we shall see him as he is" (1 John 3:2 KJV). The relationship between Christ's Sonship and our

1. The phrase, "God the Son" first comes to us in the writings of Justin Martyr (*Dialogue with Trypho*, ch. CXXVIII).

own is sometimes neglected out of fear of offending the divinity of Jesus, yet it is the opinion of this writer that the failure to adopt the New Testament's perspective on sonship that has done the greatest damage to the common Christian portrayal of the godhead. Concerning the language of sonship within the New Testament, Drane writes,

> The same image can also be applied as a theological metaphor of some substance to describe the Christian relationship to God. Here the focus is not on childhood but on the nature of Jesus as Son of God and on believers as sharing in that. A major theme of 1 John is that because of Jesus' status... Christians become "children of God" (*tekna*). Paul used similar concepts (Gal 4:5; Rom 8:15, 23; Eph 1:5)...[2].

The ability of mankind to share in the Sonship of Jesus Christ is a point which deserves more attention than it has received. In Luke's gospel, at the baptism of Christ, the Sonship of Jesus was directly connected to the sonship of Adam.

> Now when all the people were baptized, it came to pass, that Jesus also being baptized, and praying, the heaven was opened, And the Holy Ghost descended in a bodily shape like a dove upon him, and a voice came from heaven, which said, Thou art my beloved Son; in thee I am well pleased. And Jesus himself began to be about thirty years of age, being (as was supposed) the son of Joseph, which was the son of Heli...Which was the son of Enos, which was the son of Seth, which was the son of Adam, which was the son of God.[3]

The decision by Luke to include the ancestry of Jesus immediately after His baptism appears random until the reader considers the implications of the baptism itself. "Adam, which was the son of God," is the endpoint of Luke's

2. John Drane, "Sonship, Child, Children" in, *Dictionary of the Later New Testament & Its Developments*, ed. Ralph P. Martin, Peter H. Davids (IVP Academic, 1997), 1116. Here, Drane insists upon Jesus' status as "divine son," an adjective with which I would likely disagree. If by "divine son" one is attempting to describe Jesus as truly man and truly God, I find the adjective benign. However, if "divine" is modifying sonship in such a way that the Son has a pre-existent co-divinity with the Father, I suspect that it is guilty of the original sin of reading back into the Bible ideas that were developed long after it was written. The concept of a divine son who is co-eternal, consubstantial, and co-equal is one that has been addressed extensively in this paper, so I will not redress here it other than to say it a concept foreign to the NT writers.

3. Luke 3:21-23;38 (KJV).

genealogy.[4] Thus, immediately after disclosing the Son in whom God was well pleased, Luke reminded the reader of the son in whom He was not well pleased.[5] Here, the correlation between the Sonship of Christ and that of Adam is not just implicit, but explicit. This approach to the incarnation is reflected in the epistles. Paul wrote,

> Wherefore, as by one man sin entered into the world, and death by sin; and so death passed upon all men, for that all have sinned...Nevertheless death reigned from Adam to Moses, even over them that had not sinned after the similitude of Adam's transgression, who is the figure of him that was to come. But not as the offence, so also is the free gift. For if through the offence of one many be dead, much more the grace of God, and the gift by grace, which is by one man, Jesus Christ, hath abounded unto many...For if by one man's offence death reigned by one; much more they which receive abundance of grace and of the gift of righteousness shall reign in life by one, Jesus Christ.) Therefore as by the offence of one judgment came upon all men to condemnation; even so by the righteousness of one the free gift came upon all men unto justification of life. For as by one man's disobedience many were made sinners, so by the obedience of one shall many be made righteous.[6]

Romans' fifth chapter offers readers a unique insight into the apostles' view of the incarnation; Paul situated the humanity of Christ squarely in the context of His purpose as redeemer of the descendants of Adam.[7] The son in whom

---

4. This may be contrasted with Matthew's gospel, which begins the ancestry of Jesus at Abraham and works its way down the centuries to the birth of Christ. Luke, beginning at Jesus, works backwards, not to Abraham, but to Adam.

5. I discussed this topic at length in my 2023 book. Many of the central themes in this paper are drawn from discussions in that book. For more on this, see:

Steven Gill, *The Last Man: Reclaiming Father & Son Language in the Oneness Pentecostal Movement*, (Steven Gill, 2023), 80.

6. Romans 5:12; 14-15; 17-19 (KJV). This comparison and contrast style about Adam and Jesus Christ is performed again by Paul in 1 Cor. 15:20-28; 45-49. This is sometimes called "Adamic Christology."

7. Keener notes, "Paul's Jewish readers might have argued for their unique descent from Abraham the righteous (4:1-5:11), but Paul points them instead to their common descent with the Gentiles from the line of Adam the sinner...Jewish interpreters generally believed that Adam's glory, lost at the Fall, would be restored to the righteous in the world to come...Jewish writers claimed that Adam brought sin and death into the world (4 Ezra 7:118; 2 Baruch 54:15), but they also believed that each of his descendants made his or her own choice to follow in Adam's footsteps...becoming each 'our own Adam' (2 Baruch 54:19)."

For Keener: Craig Keener, *The IVP Bible Background Commentary: New Testament*, (IVP Academic, 2014), 434-435.

God was not well pleased introduced sin and death into the world, but Jesus, "the last Adam"[8] brought righteousness and justification through "obedience" (Rom. 5:19). Furthermore, He did this work, not as God, but as a man (Rom. 5:15; 1 Tim. 2:5). Of course, one co-equal person of God cannot be obedient to another co-equal person of God – but a man can be, and a perfect man *must* be.[9] In this way, the connection between Jesus' Sonship and our own is more easily understood; Adam – the first son of God – brought sin into the world through disobedience; his descendants have behaved in like manner. Adam is called "the figure of him that was to come," but in what way is he the figure? He is not a figure of Christ by his sinful behavior, but by his humanity as God's image bearer.[10] In Genesis, Adam is the first man who is the ancestor that has cursed all. Nevertheless, when Jesus came, He was called the "firstborn"[11] by the Apostle Paul, signaling Christ's supersession of Adam as the rightful ancestor of all mankind. In other words, our inheritance has now been received in a new heir; we are the sons of God, because of the work of the only begotten Son. Because He shared in our humanity, we may share in His Sonship.

Jesus' consistent submission to God the Father throughout the gospels demonstrates how He achieved the victory over Adam's failure described by Paul. Even in His final prayer before the crucifixion, the relationship between Christ's Sonship and our own is seen in His thrice-repeated request in different forms, 'let this cup pass from me.'[12] Of course, nothing of co-equality or

---

8. 1 Cor. 15:45 (KJV).

9. This also sheds light on other passages of the New Testament that are difficult to sort out from a trinitarian perspective. When Jesus came to be baptized by John, John resisted Jesus' request. "But John forbad him, saying, I have need to be baptized of thee, and comest thou to me?" (Matt. 3:14 KJV). Nevertheless, if one approaches the question of sonship with the ministry of reconciliation in mind, the response of Jesus becomes more clearly understood: "And Jesus answering said unto him, Suffer it to be so now: for thus it becometh us to fulfil all righteousness. Then he suffered him" (Matt. 3:15 KJV). Fulfilling righteousness was a work that Jesus did, and could only do, as a man – a perfect man – who is the Son of God in whom God is well pleased.

10. This is another point of distinction between humanity and the rest of creation that deserves more attention than it has historically received. No other piece of creation is said to have been created in the image of God; that honor belongs to mankind alone (Gen. 1:27).

11. "The firstborn among many brethren" (Rom. 8:29) "firstborn of every creature" (Col. 1:15) "firstborn from the dead" (Col. 1:18) "church of the firstborn" (Heb. 12:23). Interestingly, Paul is the only epistle writer to use this term.

12. Matt. 5:39; 42; 44. Of most interesting note here might be the setting. Adam, the first man, cursed humanity by an act of willful disobedience to God's commandment in a garden

consubstantiality is seen in Jesus' prayer in the Garden of Gethsemane. Instead, what is revealed is a man who, while His will conflicts with God's, is perfectly submitted to God in a way that mankind had historically not been. In Gethsemane, Jesus was in a wrestling match with His flesh; it is a wrestling match that He won. In doing so, He granted us "access by faith" (Rom. 5:2 KJV) to become "joint heirs with Christ" (Rom. 8:17 KJV). With this assurance comes a promise that, as brethren of the Son who are indeed sons, we will "reign with him" (2 Tim. 2:12 KJV) and indeed we will "judge angels" (1 Cor. 6:3 KJV) as well. In this way, Sonship may be understood as an especially human attribute. It is the characteristic that discloses the submission, ministry, and authority of Jesus Christ, and in doing so, it teaches us how we have been invited into sonship ourselves.

called Eden. Jesus, 'the last man,' restored humanity's access to God by an act of self-denial and obedience to God's commandment in a garden called Gethsemane. These contrasting portraits, perhaps, serve to underscore the ministry of Christ as the second Adam.

WEEK SIXTEEN

Trinitarian Proof Texts Revisited—Scripture, Context, and the Language of the Son

42

Jesus as the Son of Man

Andrew Herbst

INTRODUCTION

The Bible uses many titles to depict the identity and accomplishments of Jesus. For example, the Son of God term is connected to the Davidic Covenant and Christ's kingship, and the Lamb is a reference to Christ as the atoning sacrifice. This paper will focus on the Son of Man title and how it reveals Jesus as the obedient servant and heavenly judge.

THE SON OF MAN IN THE OT

The primary Old Testament (OT) reference for the Son of Man goes back to Daniel 7:13-14. The prophet saw a vision of God giving a heavenly man divine authority and a kingdom. All people and nations would serve this heavenly judge, reminiscent of the eternal Davidic throne (2 Sam. 7). The Son of Man is a different role or title from that of Messiah, but they are united through the kingship and servanthood of Jesus Christ.

THE SON OF MAN IN THE GOSPELS

Within the Gospels, "Son of Man" is the most common way Jesus identified Himself, being used around eighty times throughout all the Gospels.[1] Specifically addressing the Gospel of Mark, David Garland comments that "although the term *Son of Man* is undefined, we do learn what he does."[2] Throughout Mark's Gospel, the author reveals that the Son of Man can forgive sin (Mark 2:10), will be betrayed (Mark 14:21), suffer, die, and finally He will

---

1. Grant Osborne, *Teach the Text: Mark* (Grand Rapids, MI: Baker Books, 2014), 38.
2. David Garland, *NIV Application Commentary: Mark* (Grand Rapids, MI: Zondervan, 1998), 82.

rise again on the third day (Mark 8:31).[3] Jesus said that, "the Son of man came not to be ministered unto, but to minister, and to give his life a ransom for many," (Matt. 20:28).[4] The exalted language of Daniel 7 is not passed over, but the Son of Man must first die for all, and through His sacrifice He would be exalted in power (Mark 14:62).

THE SON OF MAN AND THE LAST ADAM

In addition, the Son of Man phrase can be joined with the Last Adam, as Oscar Cullmann points out, as the Heavenly Man restored "men to the destiny for which God had created them."[5] Jesus is the Heavenly Man, the Last Adam, living in obedience in contrast to the earthly man, Adam, who lived in disobedience (cf. Rom. 5:12-19 and 1 Cor. 15:45-47). Cullmann states that the "Heavenly Man is man as God willed him to be when he created man in his own image."[6] While there are differences between the Heavenly Man and Son of Man terms, they share a central concept: both "deal with the man who remains faithful to his divine destiny to be the image of God."[7]

Therefore, the complete covenant obedience of Jesus is essential to His fulfillment as the Son of Man and Last Adam. Jesus was able to fulfill His mission as a "ransom for many" due to His obedience as a servant. Due to this covenant obedience, Jesus could die as pure atonement for all, but if He had not been obedient, this sacrifice could not have been possible. Again, the mission of Jesus was to undo what Adam did and to obey where Adam disobeyed.

THE SON OF MAN AND THE CHRIST

Upon the question of Jesus' identity, Peter confessed that Jesus was the Christ, the anointed one, who would bring about the restoration of David's throne (Matt. 16:16 and Mark 8:29). No one, including Peter, proclaimed Jesus to be the Son of Man. Jesus affirmed Peter's confession that Jesus was the Christ (Matt. 16:16-17), but when He "began to teach them," He did not say that the Christ would suffer, but that "the Son of man must suffer…and be killed" (Mark 8:31).

---

3. Garland, *Mark*, 82.
4. Unless otherwise noted, all biblical passages referenced are in the *King James Version*.
5. Oscar Cullmann, *The Christology of the New Testament*, translated by Shirley Guthrie & Charles Hall (Philadephia, PA: Westminster Press, 1959), 142.
6. Cullmann, *Christology*, 142.
7. Cullmann, *Christology*, 151.

In Mark 8, the Son of Man is connected to the offices of Christ/Messiah and the Suffering Servant (Isaiah 53). Eckhard Schnabel confirms that, although Peter declared Jesus to be the Christ, the declaration was "not accompanied by an understanding of what the title 'Messiah' means as applied to Jesus."[8] The Jewish mindset believed that the Messiah would conquer the enemies of Israel and restore the Jewish kingdom. However, Jesus revealed that the Messiah would have a kingdom, but only after He suffered and died. Grant Osborne comments that "the Messiah as Son of Man will achieve universal dominion through suffering."[9] Thus, before the Son of Man can look like the exalted man in Daniel 7, and before the Messiah can have His kingdom, He must first become the lowly and Suffering Servant who is submitted, even unto death.

THE SON OF MAN AND THE SERVANT

Cullmann notes that while the two roles of the Son of Man and Suffering Servant were present in Jewish theology, their unified combination was not.[10] The Servant portrayed the "deepest humiliation," while the Son of Man represented "the highest conceivable declaration of exaltation in Judaism."[11] Mark's combination of the two offices reveals exaltation comes after service and submission (Mark 10:44-45). Garland relates the fact that Jesus had previously told His disciples that He would die, but "this is the only passage in Mark that tells us why he must die," He will die as a ransom.[12]

THE SON OF MAN AND HIS JUDGMENT

The night before Christ's crucifixion, the Sanhedrin attempted to find any lawful excuse to have Him killed. False witnesses gave their testimonies, and when Jesus did not respond, the high priest demanded of Jesus, "Art thou the Christ, the Son of the Blessed?" (Mark 14:61). Yet again, Jesus deferred to use Messiah or Son of God for Himself, and instead used "Son of Man" in His response. Jesus responded with, "I am: and ye shall see the Son of man sitting on the right hand of power, and coming in the clouds of heaven," (Mark 14:62).

8. Eckhard Schnabel, *Mark*, vol. 2 in the Tyndale New Testament Commentaries (Downers Grove, IL: Varsity Press, 2017), 195.

9. Osborne, *Mark*, 142.

10. Cullmann, *Christology*, 161.

11. Cullmann, *Christology*, 161.

12. Garland, Mark, 320.

At last, Daniel 7 is specifically in view. Whereas Jesus was being judged in that particular moment, He states that a time will come when He will be the universal judge. Osborne stresses that "coming on the clouds" is often associated with the return and appearance of Christ as king, and that in Mark 13:26, "He comes for His saints," but in Mark 14:62, "He comes to judge His enemies."[13] In addition, Schnabel identifies that Jesus referenced Psalm 110:1, "sitting at the right hand of the mighty one," and also Isaiah 9:6, as the Messiah is called *mighty God* or "the Powerful One."[14] All of these statements point to Jesus, the Son of Man, being exalted as Judge and King after His voluntary suffering and death.

CONCLUSION

The Son of Man term unites numerous aspects of Christ's ministry and accomplishments. It brings OT imagery into the NT and helps us understand the plan of God for salvation and judgment. The Son of Man joins together the death, exaltation, and future glory of the Servant and Messiah. In contrast to His deity, this is what the man Christ Jesus accomplished. Where the first Adam disobeyed and failed to walk in covenant with God, the man Jesus obeyed and submitted. Through His humiliation, He became a ransom for breakers of covenant, and brought the possibility for humanity to walk with God again. This is the weight of the Gospel concept of Jesus as the Son of Man. In the words of Oscar Cullmann, the Son of Man "embraces the total work of Jesus as does almost no other idea."[15]

13. Osborne, *Mark*, 283.
14. Schnabel, *Mark*, 384.
15. Cullmann, *Christology*, 137.

SELECTED BIBLIOGRAPHY

WEEK ONE

Arnold, Bill T. *Encountering the Book of Genesis.* Grand Rapids, MI: Baker Books, 2004.

Baker, David W. "God, Names of." In *Dictionary of the Old Testament Pentateuch*, edited by T D. Alexander and David W. Baker, 359. Downers Grove, IL: IVP Academic, 2003.

Cohen, Jeremy. *The Friars and the Jews: The Evolution of Medieval Anti-Judaism.* London, United Kingdom: Cornell University Press, 1982.

Coogan, Michael David. *The Ten Commandments: A Short History of an Ancient Text.* New Haven, CT: Yale University Press, 2014.

"CSB Study Bible: Notes for Genesis 1:1." *Life Bible.* Last modified, 2017. Accessed April 15, 2025. https://lifebible.com/bible.

Foster, Benjamin R. *Before the Muses: An Anthology of Akkadian Literature.* 3rd ed. Bethesda, MD: CDL Press, 2005.

Frankfort, Henri. *Kingship and the Gods: A Study of Ancient Near Eastern Religion as the Integration of Society & Nature.* Chicago: Chicago University Press, 1978.

Victor P. Hamilton, *The Book of Genesis,* Chapters 1-17, (Grand Rapids, MI: Eerdmans Publishing Co., 1990), 146.

Gaffin Jr., Richard B. "The Redemptive-Historical View." In *Biblical Hermeneutics: Five Views,* edited by Stanley E. Porter and Beth M. Stovell, 99-100. Downers Grove, IL: IVP Academic, 2012.

Gesenius, Wilhelm. *Gesenius' Hebrew Grammar: Second English Edition* Revised in Accordance with the Twenty-Eighth German Edition. Edited by E. Kautzsch and A. E Cowley. UK: Oxford University Press, 1956.

Hamilton, Victor P. *The Book of Genesis, Chapters 1-17.* Grand Rapids, MI: Wm. B. Eerdmans Publishing Co., 1990.

Hardy, H. H., and Matthew McAffee. *Going Deeper with Biblical Hebrew: An Intermediate Study of the Grammar and Syntax of the Old Testament.* Brentwood, TN: B&H Academic, 2024.

Haubold, Johannes, Adrian C. Heinrich, Sophus Helle, Enrique Jiménez, and Laura Selena Wisnom. Enuma Elish: *The Baylonian Epic of Creation.* London: Bloomsbury Academic, 2025.

Jensen, Matthew D. 2015. "Noah, the Eighth Proclaimer of Righteousness: Understanding 2 Peter 2.5 in Light of Genesis 4.26." *Journal For the Study of the New Testament* 37(4): 458–69. doi:10.1177/0142064X145581322.

Joüon, Paul, and T. Muraoka. *A Grammar of Biblical Hebrew: Third Reprint of the Second Edition, with Corrections.* Roma: Pontificio Istituto Biblico, Italy: Gregorian & Biblical Press, 2011.

Lang, Jeremy L., "From the Foundation of the World: The Establishment of the Oneness in Genesis." In *2021 ALJC General Ministry Conference Apostolic Doctrine Symposium*, edited by Nathan S. Whitley, 27-28. Memphis, TN: Assemblies of the Lord Jesus Christ, 2021.

Life Application Study Bible (NIV): Zondervan, Grand Rapids, MI; Tyndale House Publishers Inc., Carol Stream, IL, 2007, p.6.

Merwe, Christo H. J. van der, Jacobus A. Naude, and Jan H. Kroeze. *A Biblical Hebrew Reference Grammar.* 2nd ed. London: Bloomsbury T&T Clark, 2017.

Oppenheim, Adolf Leo, and Erica Reiner. *Ancient Mesopotamia: Portrait of a Dead Civilization*. Chicago: University of Chicago Press, 1977.

Oswalt, John. *The Book of Isaiah, Chapters 1-39.* Grand Rapids, MI: William B. Eerdmans Publishing Company, 1986.

Posner, Menachem. "Who was G-d addressing when He said, "Let US create man in our image?"." *Chabad.org*. Accessed March 27, 2025. https://www.chabad.org/parshah/article_cdo/aid/558595/jewish/Who-was-Gd-addressing-when-saying-Let-US-create-man.htm.

Pratico, Gary and Miles Van Pelt. *Basics of Biblical Hebrew Grammar*. 2nd ed. Grand Rapids, MI: Zondervan Academic, 2019.

Rad, Gerhard von. *Genesis: A Commentary.* Revised. London: SCM Press, 1972.

Sacks, Jonathan. *The Great Partnership: Science, Religion, and the Search for Meaning.* New York: Schocken Books, 2014.

Sarna, Nahum M. *The JPS Torah Commentary: Genesis: The Traditional Hebrew Text with the New JPS Translation*. Philadelphia, PA: The Jewish Publication Society, 1989.

"The Role of the Monarchy." *The Royal Family*. Accessed March 28, 2025. https://www.royal.uk/the-role-of-the-monarchy.

"The Royal Embassy of Saudi Arabia." *Government | The Embassy of The Kingdom of Saudi Arabia.* Accessed March 29, 2025. https://www.saudiembassy.net/government/?id=Skunk-3593-6229-42-4733.

Waltke, Bruce. *An Old Testament Theology.* Grand Rapids, MI: Zondervan Academic, 2007.

Walton, John H. *The Lost World of Genesis One: Ancient Cosmology and the Origins Debate.* Downers Grove, IL: IVP Academic, 2009.

Wenham, Gordon. *Genesis 1-15, Volume 1.* Grand Rapids, MI: Zondervan, 2014.

Westermann, Claus. *Genesis: A Continental Commentary.* Minneapolis: Fortress Press, 1994.

WEEK TWO

Baker, David W. "God, Names of." In *Dictionary of the Old Testament Pentateuch,* edited by T D. Alexander and David W. Baker, 363. Downers Grove, IL: IVP Academic, 2003.

Birsch, Nicole. "Marduk (god)." *Ancient Mesopotamian Gods and Goddesses.* Last modified, 2019. https://oracc.museum.upenn.edu/amgg/listofdeities/marduk/.

Donnellan, Victoria. "The Myth of the Trojan War." *The British Museum.* Last modified June 18, 2019.https://www.britishmuseum.org/blog/myth-trojan-war.

Dorsey, David A. *The Literary Structure of The Old Testament: A Commentary on Genesis-Malachi.* Grand Rapids, MI: Baker Academic, 2004.

Gardiner, Alan. *The Egyptians.* London: Oxford University Press, 2001.

Hamilton, Victor P. *Exodus: An Exegetical Commentary.* Grand Rapids, MI: Baker Book House, 2023.

Holden, Joseph M. and Geisler, Norman. *The Popular Handbook of Archaeology of the Bible.* Eugene, OR: Harvest House Publishers, 2013.

Hunt, Joel H. "Idols, Idolatry, Teraphim, Household Gods." In *Dictionary of the Old Testament Pentateuch,* edited by T D. Alexander and David W. Baker, 438. Downers Grove, IL: IVP Academic, 2003.

James, E. O. *The Ancient Gods.* London: Phoenix, 1999.

Livingston, G. Herbert. *The Pentateuch in its Cultural Environment.* Grand Rapids: Baker Book House, 1987.

Mark, Joshua J. "Pharaoh." *World History Encyclopedia,* October 3, 2022. https://www.worldhistory.org/pharaoh/.

Rendsburg, Gary. "Moses as Pharaoh's Equal-Horns and All." *Biblical Archaeology Society*, September 20, 2023. https://www.biblicalarchaeology.org/daily/people-cultures-in-the-bible/people-in-the-bible/moses-as-pharaohs-equal/.

Rooker, Mark, Michael A. Grisanti, and Eugene H. Merrill. *The World and the Word: An Introduction to the Old Testament.* Nashville: B & H Pub. Group, 2011.

Telushkin, Joseph. *Biblical Literacy.* New York: William Morrow and Company, Inc., 1997.

Walton, John H. *The IVP Bible Background Commentary: Old Testament.* Downers Grove, IL: InterVarsity Press, 2000.

Wilson, John A. "Egyptian Myths, Tales, and Mortuary Texts: The Theology of Memphis." In *Ancient Near Eastern Texts Relating to the Old Testament,* 3rd ed., 4–6. NJ: Princeton University Press, 1992.

WEEK THREE

Arnold A. Anderson. *Word Biblical Commentary: 2 Samuel.* Vol. 11. (Grand Rapids, MI: HarperCollins Christian Publishing, 2000), accessed March 5, 2022, ProQuest Ebook Central. https://ebookcentral- proquest-com.ezproxy.liberty.edu/lib/liberty/detail.action?docID=5607921, 112.

Barton, John. *A History of the Bible.* UK: Allen Lane; Viking, 2019.

Carson, D. A. *The Expositors Bible Commentary: Matthew.* Edited by Frank E. Gaebelein. Grand Rapids, MI: Zondervan Publishing House, 1992.

Hamilton, Victor P. *Handbook on the Historical Books: Joshua, Judges, Ruth, Samuel, Kings, Chronicles, Ezra-Nehemiah, Esther.* Grand Rapids, Mich: Baker Academic, 2008.

Hertzberg, Hans Wilhelm. *I & II Samuel, a Commentary.* translated by J.S. Bowden. Philadelphia: Westminster Press, 1964.

Joüon, Paul, and T. Muraoka. *A Grammar of Biblical Hebrew*. 2nd ed. Roma: Pontificio Istituto Biblico, Gregorian & Biblical Press, 2011.

McCarter, P. Kyle. *1 Samuel: A New Translation with Introduction, Notes & Commentary.* Garden City, N.Y: Doubleday, 1984.

Pratico, Gary Davis, and Miles V. Van Pelt. *Basics of Biblical Hebrew: Grammar.* 3rd ed. Grand Rapids, MI: Zondervan, 2019.

Roberts, J.J. "Davidic Covenant." In *Dictionary of the Old Testament Historical Books*, edited by Bill T. Arnold and H.G. M. Williamson, 208-09. Downers Grove, IL: InterVarsity Press, 2005.

Ryu, Gilsun. "Messianism and Kingship in the Gospel of John: A Comparison Between the Fourth Gospel and the Royal Psalms 2, 72, and 110." In *Journal of Religious & Theological Information*, 16:4, (2017), 125-140, DOI: 10.1080/10477845.2017.1317187.

Satterthwaite, Philip. "David." In *Dictionary of the Old Testament Historical Books*, edited by Bill T. Arnold and H.G.M. Williamson, 199. Downers Grove, IL: InterVarsity Press, 2005.

Staff, Armstrong Institute. "Mesha Stele: The Second 'House of David Inscription'."*Armstrong Institute of Biblical Archaeology*. Last modified April 22, 2024. https://armstronginstitute.org/1051-mesha-stele-the-second-house-of-david-inscription.

Staff, The BAS. "The Tel Dan Inscription: The First Historical Evidence of King David from the Bible." *Biblical Archaeological Society*. Last modified June, 2024. Accessed April 16, 2025. https://www.biblicalarchaeology.org/daily/biblical-artifacts/the-tel-dan-inscription-the-first-historical-evidence-of-the-king-david-bible-story/.

Tigay, Jeffrey H. *Deuteronomy = דברים: The traditional Hebrew Text with the New JPS Translation*. Philadelphia: Jewish Publication Society, 1996.

von Rad, Gerhard. *Old Testament Theology: Volume 1*. Translated by D. M. G. Stalker. New York, NY: Harper and Row Publishers, 1962.

Youngblood, Ronald. *The Expositors Bible Commentary: 2 Samuel.* Edited by Frank E. Gaebelein. Grand Rapids, MI: Zondervan Publishing House, 1992.

WEEK FOUR

"A New 'Reformation' That Many Don't Realize They've Joined." *Biola Magazine - Biola University Blogs*, July 2, 2025. https://www.biola.edu/blogs/biola-magazine/2015/a-new-reformation.

Arnold, Bill T., and Brent A. Strawn, eds. *The World Around the Old Testament: The People and Places of the Ancient Near East.* Grand Rapids, MI: Baker Academic, a division of Baker Publishing Group, 2016.

Chisholm, Robert Jr. *Handbook on the Prophets*, Grand Rapids, MI: Baker Academic, 2002.

Cullmann, Oscar. *The Christology of the New Testament.* Translated by Shirley Guthrie & Charles Hall. Philadephia, PA: Westminster Press, 1959.

Dunn, James D. G. *Baptism in the Holy Spirit.* Philadelphia, PA: Westminster Press, 1970.

——. *Christology in the Making: A New Testament Inquiry into the Origins of the Doctrine of the Incarnation.* Grand Rapids, MI: Eerdmans Publishing, 1989.

——. *Jesus Remembered: Christianity in the Making, volume 1.* Grand Rapids, MI: Eerdmans Publishing, 2003.

Firth, David G. "Messiah." In *Dictionary of the Old Testament Prophets*, edited by Mark J. Boda and J G. McConville, 542. Downers Grove, IL: IVP Academic, 2012.

Grogan, Geoffrey, W. *The Expositors Bible Commentary: Isaiah.* Edited by Frank E. Gaebelein. Grand Rapids, MI: Zondervan Publishing House, 1992.

Hamilton, Victor P. *Handbook on the Historical Books: Joshua, judges, Ruth, Samuel, Kings, Chronicles, Ezra-Nehemiah, Esther.* Grand Rapids, MI: Baker Academic, 2008.

Harman, Allan M. *Isaiah: A Covenant to Be Kept for the Sake of the Church.* Fearn, Rossshire, Scotland: Christian Focus, 2011.

Hilber, John W. "Israelite Prophecy in Its Ancient Near Eastern Context." In *The State of Old Testament Studies: A Survey of Recent Research*, 132–46. Grand Rapids, MI: Baker Academic, 2024.

Holliday, William. *A Concise Hebrew and Aramaic Lexicon of the Old Testament: Based on the Work of Ludwig Koehler and Walter Baumgartner.* Grand Rapids, MI: Eerdman's Publishing Company, 1988.

McConville, J G. "Micah, Book of." In *Dictionary of the Old Testament Prophets*, edited by Mark J. Boda and J G. McConville, 548. Downers Grove, IL: IVP Academic, 2012.

Nissinen, Martti. *Ancient Prophecy: Near Eastern, Biblical, and Greek Perspectives.* New York: Oxford University Press, 2017.

Pivec, Holly, and R. Douglas Geivett. *Counterfeit Kingdom: The Dangers of New Revelation, New Prophets, and New Age Practices in the Church.* Brentwood, Tennessee: B&H Publishing Group, 2022.

Smith, Gary V. "Cyrus or Sennacherib? Historical Issues Involved in the Interpretation of Isaiah 40-55." In *Bind up the Testimony: Explorations in the Genesis of the Book of Isaiah*, 175–93. Peabody, MA: Hendrickson Publishers, 2015.

Telushkin, Joseph. *Jewish Literacy.* New York: William Morrow and Co., 1991.

Rad, Gerhard von. *Old Testament Theology.* Volume 1. Translated by D. M. G. Stalker. New York, NY: Harper and Row Publishers, 1962.

——. *Old Testament Theology.* Volume 2. Translated by D. M. G. Stalker. New York, NY: Harper and Row Publishers, 1962.

WEEK FIVE

"Against the Arians, Discourse I." New Advent. Last modified, 2023. Accessed May 15, 2025. https://www.newadvent.org/fathers/28161.htm.

"Against the Arians, Discourse III." New Advent. Last modified, 2023. Accessed May 15, 2025. https://www.newadvent.org/fathers/28161.htm.

Augustinus Hipponensis, Aurelius. "On the Trinity." New Advent. Accessed May 14, 2025. https://www.newadvent.org/fathers/130105.htm.

Bauckham, Richard. *The Testimony of the Beloved Disciple: Narrative, History, and Theology in the Gospel of John.* Grand Rapids, MI: Baker Academic, 2008.

Beale, Gregory K., and Donald A. Carson, eds. *Commentary on the New Testament use of The Old Testament.* Grand Rapids, MI,: Baker Academic etc., 2009.

——. *Commentary on the New Testament Use of the Old Testament.* Grand Rapids, MI: Baker Academic, 2007.

Berkhof, Hendrikis. *Christian Faith.* Translated by Sierd Woudstra. Grand Rapids, MI: Eerdmans Publishing Company, 1979.

Bloomberg, Craig L. *Jesus and the Gospels.* 2nd ed. Nashville, TN: B&H Academic, 2009.

Brown, Raymond Edward. *The Gospel According to John: A New Translation with Introduction and Commentary.* Garden City, N.Y: Doubleday, 1984.

Bruce, F. F. *The Gospel & Epistles of John: Introduction, Exposition, and Notes.* Grand Rapids, MI: Eerdmans Pub. Co, 2002.

Dunn, James D. G. *Did the First Christians Worship Jesus?* Louisville, KY: Westminster John Knox Press, 2010.

Keener, Craig S. "John, Gospel of." In *Dictionary of Jesus and the Gospels*, edited by Joel B. Green, Jeannine K. Brown, and Nicholas Perrin, 428. 2nd ed. Downers Grove, IL: IVP Academic, 2013.

——. *The IVP Bible Background Commentary: New Testament.* Downers Grove, IL: InterVarsity Press, 2014.

Kruse, Colin G. *John: An Introduction and Commentary.* Downers Grove, IL: InterVarsity Press, USA, 2017.

Morales, L. Michael. *Exodus Old and New: A Biblical Theology of Redemption.* Downers Grove, IL: IVP Academic, 2020.

Servetus, Michael. "The Restoration of Christianity." In *On the Trinity and the Bible: An Annotated Translation of The Restoration of Christianity Books 1 and 2 on the Divine Trinity*, edited by Peter Hughes, 143-44. translated by Peter Zerner and Peter Hughes. Toronto, Canada: Blackstone Editions, 2023.

Smith, Brandon D. "Eternal Generation According to Athanasius." *The Center for Baptist Renewal.* Last modified September 21, 2021. https://www.centerforbaptistrenewal.com/blog/2021/9/20/eternal-generation-according-to-athanasius.

van Kooten G. "The Pre-70 ce Dating of the Gospel of John: 'There is (ἔστιν) in Jerusalem …a pool … which has five porticoes' (5.2)." *New Testament Studies.* 2025;71(1):29-55.doi:10.1017/S0028688524000213

Winn, Adam. "Son of God." In *Dictionary of Jesus and the Gospels*, edited by Joel B. Green, Jeannine K. Brown, and Nicholas Perrin, 886. 2nd ed. Downers Grove, IL: IVP Academic, 2013.

WEEK SIX

"Bar Kochba." *JewishHistory.org*. Accessed November 4, 2025. https://www.jewishhistory.org/bar-kochba/

Cullman, Oscar. *The Christology of the New Testament.* Louisville, KY: The Westminster Press, 1963.

Evans, Craig A. "Christianity and Judaism: Parting of the Ways." In *Dictionary of the Later New Testament & Its Developments*, edited by Ralph P. Martin and Peter H. Davids, 165. Downers Grove, IL: IVP Academic, 1997.

Gasque, W. Ward. *Sir William M. Ramsay: Archaeologist and New Testament Scholar. A Survey of His Contribution to the Study of the New Testament.* Grand Rapids, MI: Baker Book House, 1966. https://biblicalstudies.org.uk/pdf/ramsay/ramsay_gasque.pdf.

Goldingay, John. *Psalms 1-41*. Vol. 1. Grand Rapids, Mich: Baker Academic, 2006.

Green, Joel B. "Acts of the Apostles." In *Dictionary of the Later New Testament & Its Developments*, edited by Ralph P. Martin and Peter H. Davids, 12-13. Downers Grove, IL: IVP Academic, 1997.

Hemer, Colin. *The Book of Acts in the Setting of Hellenistic History.* Winona Lake, IN: Eisenbrauns, 1990.

Holden, Joseph M. and Norman Geisler. *The Popular Handbook of Archaeology of the Bible.* Eugene, OR: Harvest House Publishers, 2013.

Keener, Craig. *The IVP Bible Background Commentary: New Testament.* Downers Grove, IL: IVP Academic, 2014.

——. *Acts: An Exegetical Commentary Introduction and 1:1-2:47.* Vol. 1. Grand Rapids, MI: Baker Academic, 2012.

Kinlaw, Dennis F. *Old Testament Theology Lectures: Thirty-Six Lectures.* Wilmore, Ky: Francis Asbury Society, 2003.

Ramsay, William M. *St. Paul: the Traveler and the Roman Citizen.* Third edition. London: Hodder and Stoughton, 1897.

Ross, Allen P. *A Commentary on the Psalms: 1-41.* Vol. 1. Grand Rapids, MI: Kregel Academic & Professional, 2011.

Strassler, Robert and Richard Crawley. *The Landmark Thucydides.* New York: Free Press, 2008.

Thompson, Richard. *Acts: A Commentary in the Wesleyan Tradition.* Kansas City, MO: Beacon Hill Press, 2015.

Tigay, Jeffrey H. *Deuteronomy = דברים: The traditional Hebrew Text With the New JPS Translation.* Philadelphia: Jewish Publication Society, 2003.

Wiseman, D. J. *1 and 2 Kings: An Introduction and Commentary.* Nottingham: InterVarsity Press/IVP Academi, 1993.

WEEK SEVEN

Balla, Peter. "2 Corinthians," In *Commentary on the New Testament Use of The Old Testament*, edited by G.K. Beale, D.A. Carson, 753–83. Baker Academic, 2007.

Bauckham, Richard. *God Crucified.* Grand Rapids, MI: Eerdmans Publishing, 1999.

Bird, Michael, Ruben A. Bühner, J.rg Frey, and Brian Rosner, eds. *Paul Within Judaism: Perspectives on Paul and Jewish Identity.* Germany: Mohr Siebeck GmbH & Co. KG, 2023.

Bruce, FF. *Paul: Apostle of the Heart Set Free.* Carlisle, UK: Paternoster Press, 1977.

Capes, David. *The Divine Christ.* Grand Rapids, MI: Baker Academic, 2018.

—. *Old Testament Yahweh Texts in Paul's Christology.* Waco, TX: Baylor University Press, 2017.

Cohick, Lynn H. "Paul and Judaism." In *Dictionary of Paul and His Letters*, edited by Lynn H. Cohick, Nijay K. Gupta, and Scott McKnight, 772-73. Downers Grove, IL: IVP Academic, 2023.

Congar, Yves. "A Theology of the Third Person of the Trinity." *Church Life Journal: A Journal of the McGrath Institute for Church Life*. Last modified May 30, 2023. Accessed July 22, 2025. https://churchlifejournal.nd.edu/articles/a-theology-of-the-third-person-of-the-trinity/.

Dunn, James D. G. *Did the First Christians Worship Jesus?* Louisville, KY: Westminster John Knox Press, 2010.

——. *The Theology of the Apostle Paul.* Grand Rapids, MI: Eerdmans Publishing, 1998.

Gill, Steven. *The Last Man: Reclaiming Father & Son Language in the Oneness Pentecostal Movement*. Anderson, IN: Steven Gill: In Conjunction with Biblical Hebrew Academy Online, 2023.

Hamilton, Victor P. *Exodus: An Exegetical Commentary.* Grand Rapids, MI: Baker Academic, a division of Baker Publishing Group, 2023.

Myers, Eric. "Jewish Culture in Greco-Roman Palestine." In *Cultures of the Jews: A New History*, edited by David Biale, 168-69. New York: Schocken Books, 2002.

Plumptre, Dean. "Paul's Vow." *Bible Hub*. Accessed July 22, 2025. https://biblehub.com/sermons/auth/plumptre/paul's_vow.htm

Posner, Menachem. "The Nazir and the Nazirite Vow." *Chabad.org.* Accessed July 22, 2025. https://www.chabad.org/library/article_cdo/aid/287358/jewish/The-Nazirand-the-Nazirite-Vow.htm.

Schachterle, Joshua. "Paul's Christianity: How the Apostle Molded the Christian Faith." *Bart Ehrman*. Last modified November 17, 2023. Accessed July 22, 2025. https://www.bartehrman.com/pauls-christianity/.

Telushkin, Joseph. *Jewish Literacy: The Most Important Things to Know About the Jewish Religion, Its People, and Its History*. New York: William Morrow and Company, Inc., 1991.

Walton, Steve. "Paul in Acts." In *Dictionary of Paul and His Letters*, edited by Lynn H. Cohick, Nijay K. Gupta, and Steve McKnight, 782. Downers Grove, IL: IVP Academic, 2023.

Williams, H. H. Drake. "From the Perspective of the Writer or the Perspective of the Reader: Coming to Grips with a Starting Point for Analyzing the Use of Scripture in 1 Corinthians." In *Paul and Scripture*, edited by Stanley E. Porter, Christopher D. Land, 153–72. Brill, 2019.

WEEK EIGHT

Alexander, T. Desmond. *Face to Face with God: A Biblical Theology of Christ as Priest and Mediator*. Downers Grove, IL: InterVarsity Press, 2022.

Beale, G. K. *A New Testament Biblical Theology: The Unfolding of the Old Testament in the New*. Grand Rapids, MI: Baker Academic, 2011.

Beale, Gregory K., and Donald A. Carson, editors. *Commentary on the New Testament Use of the Old Testament*. Grand Rapids, MI: Baker Academic; Baker Academic, 2007.

Beale, Gregory K., Donald A. Carson, Benjamin Gladd, and Andrew D. Naselli, editors. *Dictionary of the New Testament Use of the Old Testament*. Grand Rapids, MI: Baker Academic; Baker Academic, 2023.

Donald J., Wiseman. "1 and 2 Kings." Vol. 9. *Tyndale Old Testament Commentaries*. Downers Grove, IL: IVP Academic, 1993.

Drane, John W. "Son of God." In *Dictionary of the Later New Testament & Its Developments*, edited by Ralph P. Martin and Peter H. Davids, 1111-1112. Downers Grove, IL: IVP Academic, 1997.

Gill, Steven. *The Last Man: Reclaiming Father & Son Language in the Oneness Pentecostal Movement*. Anderson, IN: Steven Gill, 2023.

Goldingay, John. "Psalms: Psalms 90-150." Vol. 3. *Baker Commentary on the Old Testament*. Grand Rapids, MI: Baker Academic, 2008.

Hagner, Donald Alfred. *Encountering the Book of Hebrews: An Exposition*. Grand Rapids, MI: Baker Academic, 2002.

Holden, Joseph M. and Norman Geisler. *The Popular Handbook of Archaeology of the Bible*. Eugene, OR: Harvest House Publishers, 2013.

Hurst, Lincoln D. "Priest, High Priest." In *Dictionary of the Later New Testament & Its Developments*, edited by Ralph P. Martin and Peter H. Davids, 964-66. Downers Grove, IL: IVP Academic, 1997.

Lane, William L. "Hebrews." In *Dictionary of the Later New Testament & Its Developments*, edited by Ralph P. Martin and Peter H. Davids, 450. Downers Grove, IL: IVP Academic, 1997.

LeMon, Joel M. "Egypt and the Egyptians." In *The World around the Old Testament: The People and Places of the Ancient Near East*, 169–96. Grand Rapids, MI: Baker Academic, 2016.

Peterson, David G. "Hebrews: An Introduction and Commentary." In *Tyndale New Testament Commentaries*, edited by Eckhard J. Schnabel and Nicholas Perrin, 105. Vol. 15. Downers Grove, IL: IVP Academic, 2020.

"Psalm 110 in Hebrews." *ESV Bible*. Accessed November 2025. https://www.esv.org/resources/esv-global-study-bible/chart-58-03/.

Sutton, L. "A Footstool of War, Honour and Shame? Perspectives Induced by Psalm 110:1." *Journal for Semitics*, 22(1), 51-71, 2016.

WEEK NINE

Aune, David E. *The New Testament in Its Literary Environment*. Westminster Press, 1989.

Cullman, Oscar. *The Christology of the New Testament*. 2nd ed. Philadelphia, PA: The Westminster Press, 1963.

Daniels, David. *Answers to your Bible Version Questions*. Ontario, CA: Chick Publications, 2003.

Davids, Peter. "The First Epistle of Peter." In *The New International Commentary on the New Testament*. Grand Rapids, Mich: Eerdmans, 1990.

Erhman, Bart. *The Orthodox Corruption of Scripture*. New York, NY: Oxford University Press, 1993.

Eusebius, *Ecclesiastical History*, Book VI.12., Translated by C. F. Cruse. Peabody, MA: Hendrickson Publishers, 2018.

Gorman, Michael J., ed. *Scripture and its Interpretation: A Global, Ecumenical Introduction to the Bible*. Grand Rapids, MI: Baker Academic, a division of Baker Publishing Group, 2017.

Hills, Edward F. *The King James Version Defended*. Internet archive, accessed November 15, 2025: https://archive.org/details/TheKingJamesVersionDefended.[1]

——. *Believing Bible Study*. Des Moine, IA: The Christian Research Press, 1991.

Holland, Thomas. *Crowned with Glory*. Lincoln, NE: Writers Club Press, 2000.

---

1. This book has seen multiple editions and reprints, currently the book can be found as Edward F. Hills, Text and Time: The Providential Preservation of Holy Scripture, (Reedsburg, WI: Kept Pure Press, 2024).

Jerome. *The Prologue to the Canonical Epistles in Codex Fuldensis.* Translated by Thomas Caldwell, https://faithsaves.net/wp-content/uploads/2014/04/Prologue-Canonical-Epistles.pdf.

Keener, Craig S. *The IVP Bible Background Commentary: New Testament.* 2nd ed. Downers Grove, IL: IVP Academic, 2014.

——. *The IVP Bible Background Commentary: New Testament.* Downers Grove, IL: IVP Academic, 1994.

Moorman, Jack. *When the KJV Departs from the "Majority" Text.* Collingswood, NJ: Dean Burgon Society, 2010.

Origen. *The Commentary of Origin on the Gospel of St. Matthew.* Vol. 2. Translated by Ronald E. Heine. Oxford Press, 2018.

Socrates. "Historia Ecclesiastica Book VII:32." In *Nicene and Post-Nicene Fathers, Second Series*: vol. 2. Edited by Philip Schaff and Henry Wace. Christian Literature Publishing Company, 1890. Reprinted by Hendrickson Publishers, Peabody, MA: 1995.

Walls, Muncia. *James: A Servant of God.* Medora, IN: Muncia Walls, 1997.

Webb, Robert L. "Jude." In *Dictionary of the Later New Testament & Its Developments*, edited by Ralph P. Martin and Peter H. Davids, 616. Downers Grove, IL: IVP Academic, 1997.

WEEK TEN

Aune, David Edward. *The New Testament in Its Literary Environment.* First ed. Philadelphia, PA: Westminster Press, 1987.

Bailey, Kenneth E. *Poet and Peasant and Through Peasants Eyes: A Literary-Cultural Approach to the Parables in Luke.* Combined ed. Grand Rapids, MI: Wm. B. Eerdmans Publishing Company, 1983.

Bandy, Alan S. 2011. "Patterns of Prophetic Lawsuits in the Oracles to the Seven Churches." *Neotestamentica* 45 (2): 178–205. https://search.ebscohost.com/login.aspx?direct=true&-AuthType=sso&db=rfh&AN=ATLA0001882542&site=ehost-live&scope=site.

Beale, Gregory K. *The Book of Revelation: A Commentary on the Greek Text.* Grand Rapids, MI: Eerdmans, 2000.

Beale, Gregory K., and Donald A. Carson, editors. *Commentary on the New Testament Use of the Old Testament.* Grand Rapids, MI: Baker Academic, 2007.

Drane, John W. "Son of God." In *Dictionary of the Later New Testament & Its Developments*, edited by Ralph P. Martin and Peter H. Davids, 1111-12. Downers Grove, IL: IVP Academic, 1997.

Firth, David. "Messiah." In *Dictionary of the Old Testament Prophets*, edited by Mark J. Boda and J G. McConville, 539. Downers Grove, IL: IVP Academic, 2012.

Irshai, Oded. "Dating the Eschaton: Jewish and Christian Apocalyptic Calculations in Late Antiquity." In *Apocalyptic Time*, edited by Albert I. Baumgarten, 149. Leiden, The Netherlands: Brill, 2000.

Keener, Craig S. *Revelation.* Grand Rapids, MI: Zondervan, 2000.

——. *The IVP Bible Background Commentary: New Testament.* Downers Grove, IL: InterVarsity Press, 1993.

——. *The IVP Bible Background Commentary: New Testament.* Downers Grove, IL: IVP Academic, 2014.

Kim, Seyoon. "Kingdom of God." In *Dictionary of the Later New Testament & Its Developments*, edited by Ralph P. Martin and Peter H. Davids, 634-35. Downers Grove, IL: IVP Academic, 1997.

Koester, Craig R. *Revelation and the End of All Things.* Grand Rapids, MI: William B. Eerdmans Publishing Company, 2018.

Martyr, Justin. *First Apology.* Translation taken from New Advent: https://www.newadvent.org/fathers/0126.htm

Mounce, Robert. *The Book of Revelation.* Grand Rapids, MI: Eerdmans Publishing Co., 1997.

Osborne, Grant. *Revelation.* Grand Rapids, MI: Baker Academic, 2002.

Reddish, Mitchell Glenn. *Apocalyptic Literature: A Reader.* Peabody, MA: Hendrickson Publishers, 2015.

Ryrie, Charles Caldwell. *Revelation.* Chicago, IL: Moody Publishers, 1968.

Servetus, Michael. "The Restoration of Christianity." In *On the Trinity and the Bible: An Annotated Translation of The Restoration of Christianity Books 1 and 2 on the Divine Trinity*, Edited by Peter Hughes, 25;70. Translated by Peter Zerner and Peter Hughes. Toronto, Canada: Blackstone Editions, 2023.

Walvoord, John. "3. The Letters to Sardis, Philadelphia, and Laodicea." *John F. Walvoord.* Accessed January 6, 2022. https://walvoord.com/article/261.

WEEK ELEVEN

Cairns, Earle E. *Christianity through the Centuries: A History of the Christian Church.* Grand Rapids, MI: Zondervan, 2009.

Chalfant, William. *Ancient Champions of Oneness.* Hazelwood, MO: Word Aflame Press, 1986.

Coxe, A. Cleveland, editor. *Ante-Nicene Fathers.* Peabody, MA: Hendrickson Publishers, 2004.

Engelbrecht, Edward, ed. *The Church from Age to Age: A History from Galilee to Global Christianity.* St. Louis, MO: Concordia Pub. House, 2011.

Harnack, Adolf von. *History of Dogma.* Translated by Neil Buchanan. Vol. 3. Boston: Roberts Brothers, 1897.

Heather, Peter. *Christendom: The Triumph of a Religion, AD 300-1300.* New York: Alfred A. Knopf, 2023.

Martyr, Justin. *Dialogue with Trypho.* Translation taken from New Advent: https://www.newadvent.org/fathers/0128.htm

Rea, Robert F. *Why Church History Matters: An Invitation to Love and Learn from Our Past.* Downers Grove, IL: InterVarsity Press, 2014.

Roberts, Alexander, and James Donaldson, eds. *Ante-Nicene Fathers: The Writings of the Fathers Down to A.D. 325.* Vol. 5. Peabody, MA: Hendrickson, 1995.

Tertullian. *Against Praxeas.* Translation taken from New Advent: https://www.newadvent.org/fathers/0317.htm

Volp, Ulrich. (2009). "Hippolytus." In *The Expository Times*, 120(11), 521-529. https://doi.org/10.1177/0014524609106838 (Original work published 2009).

Wormio, Christiano. "Sabellian History: The Origin and Development of the Sabellian Heretics up to the Observations Elaborated by the Ecclesiastical Authority at the Beginning of the Fifth Century." In *Sabellian History*, Edited by Eugene A. Dominquez, 54; 56-60. Translated by Juan D. Pedraza. Weldon Spring, MO: Eugene A. Dominguez, 2023.

Wright, David. "Creeds, Confessional Forms." In *Dictionary of the Later New Testament & Its Developments*, edited by Ralph P. Martin and Peter H. Davids, 256. Downers Grove, IL: IVP Academic, 1997.

WEEK TWELVE

Arnold, Clinton E. "Centers of Christianity." In *Dictionary of the Later New Testament & Its Developments*, edited by Ralph P. Martin and Peter H. Davids, 144-50. Downers Grove, IL: IVP Academic, 1997.

Bruce, F. F. "Colossian Problems, Pt 3: The Colossian Heresy." In *Bibliotheca Sacra 141*, no. 563 (1984): 195–208. EBSCOhost.

Brookins, Timothy A. *Rediscovering the Wisdom of the Corinthians: Paul, Stoicism, and Spiritual Hierarchy*. Grand Rapids, MI: William B. Eerdmans Publishing Company, 2025.

Cairns, Earle E. *Christianity Through the Centuries: A History of the Christian Church*. Grand Rapids, MI: Zondervan, 1996.

Carson, D. A. *Exegetical Fallacies*. 2nd ed. Grand Rapids, Mich: Baker Academic, 1996.

Chilton, Bruce D. "Synagogue." In *Dictionary of the Later New Testament & Its Developments*, edited by Ralph P. Martin and Peter H. Davids, 1144. Downers Grove, IL: IVP Academic, 1997.

Coxe, A. Cleveland, editor. *Ante-Nicene Fathers: Volume 1*. Peabody, Ma: Hendrickson Publishers Inc., 1994.

Durand, M., Simon Shogry, and Dick Baltzly."Stoicism." In *Stanford Encyclopedia of Philosophy*, January 20, 2023. https://plato.stanford.edu/entries/stoicism/#BodiInco.

Ferguson, E. "Tertullian." In *The Expository Times*, 120(7), 313-321. https://doi.org/10.1177/0014524609103464. Original work published 2009.

Gorman, Michael J., ed. *Scripture and its Interpretation: A Global, Ecumenical Introduction to the Bible.* Grand Rapids, MI: Baker Academic, a division of Baker Publishing Group, 2017.

Harnack, Adolf von. *History of Dogma.* Translated by Neil Buchanan. Vol. 3. Boston: Roberts Brothers, 1897.

Haykin, Michael A. G. "Biblical Exegesis in Fourth-Century Trinitarian Debates: Context, Contours, & Ressourcement."In *Reformed Faith & Practice*, June 1, 2017. https://journal.rts.edu/article/biblical-exegesis-fourth-century-trinitarian-debates-context-contours-ressourcement/.

Heather, Peter. *Christendom: The Triumph of a Religion.* New York, NY: Alfred A. Knopf, 2022.

Heick, Otto. *A History of Christian Thought.* Vol. 1. Philadelphia, PA: Fortress Press, 1965.

Irenaeus of Lyons. "Against Heresies." *Against Heresies* (St. Irenaeus), n.d. https://www.newadvent.org/fathers/0103.htm.

Keener, Craig. *The IVP Bible Background Commentary: New Testament.* Downers Grove, IL: IVP Academic, 1994.

Martyr, Justin. *Dialogue with Trypho.* Translation taken from New Advent: https://www.newadvent.org/fathers/0128.htm

——. *First Apology.* Translation taken from New Advent: https://www.newadvent.org/fathers/0126.htm

Osborne, Grant R. "Unpacking the Colossian Heresy. (Backdrops)." In *Bible Study Magazine* 8, no. 6 (2016): 24–25. EBSCOhost.

Pamphilus, Eusebius. *The Life Of The Blessed Emperor Constantine.* Translation taken from: Kessinger.

Rea, Robert F. *Why Church History Matters: An Invitation to Love and Learn from Our Past.* Downers Grove, IL: InterVarsity Press, 2014.

Robinson, Howard, and Ralph Weir. "Substance." In *Stanford Encyclopedia of Philosophy*, May 6, 2024. https://plato.stanford.edu/entries/substance/#Cate.

Rudolph, Kurt. *Gnosis: The Nature & History of Gnosticism.* San Francisco: Harper & Row, 1987.

Ryrie, Charles C. *Basic Theology*. Wheaton, IL: Victor, 1986.

Swartley, Willard M. "Intertextuality in Early Christian Literature." In *Dictionary of the Later New Testament & Its Developments*, edited by Ralph P. Martin and Peter H. Davids, 540. Downers Grove, IL: IVP Academic, 1997.

Tertullian. *Against Praxeas*. Translation taken from New Advent: https://www.newadvent.org/fathers/0317.htm

Tertullian. "Prescription Against Heretics." CHURCH FATHERS: *The Prescription Against Heretics* (Tertullian), n.d. https://www.newadvent.org/fathers/0311.htm.

Virkler, Henry A., and Karelynne Gerber Ayayo. *Hermeneutics: Principles and Processes of Biblical Interpretation*. 2nd ed. Grand Rapids, Mich: Baker Academic, 2007.

WEEK THIRTEEN

Athanasius. *Against the Arians*. Translation taken from New Advent: https://www.newadvent.org/fathers/28161.htm

Cairns, Earle E. *Christianity Through the Centuries: A History of the Christian Church*. Grand Rapids, MI: Zondervan, 1996.

"Council of Ephesus (A.D. 431)." New Advent. Accessed November 8, 2025. https://www.newadvent.org/fathers/3810.htm.

Coxe, A. Cleveland, editor. *Ante-Nicene Fathers: Volume 1*. Peabody, Ma: Hendrickson Publishers Inc., 1994.

"Doctrinal Note on Marian Titles: Mother of the Faithful, not Co-Redemptrix." *Vatican News*. Last modified November 4, 2025. https://www.vaticannews.va/en/vatican-city/news/2025-11/doctrinal-note-mother-of-the-faithful-not-co-redemptrix.html

Engelbrecht, Edward, ed. *The Church from Age to Age: A History from Galilee to Global Christianity*. St. Louis, MO: Concordia Pub. House, 2011.

Erickson, Millard J. *Introducing Christian Doctrine*. Grand Rapids, MI: Baker Book House, 1992.

French, Talmadge L. *Early Inter-Racial Oneness Pentecostalism: G. T. Haywood and the Pentecostal Assemblies of the World (1901-1931).* Eugene, OR: Pickwick Publications, 2014.

Gill, Steven. *The History & Development of the Doctrine of the Trinity.* Anderson, IN: Biblical Hebrew Academy Online, 2022.

Hanson, R. P. C. *The Search for the Christian Doctrine of God.* Edinburgh, Scotland: T&T Clark, 1988.

Heather, Peter. *Christendom: The Triumph of a Religion*, AD 300-1300. New York: Alfred A. Knopf, 2022.

Jacobsen, Douglas G. *Global Gospel: An Introduction to Christianity on Five Continents.* Grand Rapids, MI: Baker Academic, 2015.

Pamphilus, Eusebius. *The Life Of The Blessed Emperor Constantine.* Translation taken from: Kessinger.

Schaff, Philip. *Creeds of Christendom: A History and Critical Notes.* 4th ed. Vol. 1. New York, N.Y: Harper & Brothers, 1905.

WEEK FOURTEEN

Hamilton, Victor P. *Exodus: An Exegetical Commentary.* Grand Rapids, MI: Baker Academic, a division of Baker Publishing Group, 2011.

Hamori, Esther J. *When Gods were Men: The Embodied God in Biblical and Near Eastern Literature.* Berlin: Walter De Gruyter, 2008.

Heinrich, A. C., "Poem of Creation (Enūma eliš) Chapter VI. With contributions by Z. J. Földi and E Jiménez." Translated by Anmar A. Fadhil and Benjamin R. Foster. *Electronic Babylonian Library.* https://doi.org/10.5282/ebl/l/1/2

Jiménez, E. and Rozzi, G. (2024). "Story of the Flood (Atrahasīs) Chapter Old Babylonian I." With contributions by A. C. Heinrich and F. Müller. Translated by Benjamin R. Foster. *Electronic Babylonian Library.* https://www.ebl.lmu.de/corpus/L/1/1

Niehaus, Jeffrey Jay. *God at Sinai: Covenant & Theophany in the Bible and Ancient Near East.* Grand Rapids, MI: Zondervan Publishing House, 1995.

Oswalt, John N. *The Bible Among the Myths: Unique Revelation or Just Ancient Literature?* Grand Rapids, MI: Zondervan, 2009.

Routledge, Robin. *Old Testament Theology: A Thematic Approach.* Westmont: InterVarsity Press, 2008.

Smith, Mark S. *Where the Gods Are: Spatial Dimensions of Anthropomorphism in the Biblical World.* New Haven: Yale University Press, 2016.

Smith, W. Robertson. *Religion of the Semites.* London: Routledge, Taylor & Francis Group, 2002.

"Theophanies, Chariots, and Wheels within Wheels (Ezekiel 1)." Apple Podcasts, October 15, 2024. https://podcasts.apple.com/us/podcast/theophanies-chariots-and-wheels-within-wheels-ezekiel-1/id1504944937?i=1000673220794.

Walton, John H. *Ancient Near Eastern Thought and the Old Testament: Introducing the Conceptual World of the Hebrew Bible.* Grand Rapids, MI: Baker Academic, a division of Baker Publishing Group, 2006.

WEEK FIFTEEN

Gill, Steven. *The Last Man: Reclaiming Father & Son Language in the Oneness Pentecostal Movement.* Anderson, IN: Steven Gill, 2023.

Keener, Craig S. *The IVP Bible Background Commentary: New Testament.* 2nd ed. Downers Grove, IL: IVP Academic, 2014.

Martyr, Justin. *Dialogue with Trypho.* Translation taken from New Advent: https://www.newadvent.org/fathers/0128.htm

WEEK SIXTEEN

Cullmann, Oscar. *The Christology of the New Testament.* Translated by Shirley Guthrie & Charles Hall. Philadelphia, PA: Westminster Press, 1959.

Garland, David. *NIV Application Commentary: Mark.* Grand Rapids, MI: Zondervan, 1998.

Osborne, Grant. *Teach the Text Commentary Series: Mark.* Edited by Mark L. Strauss & John H. Walton. Grand Rapids, MI: Baker Book House, 2014.

Schnabel, Eckhard. "Mark, Vol. 2" in *Tyndale New Testament Commentaries.* Downers Grove, IL: Inter Varsity Press, 2017.

www.ingramcontent.com/pod-product-compliance
Lightning Source LLC
LaVergne TN
LVHW091028080826
845145LV00002B/401

* 9 7 8 1 9 6 5 5 8 4 2 5 5 *